The Body in Language

The Body in Language

HORST RUTHROF

CASSELL
London and New York

Cassell
Wellington House, 125 Strand, London WC2R 0BB
370 Lexington Avenue, New York, NY 10017–6550

First published 2000

British Library Cataloguing-in-Publication Data
A catalogue record for this book is available from the British Library.

ISBN 0-304-33805-2 (hardback)
     0-304-70580-2 (paperback)

Library of Congress Cataloging-in-Publication Data
Ruthrof, Horst.
     The body in language / Horst Ruthrof.
          p.   cm.
     Includes bibliographical references (p.) and index.
     ISBN 0–304–33805–2.—ISBN 0–304–70580–2 (pbk.)
     1. Nonverbal communication. 2. Semiotics. 3. Semantics.
     4. Language and languages—Philosophy. I. Title.
     P99.5.R88   1999
     302.2'22—dc21   99-19274
                                                                      CIP

Typeset by York House Typographic Ltd, London
Printed and bound in Great Britain by Biddles Limited, Guildford and
King's Lynn

Contents

Preface

When you look through the catalogues of the leading presses you will note that the body now turns up everywhere. From literary theory and criticism to law and sociology, from gender studies to anthropology and philosophy, the body runs through the titles like an oncoming spring tide. Perhaps this is a good thing. After all, a shift from a thinking that takes logos and principle as the basis towards a position that grants nature and the human body the status of ground can only enrich our perspective. But how radical is such a shift if it does not deal with the role of the body at the very level of description, at the level of language? Apart from some very exciting work out of cognitive science and its subspecies, cognitive linguistics and cognitive rhetoric, there is little evidence that the body is being reinstated at the base of linguistic communication. True, there is a corpus of literature in critical linguistics, following the early work of Fowler, which has persuasively addressed the presence of nonlinguistic phenomena, such as questions of ideology, in discourse. There is the influential work of Michael Halliday, which focuses on language as a socially interactive system. Other inquiries have likewise insisted on the presence of materiality and nonverbal communication in language. In none of these studies, however, have I found an explanation of the fundamental ingredients in language that make this possible.

What I want to ask is what language must be like to be able to process nonlinguistic materials so successfully. In trying to answer this question, two very different pathways seem to me to offer themselves. The one would be via principle and logos. If language is regarded as a highly abstract or even formal system we should not be surprised that it is capable of subsuming anything and everything in a certain generalized way. Alternatively, one could argue that for the body and other forms of materiality to be graspable via language, linguistic meaning must already have some kind of corporeality. If this is so, in what form does the body enter language at the semantic level? Or, what role does the body play in meaning events? My suggestion throughout this book, as in some of my earlier work, is that the body is always already part of language as discourse. The body is present in discourse in the form of nonlinguistic signs: as olfactory, tactile, gustatory, aural, visual, and many other subtle, nonverbal readings of the world. When we learn a language as part of social pedagogy, the community guides us to systemically link the sounds of language expressions with nonverbal sign complexes. For language to be meaningful, members of a speech community must be able to share, to a high degree, the way in which language and nonverbal readings are to be associated with one another. From this viewpoint, the body is present in language at the semantic level as community-sanctioned perception in the broad sense. Nor should this perceptual part of meaning exclude fantasy acts. On the contrary, I think that we gain a tremendous advantage in the description of language if we welcome mental projection, even in its most bizarre forms, as an essential component of linguistic meaning.

Acknowledgements

I would like to thank my students at Murdoch University, and especially my Honours and PhD students, who over the years have challenged my arguments and enriched my way of viewing language and literature, literary theory and the philosophy of language. I owe them a great deal and certainly more than this slim volume reveals. I also once more thank my colleagues at Murdoch and at other universities in Australia and overseas for their encouragement and criticisms. Particular thanks go to those who in various ways have contributed to the ideas expressed here: Niall Lucy at Murdoch for a thorough, critical reading of an earlier version of the manuscript; John Frow, now at the University of Edinburgh, for his critical sympathy with the thrust of the argument; and Mark Turner at the University of Maryland for introducing me to the principles of cognitive rhetoric and his willingness to welcome a voice from a critical speculative tradition. I gratefully acknowledge the research leave I was granted by Murdoch University in the second semester of 1997 and 1998. A special thank you goes to Janet Joyce, Editorial Director at Cassell, who has been a most reliable, helpful and encouraging correspondent since the inception of this book.

Chapter 7, 'The disembodiment of the signifier', relies on research on iconic representation in natural languages, a field outside this author's expertise. I thankfully list the writers from whose work I have borrowed: Coulmas, Florian (1989) *The Writing Systems of the World*, Oxford: Basil Blackwell; Davoust, Michel (1995) *L'Écriture Maya et son déchiffrement*, CNRS Editions; Diringer, David (1968) *The Alphabet: A Key to the History of Mankind*, London: Hutchinson; Frutiger, Adrian (1991) *Der Mensch und seine Zeichen: Schriften, Symbole, Signete, Signale*, Wiesbaden: Fourier; Gaur, Albertine (1984) *A History of Writing*, London: British Library; Gelb, I.J. (1965) *A Study of Writing*, Chicago: University of Chicago Press; Gimbutas, Marija (1991) *The Civilization of the Goddess: The World of Old Europe*, San Francisco: Harper; Haas, W. (ed.) (1976) *Writing without Letters*, Manchester: Manchester

University Press; Jensen, Hans (1970) *Sign, Symbol and Script: An Account of Man's Efforts to Write*, trans. George Unwin, London: George Allen and Unwin; Norman, Jerry (1988) *Chinese*, Cambridge: Cambridge University Press; Rubinger, Marcos Magalhães (1979) *Pintura rupestre: algo mais do que arte pré-histórica*, Belo Horizonte: Interlivros; Schaan, Denise Pahl (1997) *A linguagem iconográfica da cerâmica marajoara: um estudo da arte pré-histórica na Ilha de Marajó – Brasil (400–1300 AD)*, Porto Alegre: EDIPUCRS; and Weaver, Muriel Porter (1981) *The Aztecs, Maya, and Their Predecessors: Archaeology of Mesoamerica*, New York: Academic Press. My thanks also to the editorial staff at Cassell, who had all the icons selected for this chapter redrawn. I gratefully acknowledge the help I have received for Chapter 7 from my research assistant, Chris Palazzolo, who is writing his PhD at Murdoch University.

Lastly, I want to thank Peter Temple – editor, crime fiction author and friend – for his suggestions on how to make this book more accessible to the general reader.

For Dorle, once more . . .

Introduction

> When I think of hills, I think of the upward strength I tread upon. When water is the object of my thought, I feel the cool shock of the plunge and the quick yielding of the waves that crisp and curl and ripple about my body.
>
> (Helen Keller, *The World I Live In*, p. 11)

The Body in Language is a contribution to language theory, semiotics and, specifically, the theory of meaning. Its central claims can be stated simply: nonverbal signs are the deep structure of language and meaning is the event of an association of nonverbal and linguistic signs. When a meaning event occurs, the body enters language in the form of quasi-perceptual readings of the world. This may appear to be intuitively right, too naïve, or outrageously wrong. To be sure, a good deal needs to be explained before such assertions can be made coherent.

I have tried for some years to find a simple way of speaking of the role the body plays in language. It has not been easy, partly because I wanted to address as many counter-arguments as possible and partly because it takes time for a good prejudice to cure into a formula. However, the present book does not merely sum up ideas that have matured over time into a reasonably cohesive picture; it also introduces a number of new perspectives. In particular, congenial writings in cognitive science have been incorporated, as well as examples from Helen Keller's recollections of her childhood and quotations from Diane Ackerman's popular *A Natural History of the Senses*. In cognitive science, I have been particularly impressed by the 'cognitive rhetoric' advocated by Mark Turner. The book has likewise profited from his cognitive colleagues, especially from the work of Eve Sweetser, whose research on abstract terms is a mainstay of Chapter 9.

During the writing of the book, I also spent some time trying to understand why feminist writings that try to put the body into language have such a hard time arguing their case. I now believe that their difficulties have to do with the kind of language theory feminist writers have tended to embrace. On the other hand, the book shares with that literature the project of getting the body back into language. More precisely, I want to show how we can reinstate the body in our theories of language and meaning. After all, corporeality has always been part of language in all cultures. It is only our explanations about language that have lost sight of the body and the role it plays in verbal texts.

Books on meaning often begin by sorting out the various semantic roles the words 'mean' or 'meaning' play in discourse. Several such roles are traditionally distinguished. For example:

- 'What do you mean by "corporeal"?' could be rephrased by 'What do you have in mind when you say . . .?' or 'Could you give me another term for . . . ?'
- 'Don't make me angry; I mean it' suggests a firm intention.
- 'Have you seen the movie *The Meaning of Life*?' points to the role of life in the cosmos.
- 'Glances full of meaning . . . ' indicates that people are able to communicate important things without speaking.
- 'What does the word "turbocharger" mean?' asks for a verbal clarification, a picture, or some other referential explanation.
- In 'Green means on, red means off', 'means' could be replaced by 'stands for'.
- 'Your Christmas present means a lot to me' says that it is much appreciated and occupies a high rung in the speaker's value system.

Semantic theories then tend to sort out which of those uses of 'meaning' are within the scope of their inquiry and eliminate the others. No such strategy will be used here, for the simple reason that in some sense they all fall under the umbrella question of how language is able to 'mean' at all. And even in a seemingly marginal use of 'meaning', as in 'I mean it, and I won't take no for an answer', the emphasis achieved by the speech act suggests that more than an ordinary linkage between language and body is at stake. Certainly, in the picture of language advocated in this book, the body and its cognitive processes play a central role. Hence, indications of intention should not be ruled out. Indeed, nothing should be ruled out in principle, even if we can attend only to a limited number of principles and examples.

The following questions will have to be revisited: How does language relate to the world? Are meanings definitions? Are meanings concepts? Do concepts mediate between language and world? Does language play a role in the way we conceive the world? Can we only experience what our mother tongue codifies? Is language on a par with nonverbal sign systems? Do they all mean in the same way? Are nonverbal signs dependent on language or is language perhaps parasitic on nonverbal signs?

Chapter 1, 'The corporeal turn', sketches two competing trends in the way language has been viewed during the twentieth century. Around the turn of the century a way of thinking evolved which has been characterized as the 'linguistic turn' because of its focus on the medium in which we pose questions in philosophy and also in theories of language and meaning. The chapter suggests that the linguistic turn has now gone berserk and that a counter-movement, which I have termed 'the corporeal turn', has emerged to redress the balance.

Chapter 2, 'There is no meaning in language', argues that language is no more than a syntactic grid of empty sound schemata which does not mean anything by itself unless it is activated by nonverbal signs. This, the argument goes, occurs under the guidance of a semiotic community. Signifiers are shown to be meaningless by themselves, which renders the idea of an autonomous chain of signifiers problematic.

In Chapter 3, 'Meaning as quasi-perceptual', we return to some observations of Vico and Peirce relevant to a body-oriented theory of language. Findings in cognitive science are introduced to shore up a corporeal explanation of meaning, one in which quasi-perceptual processes of interpretation play a central role.

Chapter 4, 'The body in deixis and reference', faces two related tasks. One is to argue the importance of a culture's speech attitudes, or cultural deixis, especially in its implicit, yet concealed, forms. The second task is to revisit the old notion of reference – but with a difference. Both cultural deixis and cultural reference are shown to require quasi-perceptual fantasy acts for their construction. Redefined as intersemiotic, deixis and reference are reinstated as crucial aspects of the description of meaning and culture.

The following chapter, Chapter 5, 'Meaning as intersemiotic', addresses the nature of the interaction among different kinds of signs. Central to the argument here is the distinction between nonverbal sign combinations and the association between nonverbal and verbal signs. Whereas it is argued that nonverbal signs enjoy a certain limited autonomy, verbal signs are regarded as entirely parasitic on nonverbal semiosis. Nonverbal sign systems are able to stand in for one another (as do, for example, touch and smell for sight), but linguistic expressions are shown to be incapable of even a limited autonomy. On the one hand, the fact that we use them to sum up other sign systems is seen as a positive result of linguistic emptiness. It guarantees the economizing force of language. On the other hand, semantic self-reflexivity in language is not understood as merely linguistic. Once again, we need nonverbal signs to transform linguistic strings, or syntactic schemata, into meanings.

Next, in Chapter 6, 'Meaning as heterosemiotic', the book emphasizes the differences between different systems of signs. The necessary fact of inter-semiotic relations tends to obscure its functional opposite: that all signs also always stand in a more or less 'hostile' or heterosemiotic relation to one another. This suggests that the event of meaning is not a natural result of sign collaboration. Rather, the chapter suggests, we are always also dealing with a certain violence of association whenever meaning occurs.

Chapter 7, 'The disembodiment of the signifier', offers a broad-brush overview of the trajectory of signifiers from highly iconic (re)presentations to their disembodied, symbolic relations. The argument here is that the evolution of all signifiers proceeds from body-dependent marks to increasingly body-independent, conventionalized signifiers. This is claimed to apply to both oral and written signs. The notion of 'arbitrariness' is redescribed accordingly. The chapter asks the question: has corporeality, then, vanished altogether? The answer offered is No. Iconicity, it is argued, has been interiorized. It is alive and well in the signified.

Next, Chapter 8, 'The corporeality of the signified', resumes and elaborates on the claim made at the end of the previous chapter. Contrary to formal systems such as formal logic (and, to a certain degree, mathematics), the signifieds of natural language are shown to require the body to be semantically functional. At the level of the signified, we are iconic beings. This is argued with support from cognitive science and Heidegger's 'as-structure'. The chapter also attempts to explain why writers like Cixous, Irigaray, Banting and Grosz face difficulties in arguing the role of the body in a post-Saussurean conception of language.

Chapter 9, 'Social traces in abstract expressions', sets out to rebut the charge that corporeal semantics may go some way towards elucidating what goes on in concrete concepts but fails to demonstrate that the body plays any role in abstract terms and function words. In making its counter-claim, the chapter draws on observations made by Helen Keller, the work of Eve Sweetser, as well as Heidegger's analysis of the interpretive structure of assertion.

In the following chapter, Chapter 10, 'The role of the community', I deal with the question of how to avoid charges of 'mentalism' and 'subjectivism' in a body-oriented theory of meaning. The chapter argues that mental presentations are much more under social control than is generally assumed and that, vice versa, the so-called 'definitions' of linguistic expressions allegedly shared by members of a semiotic community are likewise subject to considerable variation. Both are declared intersubjective in a negotiatory sense and placed under the guidance of a community. To drive home the importance of nonverbal signification for language, the chapter redefines Wittgenstein's 'use' and 'form of life' and strengthens their interdependence.

Chapter 11, 'Sufficient semiosis', rejects the traditional approach to meaning via truth and truth-conditions. Instead, the chapter argues that in social discourse the interpretive complexities are such that truth-conditions are rendered inapplicable. It is only when natural-language examples are tailored to look like technical speech that truth-conditions look promising. What we need is a pragmatic theory of meaning that relies on social negotiation rather than definitions and exact checking mechanisms. Various kinds of semantic 'opacity' are shown to require intricate interpretive moves in aligning appropriate nonverbal signs with linguistic schemata. The question of how communication is possible at all in such a murky environment is answered by the notion of 'sufficient semiosis'.

Chapter 12, 'Semantic assumptions', begins by summing up the main axioms of the body-oriented theory of language advocated. The next step is to address the base assumptions of a number of traditional and recent descriptions of meaning. Empiricist, naturalist, behaviourist, relativist and structuralist principles are discussed, with a brief commentary on more recent positions. The chapter ends with a focus on cognitivist contributions to the debate and shows where cognitive insights collaborate with and differ from the stance taken in this book.

Finally, Chapter 13, 'Meaning, metaphysics and representation', suggests that no theory of language can escape certain metaphysical consequences. As soon as semantics comes into play, we have to decide whether we associate our theory with realist or relativist principles or want to steer a course between these or outside such polarities. This is so because meaning always implies a position as to how language and its speakers relate to the 'world'. The chapter argues that the interaction between nonverbal signs and verbal schemata works best from a position that one could term 'abductive' realism. Accordingly, we must insist on the significatory character of our nonverbal constructions of the world as well as of linguistic meaning events. At the same time, we are forced to acknowledge deep constraints inferred of necessity by cultures and reflected in the way the community guides semiotic performance. The chapter ends with a discussion of (re)presentation, with a focus on Derrida's reminder of the complexities involved in the term.

An Afterword concludes the book with a brief discussion of the much-debated possibility of a cyborg future and the question whether such a future would be incompatible with a body-oriented theory of language.

1. The corporeal turn

The linguistic turn

I want to start by questioning a powerful tradition that has dominated our thinking about language in the twentieth century. This is the widespread tendency to overestimate the role of 'linguistic definition' in language. We can crudely label this tradition 'the linguistic turn'. Briefly put, this refers to the realization that language itself needs to be carefully understood before we can deal with the phenomena it describes.

In its extreme form, the linguistic turn suggests that all philosophical problems, including those of meaning, are linguistic problems. Because the linguistic turn is motivated by a search for clarification, it has biased our view of language in two ways. One bias is the tendency to pursue definitional clarity; the other is the inclination towards resolving all language questions in terms of linguistic or, more seriously, syntactic relations.

How did these trends develop? Two thinkers at the beginning of the twentieth century bear most of the responsibility: the German Gottlob Frege and the French-Swiss Ferdinand de Saussure. Frege is generally regarded as the father of analytical philosophy, Saussure of structuralist linguistics. Most students of language know Frege as the theorist of 'sense' and 'reference'. Less well known than this distinction, and far more important, is that Frege failed to distinguish between two different kinds of 'sense'. He begins his seminal paper 'Sense and reference' (Frege, 1970) by equivocating, on the one hand, between the formal sense of the variables and constants of geometry and, on the other, the sense of natural-language expressions. In a disastrous move for the study of natural language, he proceeds without hesitation from the sense of 'a' and 'b', which are formally defined, to the sense of 'morning star' and 'evening star'. The consequences of this move still reverberate through analytical approaches as well as linguistic and popular descriptions of meaning (Ruthrof, 1993).

Then Frege took a second step, also with drastic consequences. He eliminated mental pictures that go with the meaning content of linguistic expressions. While this is, of course, consistent with a formal view of 'sense', it radicalizes Frege's description. We end up with a view of language that is too close by far to formal ideals. No wonder, then, that for the same formal reasons Frege and his successors have deplored the murkiness of natural languages.

What was the result of this illegitimate elimination of the imagined, iconic ingredients from language? We lost the perceptual and quasi-perceptual features that, I will show, play a crucial role in meaning. Language lost its semantic corporeality. Now, pure thought, Frege's 'sense', stands in for the missing body.

At about the same time, Saussure was teaching a new kind of linguistics in Geneva. The study of language was then ruled by philologists with a historical and etymological orientation. Saussure turned away from this to emphasize the systematic nature of linguistic relations, so establishing linguistics as a scientific discipline: structuralist linguistics. The brilliance of this achievement is not in question. What I seek to do here is correct some tendencies, mainly among his successors, that served to tighten the grip of the linguistic turn. Particularly important is the structuralist *intragrammatical* or *intersyntactic* emphasis, one of the mainstays of his arguments. This insists that both syntax and meaning in language are the result of the differential relations within the network of terms in a given language, independent of nonlinguistic referential relations. The destructive consequences of this emphasis for the study of meaning rival those of Frege's project.

Let me stress that these cursory criticisms of structural linguistics do not signal an intention to replace Saussure's intersyntactic strategy with one that revives empiricist referents. There are more promising solutions.

Ludwig Wittgenstein also assisted the linguistic turn, first in the *Tractatus Logico-Philosophicus*, by trying to show a homologous relation between propositional language and world, then by speaking of the 'bewitchment of our intelligence by language'. To be fair to the later Wittgenstein, many insights in his *Philosophical Investigations* (1953) and other manuscripts provide starting-points for a description of language congenial to the reintegration of the body (Wittgenstein, 1958). However, this avenue is open only if we redefine his terms 'use' and (particularly) 'form of life' from the perspective of corporeal semantics.

The papers in Richard Rorty's compilation *The Linguistic Turn: Essays in Philosophical Method* (1992) reflect the directions taken in the twentieth century by the philosophical emphasis on language. From Rudolf Carnap to Michael Dummett, philosophical problems are shown to be 'questions of language', while the theory of meaning is regarded as 'the foundation of all philosophy' (Dummett, 1973: 669). In an appendix, Rorty reviews his 25-year-old position on the question of the role of language in philosophy. Now he rejects 'the idea that philosophical problems can be dissolved by detecting the "logic of our language"' (Rorty, 1992: 373):

> insofar as the linguistic turn made a distinctive contribution to philosophy I think that it was not a metaphysical one at all. Its contribution was, instead, to have helped shift from talk about experience as a medium of representation to talk of language as such a medium – a shift which, as it turned out, made it easier to set aside the notion of representation itself.

Rorty also seems right when he observes that 'philosophers like Davidson, who speak of sentences instead of experiences, have an easier time' (373). However, the question is at what cost. Has the linguistic turn really resolved the problem of representation? Rorty appears to think so. And yet, to replace talk of 'experiences' by talk of 'sentences' solves only the problem of removing the ambiguity between 'sense-impressions' and 'belief' by making language self-referential. Unfortunately, the posited univocality of the 'sentence' is achieved at the dual cost of (a) treating natural language sense as if it was formal sense and (b) eliminating nonverbal ingredients (sensory readings of the world) from linguistic expressions.

It is worth stressing, though, that Rorty's comments on 'the death of meaning at the hands of Quine, Wittgenstein, Davidson and Feyerabend' are of a different order from that of the 'fatality of meaning' announced by Jean Baudrillard. What has died is an empiricist orthodoxy in which meanings were secured by verification procedures and truth conditions. Much the same can be said about Davidson's remark that 'it is good to be rid of representations', for what Davidson has in mind here are representations guaranteed by a 'correspondence theory of truth' (Rorty, 1992: 372). Giving up thinking about representations may indeed result in abandoning our 'interest in the relation between mind and the world or language and the world' (372) if that world is conceived as given rather than mediated by signs other than language.

Playing into the hands of the linguistic turn for a moment, one could say that perhaps the problem with representationalism and its critique is a particular usage of the term 'representation' as a kind of copying. If this is so, the problem appears differently in English from its non-English versions. Indeed, in 'Sending: on representation' (1982) Jacques Derrida has drawn our attention precisely to this point that the talk of representation as well as its critical opposition are in need of semantic-philosophical scrutiny. I will return to Derrida's remarks at the end of the book. When Frege eliminated as merely subjective the 'idea' or 'image' that may accompany a concept he used the German *Vorstellung*, a putting in front of oneself or a mental projection. Unlike re-presentation, *Vorstellung* is not tied to copying or any other form of repetition. *Vorstellungen* can vary from fairly close presentations to the most experimental distortions and indeed to entirely free inventions. Not that this would have satisfied Frege's need for a *Begriffsschrift*, a purely logical form of notation. But the semantic latitude of *Vorstellung* provides the kind of concept that would allow perceptual and quasi-perceptual realizations of the world to be a part of language.

The corporeal turn

From the very beginnings, Edmund Husserl's phenomenology, in spite of its idealizing tendency, carried within itself the seeds of the return of the body. True, the body appears mostly as a visualizing agency, a feature shared incidentally by the new disciplines of cognitive science. Yet without visual-ization as the perceptual ground from which consciousness arises and to which Husserl frequently refers, phenomenology could not do its work. Theme and horizon are first defined in terms of seeing and then transposed to other perceptual acts, as well as to acts of cognition and reflection. The definition of the phenomenon, as for instance of the apple-tree-as-it-appears-to-me, rests on visualization. So do Husserl's recollection, retention, protension and future projection. Various forms of reduction are performed in quasi-perceptual terms. Both the imaginative variation of objects and the realization of their adumbrational aspects in phenomenological reduction are derived from visual acts. Appresentation, the imagining of habitual but absent aspects of reality, is a quasi-perceptual procedure (Husserl, 1973). Sedimentations are likewise typified instances of perceptual experience, as is the totality of the typified lifeworld.

Clearly, the body cries out to become the focus of phenomenology. What bars Husserl from achieving the corporeal turn is his arithmetic and geomet-rical leaning, the logic in his autobiography, which finds its most succinct expression in the search for the eidos or underlying essences (Husserl, 1969). This search would not have proved detrimental had it remained restricted to the description of formal domains. Disaster struck, however, when Husserl attempted to find the eidos everywhere, and especially in language. There simply is no eidos in the expression 'late capitalism' or 'gender bias'. We now know roughly what it means here and now. Somewhere else, a few years later, spoken by other people, the phrases have taken on different meanings, ever so slightly perhaps and sometimes obviously so. Semantic drift rules out eidos and for that matter any other idealization. It is well known that in his later years Husserl became increasingly aware of the irreconcilable gulf that he had himself created between phenomenological description and the vivacity of the lifeworld, of which language is a fundamental ingredient. Various, substantive corrections of Husserl's ideality emerged from phenomenology itself. Think of Max Scheler's contributions to ethics, Alfred Schutz's to social philosophy, Roman Ingarden's and Mikel Dufrenne's to aesthetics, Heidegger's to the philosophy of Being, or Merleau-Ponty's to the phenomenology of perception.

One could construe a theory of the role of the body in Heidegger's philosophy by starting with such notions as the 'totality of involvements', 'Being-in-the-world', 'Being-towards-death', or *'Dasein'*. In doing this, one could draw on his view of the person as 'a performer of intentional acts' (Heidegger, 1962: 73) and his existential definition of what it is to be human. Arguing against traditional accounts of corporeality and spirituality, Heidegger rejects the idea of a human person 'as a spiritual Thing which subsequently gets misplaced "into" space' (83). For 'not until we understand Being-in-the-world as an essential structure of Dasein can we have insight into Dasein's *existential spatiality*' (83). Thus, 'man's "substance" is not spirit as a synthesis of soul and body; it is rather *existence*' (153). Yet according to Heidegger's overall emphasis, the body plays no more than a minor role in poetically and philosophically thoughtful existence.

Given that the corporeality had been so held in check in the Husserlian tradition, it was only to be expected that sooner or later the body should play a more prominent role. And so it does in most of Merleau-Ponty's writings. Corporeality comes to the fore in Merleau-Ponty as the body's integration into the world in the form of a post-Heideggerian, yet more sensuous being-in-the-world. Merleau-Ponty's 'primacy of perception' extends to Husserl's 'appresentation', the presentation to ourselves of hidden aspects of the lifeworld. Accordingly, things that are 'behind my back' are available to us in a kind of 'visual presence' (Merleau-Ponty, 1962: 6). In Merleau-Ponty's scenario, all 'elementary perception' is always 'already charged with meaning' (4). Indeed, perception is not only some kind of passive synthesis but rather 'just that act which creates at a stroke, along with the cluster of data, the meaning which unites them', so that perception 'causes them to have meaning' (36). Husserlian consciousness, then, is de-idealized to the extent that it is regarded as 'being towards the thing through the intermediary of the body' (139). For it is the realization of our corporeality that forces us 'to acknowledge an imposition of meaning that is not accomplished by a universal constituting consciousness' (171). We are directly linked with the things that make up our world by way of our body's 'own ontogenesis'. For Merleau-Ponty, 'it is the body and it alone' which is able to 'bring us to the things themselves' (Merleau-Ponty, 1968: 135f.). He speaks of 'the emergence of the flesh as expression' (1968: 145) which permits our access to things in a certain way: 'the thickness of the flesh between the seer and the thing is constitutive for the thing of its visibility'. The same applies to the relation between the one who does the seeings and his or her 'corporeity'. Indeed, 'it is their means of communication' (1968: 135).

Bodily extension in space and the body's kinetic scope function as first base for spatial representation. Hence, Merleau-Ponty regards 'motility' as the 'primary sphere in which initially the meaning of all significations in the domain of represented space is engendered' (1962: 51). At the same pre-cognitive level at which bodies move about in the world we also find his notion of desire, which 'comprehends blindly by linking body to body' (1962: 157). Awareness of my body grants a certain immediacy of primary significa-tion: 'my body immediately signifies a certain landscape about me' and 'my fingers a certain fibrous or grainy style of the object'. Here, Merleau-Ponty draws a distinction between two different kinds of meaning, to which we must return, the primary meaning generated by corporeal presence and 'languagely' meaning, the 'immanent meaning' of language (1964c: 88f.).

Another contribution to the corporeal turn is Merleau-Ponty's observation that although language has some 'inner content', we must not equate this with 'self-subsistent' or 'self-conscious thought'. Language, instead of expressing thoughts, is a subject's act of 'taking up a position in the world of meanings' (1962: 193). When this happens, 'it is the body which points out, and which speaks' (197). In agreement with phenomenological practice, meaning is not restricted to linguistic expressions but is a part of every perceptual performance by which we constitute our world:

> perception is just that act which creates at a stroke, along with the cluster of data, the meaning which unites them – indeed which not only discovers the meaning which we have, but moreover sees to it *that they have a meaning*. (36)

Merleau-Ponty distances himself from the headier Husserl by pointing out that it is the experience of the body that makes us realize that there are meaning acts which are not the result of a universal constituting conscious-ness. The conceptual meaning of words, he says, 'must be formed by a kind of deduction from a *gestural meaning*, which is immanent in speech' (179). Hence, the generality of a word 'is not that of the idea, but that of a behavioural style "understood" by my body' (403). The word, for Merleau-Ponty, is not

> inspected, analysed, known and constituted, but caught and taken up by a power of speech and, in the last analysis, by a motor power given to me along with the first experience I have of my body and its perceptual and practical fields. As for the meaning of the word, I learn it as I learn to use a tool, by seeing it used in the context of a certain situation. The word's meaning is not compounded of a certain number of physical characteristics belonging to the object; it is first and foremost the aspect taken on by the object in human experience, for example my wonder in the face of these hard, then friable, then melting pellets falling ready-made from the sky. (403)

This position, together with his emphasis on 'being-in-the-world', could be seen as the moment when the 'linguistic turn' meets up with the 'corporeal turn' as a corrective. And indeed, much of the *Phenomenology of Perception* (1962) as well as *The Primacy of Perception* (1964a) supports such a reading. One could expect, then, that a semantics which takes the body as its ground, though not its cause, would regard Merleau-Ponty's work as that of a founding father (Froman, 1982). Why this is not so has to do with his preoccupation with the unique position that human perception takes in the order of things, the belief that 'a word has a meaning' (1962: 177), the separation of the body as 'sensible' from the body as 'sentient' (1968: 136) and, most importantly, a hankering after a deep logos unwarranted in a corporeal theory of meaning.

When we read that 'a dog's gaze directed towards me causes me no embarrassment', we may be inclined to reply, 'What an insensitive bastard!' (1962: 361). Surely, under certain circumstances we respond to the gaze of animals with more than the cool, descriptive and bracketing attitude of a phenomenologist. Minute as his remark is, it suggests, together with a good deal of comparable evidence, that Merleau-Ponty's phenomenology of perception is an exclusively humanistic way of viewing the world, incompatible with a broader view of the cognitive processes of living organisms. If this is so, his orientation towards the body is far less valuable than it promises to be. For any theory of meaning that goes beyond the linguistic must be able to accommodate in some form the findings of cognitive science and in particular the typical mapping processes which humans appear to share with at least some other animals.

A more serious reason for disqualifying Merleau-Ponty's contribution to a corporeal semantics is his nostalgia for a deep logos underlying everything, including the primacy of perception. In a comment on Husserl's procedure he approvingly explains that

> our existence is too tightly held in the world to be able to know itself as such at the moment of its involvement, and that it requires the field of ideality in order to become acquainted with and to prevail over its facticity.

It is via Husserl's essences that we are able to reflect on 'all the living relationships of experience'. In this perspective, 'it is the office of language to cause essences to exist in a state of separation which is in fact merely apparent, since through language they still rest upon the ante-predicative life of consciousness' (Merleau-Ponty, 1962: xv). Language is able to do this because there is a prior logos to which it relates, the 'Logos of the perceived world' (1964a: 10). This 'pre-existent Logos is the world itself' (1962: xx). Only metaphorically speaking, one should add.

In the end, Merleau-Ponty is unable to free his phenomenology from Husserlian, eidetic convictions. In spite of his emphasis on the body and our being-in-the-world, perception nevertheless remains a 'nascent logos' (1964a: 25). As to language, he conceives of an expression as 'perfect to the extent that it is unequivocally understood'. Language is a case in which we observe the 'surpassing of the signifying by the signified' (1964c: 90). But we have here a signified that is less corporeal than eidetic. Univocality, strictly a feature only of formal signs, is also a linguistic possibility in Merleau-Ponty because 'the being of language' is to be conceived of as 'logic in contingency' or 'incarnate logic' (1964c: 87f.). The upshot of this hankering after an overarching essence is revealed in *The Visible and the Invisible*, where he assures us that 'there is an essence beneath us, a common nervure of the signifying and the signified' (1968: 118). And this is why Merleau-Ponty (1964b) cannot bring himself to embrace entirely the notion of thought as corporeal. Instead, he seems to be torn between two irreconcilable alternatives, his own corporeal insights and a logocentric philosophical tradition. And so he opts for the in-between of an '*almost* carnal existence of the idea' (207). For the same reason, and in spite of his corporeal emphasis, he speaks of thought and perception of space as being 'liberated' in the end from our primary 'motility and being-in-space' (51).

We find, then, that Merleau-Ponty's corporeal turn founders on his retreat to something less or more than the body and an all-embracing essence which underlies everything and appears in contingent guise in human speech. Contrary to his much-celebrated insistence on the primacy of the body, at a closer look logos still rules. This is where a radical emphasis on corporeality differs: here logos is always construable after the fact. Such is the nature of human consciousness and such must be the 'stuff' of the universe, that we are able to signify in a wide variety of discursive practices: generalization as well as formalization, poetic speech and realist presentations, culture-specific descriptions and scientific observations, human-scale response and readings by the most sophisticated instruments. By employing different kinds of signs we signify the world. The later Wittgenstein's position on these matters is congenial when he tells us that mathematics should be regarded as an anthropological phenomenon (Wittgenstein, 1978: 399), as should doing logic and proofs (352f. and 61). To say, as Merleau-Ponty does, that logos is there in the first place or as primary ground is no more than a leap of faith, an unwarranted move – shared, one might add, by some prominent physicists. We must look elsewhere.

For some time now, the body has been a dominant feature in feminist theorizing. And to the degree that it has, we could speak of a feminist corporeal turn, were it not for the fact that such writing has had a difficult time finding convincing arguments that would allow the insertion or reinstatement or, more appropriately, the rediscovery of the body in language. The motivation for and even necessity of such moves are not in question. What I want to draw attention to is the problematic of the precise theoretical point, avenue or process by means of which the body can be shown to be in language.

The most relevant work in this respect is that of Julia Kristeva, Luce Irigaray and Hélène Cixous. Yet all three shy away from the ultimate step of designing a theory of language based on the body. I will explain why I think this is so in Chapter 8. Here I want to say only that these difficulties have to do with the structuralist leaning these writers share on questions of meaning. The work of Julia Kristeva on language is, of course, exemplary and path-breaking. I will have more to say about her position in relation to linguistics, summed up in her *Language the Unknown: An Initiation into Linguistics* (1989). What interests us here is Kristeva's insights into the role of corporeality in signification. Her wilful use of the term 'semiotic' to characterize fermenting creativity in contrast to symbolic control can be seen as an entry point to an alternative attitude to language in opposition to formal and empiricist semantic assumptions. In particular, Kristeva's description of what she terms the *genotext* adds a new dimension to language theory. The genotext includes 'semiotic processes but also the advent of the symbolic'. It

> includes drives, their disposition and their division in the body, plus
> the ecological and social systems surrounding the body, such as objects
> and pre-Oedipal relations with parents. . . . Designating the genotext in

a text requires pointing out the transfers of drive energy that can be detected in phonematic devices ... and melodic devices, in the way semantic and categorial fields are set out in syntactical and logical features, or in the economy of mimesis (fantasy, the deferment of denotation, narrative, etc.). The genotext is thus the only transfer of drive energies that organizes a space in which the subject is not yet a split unity that will become blurred, giving rise to the symbolic. (Kristeva, 1986: 120f.)

Importantly, 'the genotext is not linguistic' but acts as 'language's underlying foundation' (121). Though Kristeva has found a way of accounting for the presence of the body in signification, she bars it from entering the symbolic order, language as social communication. The body remains a preliminary, even if foundational, condition for linguistic structures. From the perspective of linguistic meaning, the genotext remains subservient to the phenotext. Such is her commitment to the tenets of structural linguistics, in spite of her critical comments on that very tradition. So it is perhaps not surprising that Kristeva's most significant contribution to the 'corporeal turn' is not to be found in her work on language, but rather emerges from her psycho-analytical practice. In her book *In the Beginning Was Love: Psychoanalysis and Faith* (1987), Kristeva embraces the body much more readily as an aspect of meaning. And although her remarks are made in the context of her psycho-analysis, I suggest that they are of the utmost importance to a reorientation in semantics. Starting from the innocuous premise that 'the object of psycho-analysis is simply the *linguistic exchange*' (1), she moves on to make startling claims. In psychoanalysis, she says,

language works with signs that encompass representations of at least three types: representations of words (close to the linguistic signifier), representations of things (close to the linguistic signified), and repre-sentations of affects (labile psychic traces subject to the primary processes of displacement and condensation, which I have called *semi-otic* as opposed to the *symbolic* representations inherent in, or derivative of, the system of language). (Kristeva, 1987: 4)

It would seem that Kristeva is advocating a broad view of (re)presentation, from near repetition to imaginative extensions. Importantly, without any acknowledgement of such representations the analyst could not do her job. I suggest that what applies to Kristeva's psychoanalytic situation equally holds in ordinary language use. Indeed, she concludes by looking at lan-guage precisely in this way. We 'develop a powerful model of the human in which language *is not divorced from the body*; "word" and "flesh" can meet at any moment, for better or for worse' (6; emphasis added). More radically, I propose to change this 'can' rule into a mandatory relation. Word and flesh are not only occasionally aligned but always and of necessity so. Likewise, what Kristeva has to offer psychoanalytic interpretation could be broadened to apply to all processes of meaning-making: 'From this tissue of meanings, ranging from prelinguistic emotional traces to linguistic representations and, by extension, to ideologies (symbolic representations), the analyst attempts to interpret the essential discourse of his patients, that is, their symptoms and fantasies' (6). Yet far from fantasies being some sort of sickness to be healed, fantasies, as I shall argue, are a *sine qua non*, a condition without which we could not walk, let alone speak. They are not only 'truths of the speaking subject' but the general ground on which all language depends. Again and again, Kristeva addresses fundamental principles that contradict orthodox semantic assumptions. For example, she speaks of 'emotions too subtle for words' (6), thus implicitly challenging the dominant conception that our most differentiated experiences are those coded in language. This supports the observation of communities in which only a very limited number of colour terms are in use, even though a finely differentiated scale of colours is registered by nonlinguistic means. More on this subject later.

Patients' fantasies, in Kristeva's practice, are regarded as 'references to the past' which she tries to transform into beneficial 'new configurations' (7). This kind of investigation leads her to the deep corporeal ground of human signification. 'At the extreme limit of the psychic traces,' she writes, 'beyond the *representations* of words or things, we find the ultimate *marks* of the biochemical processes that take place in a subject interacting with another subject'. For Kristeva, such marks are always already involved in the semiotic processes of 'desire and communication' as pre-signs (8). It should not come as much of a surprise that this kind of search in the end should deal with preconditions of language, one of the most prominent research enterprises in recent years in cognitive science and cognitive linguistics. Not that Kristeva could in any way be directly associated with such research. Nevertheless, we cannot but note how her corporeal emphasis in language produces results compatible, to a certain extent, with cognitive insights.

As speaking beings, always potentially on the verge of speech, we have always been divided, separated from nature. This split has left within us traces of the pre- or translinguistic semiotic processes that are our only access to the species memory or the bioenergetic neuronal maps. These semiotic processes (archaic traces of the links between our erogenous zones and those of the other, stored as sonorous, visual, tactile, olfactory, or rhythmic traces) diachronically constitute a *pre-subject* (the *infans*). (8)

Psychology of a very different kind has recently begun to make its mark in the discussion of semantic processes from the perspective of corporeality. Since the demise of strict behaviourism, a broad front of psychologists has turned cognitive and so has been in a position to look at the inside behaviour of cognition, the cognitive processes themselves. Even in this turn to cognition, approaches to meaning vary from computational models to experimentation with visual creativity. But, as Jerome Bruner shows, psychology, when it focuses on meaning, 'inevitably becomes a cultural psychology' and so 'must venture beyond the conventional aims of positivist science with its ideals of reductionism, causal explanation and prediction' (Bruner, 1990: xiii). Leonard Bloomfield's behaviourist frame of analysis is hardly recognizable in the cognitivist formulation, which sees its task as 'so compellingly important that it deserves all the rich variety of insight that we can bring to the understanding of what man makes of his world, of his fellow beings, and of himself' (xiii). While most traditional theories of language have found it difficult to accommodate mental projections of the world, cognitive science appears to be offering a new corporeal turn. As Rollins observes, traditionally 'mental images fall between the cracks of scientific explanation' because they are 'formal configurations without formal rules' (Rollins, 1989: 31). Now cognitive linguistics is beginning to open its perspective to our mental world. However, as it does so it is not yet able to address the body in its entirety but favours its visual mechanisms. At the forefront of its research are visual, *cognitive maps*.

In *Changing Visions: Human Cognitive Maps, Past, Present and Future* (1996), Laszlo *et al.* bring cognitive research up to date, defining cognitive maps as 'mental representations of the world in which we live'. Cognitive mapping is seen as an activity by which we construct 'dynamic models of the environments in which we carry out our daily lives'. As a result, the world of objects as well as our social environment is a web 'woven of individual cognitive maps' (3). The authors reconcile 'the constancy of the perceived world', retinal optics, neural chain reactions and interpretive labour to form an overall picture of pattern recognition (4f.). This stands in contrast to explanations based on narrow bottom-up computational processes whose 'computational cost' renders them unlikely candidates for a satisfactory explanation of how we process information. According to cognitive scientists, the human brain is simply not equipped 'to carry out multiple operations in the space of nanoseconds' (5).

Instead, cognitive science offers an approach in which basic models of neuron activity are combined with a top-down approach according to which previously stored contexts greatly narrow the search to 'objects most likely to be seen' (5). Visual presuppositions then predetermine what is likely to be cognized as a 'search image controls the action of the brain while looking for a given object' (16). This allows for errors in our nonverbal readings of the world. Just as a preconceived string of verbal signifiers can block communication, so too can a search image impede the recognition of unexpected visual information. What are termed 'secondary characteristics' in cognitive science, such as 'colour and taste, values and morals' (93), are all 'readings' in semiotic terms. And although cognitive science so far has favoured visual readings, the creation of our three-dimensional spatial experience by the interaction of different sensory readings can be extended to allow for other nonverbal dimensions. Applying the principle of semiotic corroboration, one could say the more nonverbal readings of a different kind, the more real our world. Moreover, cognitive science has opened its doors to the role of fantasy in our mental construction of our environment. Here it is 'the frontal lobe, the most recent evolutionary development of the neocortex, that is uniquely involved in creating images of the future, and with projecting ourselves as active agents into those images' (101). As neuropsychiatrist Gordon Globus and his co-workers assure us, the human brain is able to fantasize endless varieties of alternative worlds, a 'virtual holoworld of possible worlds' (Globus *et al.*, 1976: 378). The question is whether cognitive science is able to transfer the role that acts of fantasy play in ordinary cognition also to its description of language. For a semantics grounded in the body, fantasy acts are of course crucial as an ingredient of meaning. For an answer to this question let us turn to the cognitive branch of the philosophy of language.

In *The Body in the Mind: The Bodily Basis of Meaning, Imagination, and Reason* (1987), Mark Johnson reaffirms the centrality of the imagination and the body for human cognition: 'Without imagination, nothing in the world could be meaningful. Without imagination, we could never make sense of our experience. Without imagination, we could never reason toward knowledge of reality' (1987: ix). And without the body we could not imagine anything; the forms of our imagination 'grow out of bodily experience' (xiv). It also follows that the imagination so grounded in the body is 'central to human meaning' (172). Image schemata, by which we process the particulars of the world, and the 'metaphorical projections' which we are able to mould with their help, are seen as 'experiential structures of meaning' that are important in our construction of daily reality as well as of 'most of our abstract understanding and reasoning' (xvi). And so, understanding is best described as 'a historically and culturally embedded, humanly embodied, imaginatively structured event' (175). Using a near-Heideggerian way of putting it, Johnson calls understanding 'one's way of being in, or having, a world' (137).

Johnson's body-oriented philosophy offers a post-Kantian view of understanding reworked from the perspective of cognitive science. What comes out is a bottom-up description of mental processes such as meaning constructions and their imaginative extensions, well equipped to critique linguistic and philosophical perspectives. In particular, Johnson takes issue with the dominant assumptions of the propositional nature of language and what goes with it: tight reference, truth-conditional arguments, and definitional sense. Attractively, he replaces this 'objectivism' by a preference for analogue reasoning grounded in imagination. This is compatible on a number of fronts with the way corporeal semantics argues its case. That there are nevertheless a number of disagreements is not of importance here, but I will address some of them at a later stage (Chapter 12).

In cognitive linguistics and especially in the work of John Lakoff and his co-authors, Mark Johnson and Mark Turner, cognitive science made its powerful entry into the study of language and meaning. To keep matters brief, I single out in summary fashion the recent research by Mark Turner. What he terms 'cognitive rhetoric' is closely related to the interests of Lakoff, Sweetser, Fauconnier and Johnson. What is remarkable about his work is his extension of cognitive science and semantics to literary meaning and its feedback effect on the description of ordinary language. In agreement with his colleagues, Turner offers a cognitive linguistics that 'allots the key role to semantics'. His *Reading Minds: The Study of English in the Age of Cognitive Science* (1991) is an impassioned plea for a revival of the teaching of English literature from the perspective of language and its cognitive structures. This is to be achieved by refocusing our attention on the cognitive processes of meaning, which find their most sophisticated form in literature. At the centre of this study is the body and the role it plays in the way we understand both language and world.

Turner makes the startling observation that 'understanding the unusual is simple – a slight extension of understanding the obvious'. Using the description of habitual processes of deciphering the world as presented in cognitive science, Turner shows how literary language is grounded in the very same structures of perception. He writes:

> It should be remarkable that we can see a connection between the visual image of our hands and the linguistic construction 'Harvard Yard in April: April in Harvard Yard'. It should be even more remarkable that such a mysterious recognition is conducted unconsciously, automatically, and effortlessly. (68)

Emphasizing the role of symmetry in our constructions of world and language, Turner reminds us that 'we have a felt, embodied understanding of bilateral symmetry, and we employ this schematic understanding constantly, moment to moment, in every aspect of our existence, to make sense of the world and to interact with it' (70). Given this leaning, it is not surprising that Turner would reject the orthodoxy of separating 'syntax from meaning, language from other cognitive systems, grammar from the lexicon, semantics from pragmatics, and literal from figurative language' (20f.). Literary language, like the language of everyday life, is based on 'shared human conceptual patterns', which in turn can be given satisfactory explanations only when we embrace the notion of the mind as corporeal:

> The brain is what knows about the body. The brain manipulates the body. Brain patterns are the body's meaning and the body's understanding. To say that a human being is a mind that is a brain is not to leave out the body. (35)

Turner's bottom-up approach, however, does not favour the study of narrowly referential language. Quite the contrary: he prefers a cognitive review of the most elaborate literary tropes. And far from leading to a reduction of literary uses of language to base propositions, Turner celebrates the complexities of linguistic experimentation. His pedagogic aim is a broad one, namely the revitalization of English Literature. Whether his ambitious goal of creating a new umbrella under which to unite the current theoretical diversity in the study of English and Cultural Studies can be accomplished from the premises of cognitive science and its rehabilitation of the body will have to be seen.

To grant the corporeal turn its due in the description of language we must allow for certain features which we intuitively feel to be important: that we communicate meanings; that they somehow relate to the world we live in; that language coheres as a system; that language is not a private affair but that we are taught how to use it; and that our sensory readings have something to do with the way we express ourselves. Traditional theories of meaning do a good job in explaining some of these observations. A semantic theory that is based on the assumption that meanings are governed by definitions is able to explain how it is possible to communicate but is not very convincing when it comes to explaining how such definitions link up with the world we experience through our sensory readings. An empiricist and naturalist semantics that declares meaning to be the linking of language and world runs into difficulties in showing how a sign system such as language can be associated with a physically given world without mediation. For as soon as we allow the idea of mediation into our equation we note that the world, as a culture sees it, is closely related to the signs that culture uses, including those of its language. In naturalist semantics this circularity should be regarded as a flaw. There are other assumptions about meaning that characterize a number of different kinds of semantics which I will address later (Chapter 12). Here I only want to clarify briefly a crucial question, one that is at the heart of much of what follows.

The question is how we can best describe the relation between how we 'grasp' and 'see' the 'world' on the one hand and how we speak about the 'world', on the other. The many quotation marks suggest that these seemingly simple terms hide unexpected difficulties. By 'seeing the world' I refer to the many ways in which we are in bodily contact with our environment: through touch, smell, taste, our sense of gravity, of heat, of proximity and movement, of time, sound and sight. Somehow our brain enables our mind to reconcile these various readings into a more or less coherent 'world'. So by 'world' we do not mean the 'stuff' that gives rise to the most contradictory pictures such as a table seen and a table scanned by an electron microscope, the one a familiar Gestalt, the other a net of holes and moving particles. By 'world' we mean the human-scale construction of our environment – a construction which is in the first instance nonverbal.

As I will try to demonstrate, the linkage between language and our nonverbal construals is at the heart of meaning. Yet before this connection can be made persuasive, I must first show that words and linguistic expressions in their customary syntactic sequence are no more than an arbitrarily agreed-upon set of markers for speaking and writing. By themselves they are meaningless schemata. In this sense language is empty and makes no sense at all. This is the topic of the next chapter.

2. There is no meaning in language

What does the title of this chapter mean? Does it mean that I agree with theorists who have removed meaning from linguistics, who, in Roman Jakobson's words, have made meaning 'a no man's land'? (Jakobson, 1971e: 567).

No. What I am saying is that language as a set of linguistic expressions does not mean at all. There is no meaning in language, no meaning in the dictionary. Language in this sense is as arbitrary as any set of symbolic signs. As Ferdinand de Saussure assures us, 'The bond between the signifier and the signified is arbitrary. Since I mean by sign the whole that results from the associating of the signifier with the signified, I can simply say: the linguistic sign is arbitrary' (Saussure, 1974: 67f.). Here, Saussure draws three far-reaching conclusions. First, since the relation between signifier and signified is arbitrary, therefore the sign as a whole and, by implication, the signified must also be arbitrary. Second, he infers that arbitrariness is also the typical character of semiosis in general and, third, that language is particularly well suited to demonstrate this. Hence, in Saussure's view, 'linguistics can become the master-pattern for all branches of semiology' (68).

This position has two main drawbacks. For one, it makes it virtually impossible to find a place for nonverbal readings, such as tactile or aural mappings of the world, inside our linguistic, conceptual frames. Moreover, once we have declared our master theory of investigation to be language we will find it extremely difficult to discover anything in nonverbal semiotic domains that is not already prefigured in language. In other words, we will only rediscover quasi-linguistic characteristics. Yet to understand how tactile or olfactory semiosis works it seems a dubious starting-point to suggest that they must operate like linguistic signs. To apply a *reductio ad absurdum* to this problematic, we could ask what the haptic and olfactory equivalents are to noun phrases, present participles, the passive voice, and so on. We should avoid this kind of linguistic imperialism that blinds rather than enlightens.

We must remain open to the possibilities that nonverbal signs operate differently from their natural-language relations. So arbitrariness is not as clear-cut as structuralist linguistics has us believe. We will return to this question later.

As to semantics, we must also tread carefully when we encounter the structuralist conviction that meanings are the result of the differential relations between terms. For we note very quickly that there is no meaning in the differential relations between signifiers and their explanation via other signifiers when we look at a foreign-language text, say Malay, or hear it spoken. We 'know' that it is a language, so we know that we are dealing with systemically related signifiers, but the signifiers remain meaningless. This is as obvious as it is baffling. For as soon as we start an explanation we find ourselves in the deep and murky waters of folk myth and controversial semantic theories. We must proceed with great care. Once we do, we will realize that we must seriously qualify the idea that 'in a syntagma a term acquires its value only because it stands in opposition to everything that precedes or follows it, or to both' (Saussure, 1974: 123).

This is so, no doubt, if you know the language, which begs the question of meaning. One can demonstrate the validity of the 'intragrammatical' or syntactical, relational argument only by tracing the steps that are necessary in order to ascend from the cognition that we are dealing with signifiers to the level of the signified. In other words, we must show how the sounds of linguistic expressions become meaningful in a social sense. To anticipate the solution in summary form, the very Saussurean sign as a relation between signifier and signified can come about only when we exit language, when we combine the empty schemata of linguistic expressions with nonverbal signs. This not only flies in the face of the structuralist tradition but likewise challenges a series of other semantic orthodoxies.

Let me remind the reader of the famous case of the blind and deaf Helen Keller, to which I will refer frequently in this book. We learn from her written documents that only once the relationship was established between her sense interpretations of her surroundings and language in the form of tactile spelling into her hand was she able to deal with language in a semantic sense. Once that was achieved, learning to speak proved a relatively simple affair. I say this, because this is precisely how Ms Keller herself later describes the process. Nothing linguistic can be easy for a person who is both entirely blind and deaf. The point is that Helen took years to proceed from simple signs and pantomime to being able to read and write, while she learned to speak within only eleven lessons. Within one hour, the child had acquired six phonemes and within a few weeks she was able to use entire phrases:

the delight I felt when at my call Mildred ran to me or my dogs obeyed
my commands. It is an unspeakable boon to me to be able to speak in
winged words that need no interpretation. As I talked, happy thoughts
fluttered up out of my words that might perhaps have struggled in vain
to escape from my fingers. (Keller, 1954: 60)

The eager pupil is astonished 'to find how much easier it is to talk than to
spell with the fingers'. And all this in the face of this immense obstacle of
having to sense other people's responses by tactile readings. 'I had to use the
sense of touch in catching the vibrations of the throat' (60).

   The problem with this sort of phrasing is that depending on what we take
language to include and what 'in' precisely stands for we could be saying
something outrageously wrong or offering a proposition to be taken seriously. So let us try to clarify. Let us use the term 'language' in the strict sense
of a natural language like Japanese or French or an artificial language, such as
various kinds of symbolic logic. This means signification systems with
recognizable, fairly complex syntactic structures. For the sake of clarity we
must also avoid the widespread metaphorical use of the term 'language' to
cover all forms of communication. So the signifiers 'language', 'signification'
and 'communication' are used here not even as rough synonyms. Language
is a form of communication, but not all communication and signifying
systems are languages. The reason for this separation is not mere pedantry.
For if we talk of the language of painting, the language of gesture, body
language, the language of touch and so on, we have blurred the very
distinctions that will prove essential for a clarification of how language as a
collection of linguistic expressions is related to as well as dependent on
nonverbal signification (Sebeok *et al.*, 1981).

   As Diane Ackerman observes in *A Natural History of the Senses*, touch is able
not only to comfort but also to heal, and 'touching is just as therapeutic as
being touched; the healer, the giver of touch, is simultaneously healed' (1991:
121). There appears to be a certain independence of nonverbal signs which
we do not find in language. Linguistic signs are always parasitic on nonverbal signification. No matter what expressions we use, if they are not
spoken soothingly, they will not comfort. The nonverbal deictic additions to
linguistic schemata make all the difference. In German you say '*der Ton macht
die Musik*', the intonation is what is important in music. In language, sound
acts both as primary signifier and as corporeal 'colouring'. Other such
metalinguistic additions are body stance, ways of looking, breathing and so
on, all of which cannot be separated from the description of natural language
without an unwarranted and illegitimate reductionism. These are well-
established principles in any pragmatic approach to language. However, as

we shall see, in addition to such necessary metalinguistic signs language is *parasitic* on nonverbal signification in an even more crucial sense: language needs nonverbal mental projections to mean at all.

What the expression 'there is no meaning in language' suggests is that linguistic signifiers even in standard grammatical order are in themselves no more than empty grids or sound patterns which attain meaning only under very specific circumstances. This is how, for example, speakers of Italian might confront, say, an Indonesian dictionary. They would be able to produce the sounds of the language so that Indonesians would understand what was being read. In this situation the native Italians are able to perform no more than the rough intonation and syntax of the language, while the Indonesian listeners are able to move to the level of semantics or meaning. Different theories of language give different explanations of how precisely the Indonesian native speakers are able to do this. Uncontroversially, we could say that language consists of sounds in a certain syntactic order plus something else. It is this 'something else' to which this book will give a 'corporeal' answer. Let us say at this point that the Indonesian speakers are able to construe meanings because the community has taught them what sort of world they should imagine when they hear certain sound sequences. If this kind of explanation feels intuitively right, we need to remind ourselves that it does not concur with orthodox semantic theories.

Our Italian friends, we could say on the other hand, have produced no more than empty signifiers. They know by the conventions of dictionaries that what they are speaking is a natural language. So they know that they are dealing with signifiers rather than with non-signs (if there is such a thing). This is a situation in which signifiers are strictly separated from signifieds. Likewise, for me, a Japanese script is a series of signifiers without signifieds. Empty signifiers, though, have been claimed to occur not just under the sort of circumstances construed here. There is a tendency in some recent theorizing to claim that signifiers are empty even for the native speaker of language. We need to look at this radical claim.

There seem to be two versions of the argument. One, which I call metaphorical, suggests that the movement from signifier to signified, from phrase to concept, never quite delivers the goods. Jacques Derrida has made a major contribution to this perspective by rejecting the assumed saturation of the sign by a stable meaning or *presence*. Instead, following Peirce, he has shown that we always find ourselves in an endless chain of signs. But while he has removed the assumed stability of the signified he has not done away with meaning altogether. To express the point technically, he has destabilized the phenomenological noema while retaining its noetic directionality. What is often forgotten, though, is that the relativization introduced by the stronger emphasis on the double differentiation of temporal and spatial differing is only a sharpening of something Husserl himself had already emphasized. The 'now' of conceptual realization is no more than an idealization. Husserl speaks of a 'continuum which is continuously modified' so that 'the pure now' of perception 'is just an ideal limit, something abstract which can be nothing for itself' (Husserl, 1966: 62f.). What Derrida adds is to tell us that even the heuristic use of such an idealized 'now' is misleading. Whenever we signify anything, we do know what our 'gaze' is directed towards (directionality), but the precise circumscription of the concept itself remains forever deferred. We know what we are talking about, but when we begin to pursue the specific qualities of the signified 'object', we find that we could continue our signifying acts for ever. This is why one can say that we stand in a metaphorical relation to what we signify. Signification in natural language at least is a process characterized by *différance*, the condition of difference, and *metapherein*, a process of being carried away (Derrida, 1973; 1978).

In this move, Derrida also elaborates Heidegger's 'as-structure'. For Heidegger, understanding is a process in which we always grasp something as something else. Theoretically at least, this implies the possibility of an infinite chain of signs pervading the entirety of a culture from ever new perspectives. However, it would be a mistake to conclude from this that such a chain consists only of signifiers without any signifieds. As long as we keep in mind the tentative and fleeting nature of the signified, this picture is consistent with the facts of cognition and ultimately the idea of a cohesive, even if gradually changing, lifeworld. What we have is directionality without finality rather than the radical demise of the signified.

From this perspective, the Lacanian leap to the collapse of the signified into the signifier does not appear to be warranted (Lacan, 1974). If the signified is to be equated with desire and desire cannot ever be fulfilled, that does not mean that we are unable to fantasize. Simply because we cannot hang on to our fantasies does not mean that they do not play a powerful role in cognition. Indeed, the signified may be very well described as the fantasies that a culture attaches to linguistic signifiers. Or, to adopt a revised Lacanian perspective, the signified is the imaginary in the shadow of the symbolic order.

Again, then, to say that language is an empty schema does not mean that signifiers can be substituted for signifieds. The converse appears to be the case. Signifieds cannot be cashed by further merely linguistic ingredients. To mean is to step outside of language. The remainder of the book is an attempt to justify this claim.

An argument related to the endless chain of signifiers can be found in

Deleuze and Guattari, who otherwise have a great deal to offer to a corporeal semantics. On the topic of the 'asignifying sign' and the 'declination' of the signified, though, it is difficult to take them by their word. An asignifying sign is a concept difficult to grasp. A sign is a sign by virtue of a cultural, social rule that gives it a directionality. This directionality typically links different significatory domains. So one could say that a musical notation is a sign that directs a musician towards performing a sound in a certain way. It is not semantic, to be sure, but not asignifying either. Taken literally, a string of asignifying linguistic signs would amount to no more than syntax. And as long as there are no social agreements as to how to associate such a syntax with specific semantic values we are indeed dealing with mere signifiers, or asignifying signs. Surely this is not what Deleuze and Guattari have in mind.

Take Guattari's description of the Concorde, which is made up of 'several universes of reference, each with its specific mechanisms': there is a 'dia-grammatic universe' of blueprints and plans which is aligned with 'technological universes', 'industrial universes', a 'collective imagination', a 'desire to make it happen', as well as 'political and economic universes', so that the production of the plane can be guaranteed and profits secured (even if this turns out to be an illusion). The final production of the Concorde is accomplished, according to Guattari, 'through the conjunction of asignifying signs' (Goodchild, 1996: 49f.). What is happening here? It would seem that what we can observe in this complex network of sign relations is a surplus rather than a poverty of signifieds, an explosion rather than an implosion of the sign. How can we say that those compound webs of significatory practices result in asignification? Geometrical signs interact with technical instructions, mathematical codes, signs marking industrial processes, com-plex social interactions, financial calculations, economic networks, political agendas, and so on. How can such a 'rhizome' be anything but signifying in the most elaborate manner? We are certainly always dealing with signifiers in the first instance, but if we could not associate them with specific non-verbal construals – that is, signifieds – then we would not be in a position to understand, let alone debate, the matter.

Surely, Guattari must have some other aim that does not come across well in translation. One suspects that whenever French theoretical metaphors are translated into analytical English, things go wrong. Only formal variables and constants can be said to be asignifying. They do not signify unless they are provided with a secondary formal system or other referential relations that point outside their formal grammar. By themselves they are mere place-holders embedded in formal syntactic strings. By contrast, natural-language signs are what they are for the speech community by virtue of the culturally controlled manner in which they guide speakers to fantasize a world and its relations. Having struggled through Guattari's complex semantic network, and not just syntactic operations, to get to the point of seeing how the project of building the Concorde emerges out of signs, the reader cannot but conclude that Guattari understands the term 'asignifying' other than in its technical sense. It appears that 'asignifying' alerts us to the dynamics of significatory 'declination' as well as to the infinite regress of meaning theorized a century ago by Charles Sanders Peirce.

'Declination' appears to imply the weaker thesis that we never quite achieve a full signified. This is familiar from Derrida's work and is summed up in Deleuze and Guattari by the observation that there is 'always a declination of the sign away from its signified' (Ruthrof, 1997c: 249f.). This is a very different claim from what we have just discussed. That signifieds are never fulfilled, are always deferred, carried away and are in a sense no more than metaphoric presentations is persuasive. From the perspective that wants to reinstate the body in language one could say that linguistic expressions are directional pathways to nonverbal fantasies about the world. In one sense, 'declination' rules out the asignifying sign. For if a sign were not to signify we could not say from what something was declining. Declination entails that we can distinguish different signifieds, even if such signifieds are unstable and highly tentative entities. A minimal requirement for declination would seem to be a certain directionality. We need to know at least roughly what to look for, smell for, listen to, grope towards, be sensitive to, and so on. Directionality is part of the social contract of signs. Phrased in this fashion, 'declination' looks like a good way of describing the tentative relation that exists in the formation of signs between signifiers and signifieds and the construal of a world.

A second kind of argument is a more radical one: meaning is dead. In this case signifiers are indeed empty. This is a position we find most unambiguously expressed in the later writings of Jean Baudrillard. Much of this work celebrates the perceived collapse of social semantics into the surface of the syntax of signifying systems. Beyond Derrida and Deleuze/Guattari, Baudrillard abandons altogether the dialectic of signifier and signified. All we now have is signifiers, while meaning is not only dead but 'fatal' (1984: 38f.). As a consequence we live in a world characterized by 'reversibility and indetermination'. Communication has become a 'closed circuit' because the social contract of how to associate signifiers with signifieds in a cohesive manner no longer exists (1987: 71). It follows that now we can no longer know how the sounds of linguistic expressions are to be consistently aligned with our nonverbal realizations of the world. In other words, the social, semantic contract is replaced by 'a pact of simulation, sealed by information and the media' (1979: 221f.). Having stipulated the collapse of the gap between signifier and signified as a 'circularity of all media effects', Baudrillard speaks of the 'impossibility of any mediation' and hence of the demise of the medium itself (1983: 102f.). Having eliminated the signified and so also meaning and the entire semantic level in language and nonverbal signs, Baudrillard is left with a purely syntactic world. Here, then, we have an extreme version of the idea that language is empty and meaningless.

Given such excess in phrasing, it is not surprising that Baudrillard's picture of language and world runs into massive contradictions. From his earlier and more sober studies of the culture of regulated consumption he still wants to hang on to something that looks like a critique of the 'immorality of capital' (1983: 27) and 'the neo-capitalist cybernetic order that aims now at total control' (1983: 111). At the same time he still wishes to assure his readers that 'strategic resistance' by the people is nevertheless possible. Unfortunately, none of this makes sense in the meaningless syntax of mere simulation. And even if resistance could be argued in his scheme, what would it mean in a 'process without subjects'? (1987: 75).

Neither can language be empty in the way Baudrillard puts it, nor can he argue any kind of ethics, critique or political message in the scenario of signs he offers. Indeed, the very contradictions in his writings can be traced to the negation of semantics by his collapsing all signifieds into the plane of signifiers. Assuming that we could read at all in this view, how could we judge what he terms 'the promiscuity of concepts' without distinguishing between them? (1990: 178). How could we realize that the entire world is 'a control screen' if we could not imagine possible mechanisms of control? (1990: 66). Yet, faithful to his own 'fatal strategy' of having eliminated the level of semantics, Baudrillard refuses to address the ground from which such postmodern surfaces arise (1990: 57). They seem to be self-generating: signifiers begetting more signifiers, mere syntax producing ever more syntax. What has happened here and why has what Baudrillard says been so influential? Apart from the seductive metaphoricity of his prose, the emphasis on mere signifiers answers a justified scepticism towards the assumed stability of meanings. At the same time, Baudrillard's celebration of the surface of signification neatly reflects the bit stream character of media messages. However, there is a fatal flaw in equating surface phenomena with their production and ground. To note the speed of the surface stream of signs is one thing, to draw the conclusion that therefore 'every event is today virtually inconsequential', that it allows 'all interpretations' and that therefore we must speak of the 'equiprobability of all causes and of all consequences', is quite another. To conclude that therefore we are dealing with mere 'aleatory imputation' is demonstrably wrong (1990: 17). The thousands who were mutilated, burned and bulldozed into the ground during the Persian Gulf War would not have understood Baudrillard's glib rhetoric of the Gulf War as no more than a media event, of the Gulf War not having taken place at all. Nor, in his very own terms, should that matter. Having got rid of semantics, and so of anything that allows us to judge states of affairs or construe a world, Baudrillard is left with the syntax of the dice. The chess analogy of language that we find in structuralist linguistics since Saussure and elsewhere is misleading. Only part of language is like chess. Language is like chess only as far as its syntactic relations are concerned (Saussure, 1974: 22f., 88, 110; Wittgenstein, 1953: 1, 31).

We need a very different story. If language is empty, it is so in an altogether different sense. Language is empty, it remains without meaning, if it is not associated with its Other, the nonverbal. If we had not learned from earliest childhood, perhaps to some extent even prenatally, how to associate linguistic sounds with nonverbal materials, we would have no meaning. The question is in what form this Other of language functions in the process of the activation of empty linguistic schemata. The remainder of the book will elaborate this problematic. Here we need only point to the necessity of such a process and its rough features. As I have argued above, language as a mere sequence of signifiers cannot mean. We have to add something to make language mean. This additional ingredient moves language from the level of signifiers to that of signifieds, from the plane of syntax to that of semantics. How does this happen?

No matter how wobbly our linguistic meanings are, they are realized by the speakers of the language as *directional*. If we unfold the process that underlies this seemingly simple phenomenon we note at least the following twelve characteristics.

1. While the sounds of a foreign language are recognized as signifiers, their signifieds are hidden from us. As such they remain empty. Yet they look organized and hence under social control.
2. In a language known to us, the sounds of linguistic expressions appear as schemata for something other than themselves; they appear to cover a certain 'terrain' of the perceived world.
3. When we make sense of linguistic sounds we realize that these schemata are directional; they consistently point to the 'same' aspects of our world. Their consistency suggests that semantic directionality is socially guided.
4. When we associate language with portions of our world we appear to be following cultural instructions as to how to fill linguistic schemata with nonverbal readings of the world.

5. Such nonverbal construals of the world (as our world) consist of signs from distinct systems: olfactory, gustatory, tactile, proxemic, kinetic, thermal, aural, gravitational and visual, as well as nonverbal interpretations of viscosity, softness, depth, harshness, and infinite variations of such readings.

6. The majority of those readings reinforce one another; others appear to be contradictory.

7. What counts as appropriate activations of linguistic schemas by nonverbal signs is socially regulated.

8. What counts as a sufficient degree of nonverbal elaboration of language is guided by genres and other macrostructural constraints.

9. As a result, meaning is an event, always under erasure, but nevertheless a recognizable event.

10. As a consequence of the character of variability of nonverbal materials needed to activate language, semantic drift is a necessary feature of natural languages.

11. Because of the dependence of meaning on nonverbal signs, language is fundamentally parasitic.

12. As a result of the schematic nature of linguistic signs, language is at the same time exceptionally well suited to subsume and order nonverbal signs. Generalization and formalization are expressions of the schematic character of language. Therein lies its economy and dominance as a sign system.

In itself, then, language as an ordered sequence of words is indeed empty. It is mere syntax, mere sequences of words. Only when language is combined with something other than linguistic signs is it able to mean. This Other of language is not the world as a set of unmediated data, but rather a fabric of nonverbal signs out of which cultures weave the world the way they see it. When this happens, language is no longer empty but *directed*. Meaning is understood in a phenomenological as well as Derridean manner 'in the sense of direction' (Derrida, 1978: 24). In phenomenology, directionality means socially controlled acts; in Derrida it is multiplied and so produces dissemination.

We can imagine the *directionality* of language as one of two axes. On one axis we can imagine how combinations of linguistic expressions and nonverbal readings are negotiated between two limiting boundaries, full *determinacy* and total *indeterminacy*. Neither is a pragmatic possibility for natural language. Determinacy marks the boundary to formal systems. To the extent that logical features are employed in ordinary discourse we become aware of their alterity. By contrast, radical indeterminacy sense-limits language off against situations in which the social semiotic breaks down altogether. In this case, all meanings are possible and none can be negotiated.

The second axis of the *directionality* of language can be viewed as the axis of directed *underdetermination*. Accordingly, all sign systems are forever more determinable. This has been known since Kant's dual observation that our concepts do not have 'secure boundaries' and that the 'analysis of my concepts is never complete' (Kant, 1965: A 727f.). Since Kurt Gödel we can also include logical systems to the extent that their full description via proofs is forever deferred to the next higher or meta system. For natural language this means that we can carry on forever adding further nonverbal signs to our linguistic schemata, a case of infinite semiosis. In practice, the activation of language schemata by nonverbal readings is terminated according to need on the one hand and pedagogic and political control on the other. Who or what provides the instructions for this double directionality or what controls directionality is the topic of Chapters 10 and 11.

The more playful the discourse, the broader the spectrum of variation of what sort of nonverbal material we bring to bear on words and expressions and the longer we continue to let our imagination unfold the networks of nonverbal signs. Both axes are explored at leisure. In technical discourse, or social discourse filled with technical expressions, we have been taught to act in the opposite manner. We curtail the variety of nonverbal readings to those that are immediately relevant and stop the imaginative chain at the minimum of semantic agreement. By explaining the difference between social discourse and technical speech in this way, we avoid the definitional path, which is available only as far as logical, formal signs are concerned.

This corporeal approach to directionality finds itself located between two very different projects. It has its roots in phenomenological inquiry and the semiotics of Peirce, while its findings appear compatible to a considerable extent with the research in cognitive science and its offshoots in cognitive linguistics and cognitive rhetoric. I end this chapter with a brief indication as to how these fields view the relation between language and the nonverbal. Gilles Fauconnier, for example, distinguishes the reading potential of a sentence from actual readings that occur as a result of its activation by mental-space configurations:

A sentence in itself has no fixed number of readings. It has a potential for generating connections in mental-space configurations. The number of readings will be a product of this potential and the spaces available (and accessible) in a particular context. (Fauconnier, 1997: 54)

Sentences, in his view, are not exactly empty, nor are they fixed. But they only acquire a specific reading once they are combined with nonlinguistic schemata. In this sense, meanings are likewise regarded as directional. In spite of this directionality, however, Fauconnier notes that meaning constructions are 'highly underspecified by language' (8). I want to go further. Language does not mean at all, unless ingredients are brought to bear on it that provide the kind of specificity which we associate with meaning: nonverbal signs.

Cognitivists also see language as tightly secured to nonlinguistic cognitive processes. As Eve Sweetser observes, 'our linguistic system is inextricably interwoven with the rest of our physical and cognitive selves' so that 'there is no point in pretending the autonomy of language if such a pretense obscures real explanatory possibilities' (1990: 6). If language were autonomous, like a calculus, it could not mean. On this general point, cognitive scientists and cognitive linguists pursue goals congenial to the present project. Yet they do not debate the 'point' where precisely meaning resides and how meaning itself has to be described. This is a task at the heart of a semantics that places the body at the centre of language. Now that we have eliminated the possibility that linguistic signs can mean without corroboration by nonverbal signs, we must turn to the way perceptual interpretations can be said to do their job in the process of meaning as event.

3. Meaning as quasi-perceptual

The silent worker is imagination which decrees reality out of chaos.
(Helen Keller, *The World I Live In*, p. 13)

It is ... beyond our power to enter into the vast imagination of those first men, whose minds were not in the least abstract, refined, or spiritualized, because they were entirely immersed in the senses, buffeted by their passions, buried in the body.
(Giambattista Vico, *The New Science*, [378], p. 118)

There is a view of language that regards nonverbal significations as 'parasitic formations, optional superstructures imposed upon spoken language and implying its earlier acquisition' (Lotz, 1951: 87f.). Corporeal semantics is built on quite different assumptions. Here, nonverbal readings of the world are primary in terms of human evolution as well as 'synchronically', in terms of cognition. We are in the world as a totality, not just as sentences. Moreover, we note the priority of the nonverbal when we are half awake, sensing the way our body weighs on the bed well before the chainsaw of syntax has had time to rattle our minds. There are many other moments during our waking lives when the body demands its rights unencumbered by linguistic processing. The idea that we experience the world as differentiated only because of language is a wild prejudice. If this were so, we would be the only organism capable of making fine distinctions in our environment, an unlikely scenario given the split-second and spatially acute performances of other animals (Sebeok, 1986). The simple mapping explanation sometimes put forward to allow for ingenious survival techniques of nonhuman species is no more than a last-ditch theological prejudice. And why should mapping not also play a significant role in human cognition? As recent research shows, the body is reclaiming its central place in evolution, especially in such evolutionary products as language and the human imagination. Let us say, then, that *nonverbal signs are the deep structure of language.*

The other of language

In order to clarify the difference between an intralinguistic or syntactical view of language and one in which semantics requires quasi-perceptual processes I would like to sum up and critique the by now famous example of the Chinese room advanced by John R. Searle (1984: 30ff.). Most of the responses to Searle's thought-experiment either support or reject his argument. From the perspective of corporeal semantics, he appears to be right, except that he does not pursue the possibility of a programme that imitates mental states, which complicates the issue at hand. As it stands, Searle offers strong support for the claims made in the previous chapter. The rough outlines of his reasoning are as follows. Imagine that you do not understand Chinese and find yourself in a closed room with a rulebook that tells you how to manipulate Chinese symbols. Imagine that you are asked to respond to given symbols by selecting other symbols according to prescribed rules. You do not know that the characters to which you are responding are actually questions and that the symbols you are instructed to offer as a response are corresponding answers. Searle's experiment could also be conducted with Chinese sounds on the assumption that the person in the Chinese room has a very fine ear and so is able to pronounce Chinese words reasonably well. In this situation a Chinese speaker would be unable to decide whether or not you are actually capable of understanding Chinese. The very same principles, argues Searle, apply to a digital computer programmed to respond to Chinese symbols. Both the person in the experiment and the computer do no more than repeat syntactic instructions. Neither is able to move from the level of syntax to the level of semantics. According to Searle, to operate at the level of semantics we have to have something in addition to the formal symbols. Understanding a language, he says, involves having mental states which provide syntax with meaning.

So far, Searle has made the kind of case put forward in the last chapter, an argument why language signs on their own are semantically empty. Hence the Chinese room experiment is a perfect example for illustrating the transition from a syntactic to a quasi-perceptual, semantic view of meaning. Imagine the following extension to Searle's hypothetical situation. In addition to a computer programmed to manipulate Chinese characters (or sounds), we have another program which drives a robotic device capable of simulating various perceptual operations. Imagine that it has optical processing facilities, tactile sensors, olfactory measuring techniques, and perhaps some other sensors beyond human capability, such as infrared and X-ray vision, electron microscope optics and so on. Imagine also that the computer is programmed in such a way that it can match its various pattern recognitions systematically with syntactic strings of Chinese symbols. Finally, the computer has been preprogrammed to recognize a large variety of objects in the world. Thus when it touches a cup it could show the cup on the screen, provide an additional schematic chart, an X-ray picture, a written text describing its measurements and other features, and at the same time provide a spoken commentary on its activities.

In this new scenario, Searle's critique loses much of its sting. The computer is still digitally steered, but its Chinese syntax now fulfils one of the main ingredients demanded for a semantic. Not only has the computer a functioning syntax, its syntax is also *about* something. Furthermore, by means of its associated robotic devices, the computer now interacts with the actual world that it describes in different ways. The computer now has more than mere symbols, it also has a content. Searle would object perhaps that this very content is itself formally constituted. But here the edges of the argument begin to blur. The computer was, of course, programmed to link world and language in a particular way. The crucial question here is whether we are not likewise 'programmed' to combine linguistic expressions with nonverbal readings that make up our world. Does not culture fulfil in principle the same function? Is the difference not merely one of pedagogic complexity?

The body and quasi-perceptual grasp

These are difficult questions and we must leave it to science fiction to fantasize possible as well as impossible solutions. What is of interest to this chapter is the point that perceptual and quasi-perceptual readings – that is, signs – appear to offer a way out of the syntactic bind. To open our perspective a little, let us go back in the history of language theory for a moment to some of the observations concerning the body and language made by Giambattista Vico. In his *New Science* we are offered an evolutionary picture in which humans were at first 'almost all body and almost no reflection', entirely given to 'vivid sensation in perceiving particulars, strong imagination in apprehending and enlarging them, sharp wit in referring them to their imaginative genera, and robust memory in retaining them'. These early faculties of the mind, Vico speculates, must have 'their roots in the body and draw their strength from it'. This corporeal emphasis goes well with Vico's iconic view of the origins of language, which he says 'must have begun with signs, whether gestures or physical objects'. Even the very notion of logos, he observes, suggested to the Greeks not only language but also 'things'. So language in its early stages must have been 'a fantastic speech making use of physical substances endowed with life' (Vico, 1968: [401],

127f.). From both the perspective of cognitive science and the kind of intersemiotic, corporeal semantics advocated here, Vico's insistence on the active presence of the body in language is what we need. Not only is it likely that the body played an important part in the evolution of natural languages, it would be difficult to deny that that continues to be the case. Vico certainly thought that humans are such that even when they engage their imagination in the service of spiritual matters they have to give the body its due:

> when we wish to give utterance to our understanding of spiritual things, we must seek aid from our imagination to explain them and, like painters, form human images of them. But these theological poets, unable to make use of the understanding, did the opposite and more sublime thing: they attributed senses and passions . . . to bodies, and to bodies as vast as sky, sea, and earth. Later as the vast imaginations shrank and the power of the abstraction grew, the personifications were reduced to diminutive signs. Metonymy drew a cloak of learning over the prevailing ignorance of these origins of human institutions, which have remained buried until now. (Vico, 1968: [408], 131)

Vico understood language as having emerged from poetic speech characterized by tropes of which metaphor, metonymy and synecdoche were the three original and dominant ones. Irony, the fourth major class of figures of speech, is regarded as a latecomer in this series ([404–408], 131). According to Vico, this must be so because irony 'could not have begun until the period of reflection'. For 'it is fashioned of falsehood by dint of a reflection which wears the mask of truth' ([408], 131). The earlier tropes are shown to share the same basic structure of a concrete origin pointing towards a more abstract idea. Vico held that it was typical of all languages that expressions referring to inanimate objects were 'formed by metaphor from the human body and its parts and from human senses and passions' ([405], 129). As to metonymy, Vico notes the structure of the substitution of 'cause for effect', which he says has 'produced in each case a little fable', such as 'ugly Poverty, sad Old Age, pale Death' ([406], 130). Finally, synecdoche too reflects the general process of evolution from corporeal particulars to abstraction. For Vico synecdoche is a form which developed into metaphor by a process of transformation from specifics to universals.

> *Tectum*, roof, came to mean a whole house because in the first times a covering sufficed for a house. Similarly, *puppis*, poop, for a ship, because it was the highest part and therefore the first to be seen by those on shore; . . . a ship was called a sail. Similarly, *mucro*, point, for sword,

because the latter is an abstract word and as in a genus comprehends pummel, hilt, edge, and point; and it was the point they felt which aroused their fear. ([407], 130)

All tropes, then, are 'necessary modes of expression' in early societies. Only later do these concrete expressions become 'figurative' when abstract terms were invented to signify genera, species and part–whole relations. From this, Vico concludes that contrary to the ruling view of the grammarians of his time, poetic speech precedes prose in the evolution of language ([409], 131). Let me conclude this excursion to Vico with a quotation reiterating his belief in the foundational role of the body in language. Note that some of the examples have been altered by the editors for the convenience of English-speaking readers:

> Thus, head for top or beginning; the brow and shoulders of a hill; the eyes of needles and of potatoes; mouth for any opening; the lip of a cup or pitcher; the teeth of a rake, a saw, a comb; the beard of wheat; the tongue of a shoe; the gorge of a river; a neck of land; an arm of the sea; the hands of a clock; heart for centre (the Latin uses *umbilicus*, navel, in this sense); the belly of a sail; foot for end or bottom; the flesh of fruits; a vein of rock or mineral; the blood of grapes for wine; the bowels of the earth. Heaven or the sea smiles; the wind whistles; the waves murmur; a body groans under a great weight. The farmers of Latium used to say the fields were thirsty, bore fruit, were swollen with grain; and our rustics speak of plants making love, vines going mad, resinous trees weeping. ([405], 129)

In his examples, Vico points out, humans have made themselves 'an entire world'. This should not be surprising, he suggests, for when 'man' faces difficulties in understanding things he makes 'the things out of himself and becomes them by transforming himself into them' ([405], 129f.). Whether it is this interpretive difficulty or whether it is a necessary evolutionary process cannot be legislated. What we can observe with the help of Vico's observations is that language even after a very long time, say half a million years (give or take a couple of hundred thousand years), still retains the epistemic, iconic perspective of the human body, our human scale, in the descriptions of the world. And although abstraction in the form of both generalization and formalization covers and so absorbs and veils corporeal content, natural languages still reveal the primacy of the body (Danesi, 1993; Danesi and Nuessel, 1994). I will address the corporeality of abstract terms separately in Chapter 9.

Mental images in cognitive science

On the assumption that the route suggested by Vico is promising and that the imagination does play a fundamental role in semantic processes, we must turn to the topic of perceptual and quasi-perceptual readings. The best support for such a position available at the moment can be found in the literature of cognitive science. In *Principles of Mental Imagery* (1989) Ronald Finke distinguishes mental imagery from retinal images and iconic images, or short-term retention of visual information in sensory mechanism. Mental images he defines as 'the mental invention or recreation of an experience that in at least some respects resembles the experience of actually perceiving an object or an event, either in conjunction with, or in the absence of, direct sensory stimulation' (Finke, 1989: 2). Contrary to propositions, mental images bear a certain structural resemblance to perceived objects 'such that relationships among an object's parts can be both preserved and reinterpreted' (138). This principle does not have to be accepted in any strictly realist fashion, of course; it suffices for our purposes to rely on the experimentally supported evidence. What is more interesting for the argument on meaning is that no matter how accurate a reflection of perceived reality, such imagery covers a wide range of possibilities of mental reflection available for the language user. That Finke should focus on mental imagery that is 'meaningful and well organized' is not surprising given his scientific starting-point (14f.). However, for a broader view it is important to grant room also for mental imagery in need of interpretation. Think of the mental imagery of dreams, including nightmares, which appear to be 're-created' in some way out of experiential materials. Whether this occurs in the Freudian manner via 'dreamwork' or in some other fashion does not have to be decided for the purpose of establishing the fact and role of such images in language. Although Finke allows for 'distortions in cognitive maps' (81–84), we need to move to centre stage the possibility of fragmented, distorted, as well as well-organized imagery and certainly the requirement of interpretation.

In his more recent *Creative Imagery: Discoveries and Inventions in Visual-isation* (1990) Finke extends his findings to the recognition of 'unexpected patterns that "emerge" as [people] construct and transform images' (Finke, 1990: 18). As a rule, however, imagined objects are typically interpreted very much like actual objects. For this observation Finke cites a host of cognitive literature (18). Applied to language, something Finke does not do, this allows for both an inferential, realist version of semantics and the suggestion that the process of activating linguistic schemata by way of nonverbal readings is also complicated by representational creativity or confabulation. This means that the event of meaning as a process of assembling mental images and their nonvisual parallels is affected by creative extensions. Meaning, then, is certainly much less fixed than a definitional or empiricist or naturalist semantics would allow. Although the process of meaning activation happens at extremely fast speed in habitual meaning events, it can at any point be modified by creative transformations of the nonverbal material engaged. This flies in the face particularly of propositional theories, which are among the main targets of Finke's research. As he assures us, 'the past two decades of image research have shown that propositional theories simply cannot account for a vast majority of findings of imagery experiments' (19). In particular, it is 'the essential spatial character of human cognition' that is at odds with propositional theories (171). These findings are persuasive and should be incorporated into theories of meaning. The spatial emphasis, although not to be dismissed, may be the result of his preoccupation with vision. Nevertheless, even our sense of time as well as our readings of smell, touch, gravity, thermal change and a host of others cannot be entirely dissociated from spatial (re)presentation. So this all points to a unitary nonverbal construction of our world in which language plays a meta-structural and economizing role. This is so, however, if and only if language is activated by nonverbal signs.

As to how meaning works, the principle of a significant relation between language and nonlinguistic processes is supported by a growing number of cognitivists. In *From Etymology to Pragmatics* (1990) Eve Sweetser strongly agrees with 'semanticists who consider meaning to be rooted in human experience: experience of the cultural, social, mental, and physical worlds'. In her studies, 'the apparently disorderly domain of linguistic meanings' is typically 'shown to be structured around speakers' understanding of a cognitive domain' (Sweetser, 1990: 12). This is compatible with the view that understanding occurs outside language, as well as in language once it is activated by nonverbal readings. The claim, then, is that there is a nonverbal and also a corporeal, linguistic kind of understanding of our world.

Another cognitivist, Gilles Fauconnier, supports the crucial role of cognitive maps in *Mappings in Thought's Language* (1997). He points to the by now 'impressive evidence for the key role of mental spaces and mappings in signed languages' (Fauconnier, 1997: 190). According to Fauconnier, mappings are understood in terms of 'a correspondence between two sets that assigns to each element in the first a counterpart in the second' (1 n.1). Such mappings he regards as central to our 'faculty of producing, transferring, and processing meaning' (1). Thus, when language reflects the world it does so not directly but via 'elaborate human cognitive constructions and construals' (8). What is attractive here is the centrality of nonverbal constructions. Yet 'mapping' remains an umbrella term, largely supported by visual evidence.

What is lacking is the specificity of, for example, an olfactory instance of mapping in relation to a linguistic expression. How in such a case does meaning accrue to the signifier?

Fauconnier also at times reverses the procedure, so that language operates as an ordering system for nonverbal acts. But then we are not sure whether the nonverbal was needed for language to mean in the first place. 'Language is actively involved in setting up construals, mappings between domains, and discourse configurations, with the fundamental properties of accessing, spreading, and viewpoint' (99). Yes, but what process does 'involved' refer to? If language is 'involved in setting up' something then it must have certain characteristics. What are they? The picture of language envisaged here is still tentative. Are its syntactic properties autonomous? More importantly, how does semantics kick in? And when? Are there nonverbal preconditions when that takes place? Some of these questions are pursued further in *Spaces, Worlds, and Grammars* (1997), co-edited by Fauconnier and Eve Sweetser. I have already referred to Mark Johnson's innovative arguments in *The Body in the Mind* (1987). Mark Turner's work on 'cognitive rhetoric' in *Death Is the Mother of Beauty* (1987) and *Reading Minds: The Study of English in the Age of Cognitive Science* (1991) addresses the question of how foundational the connection between verbal and nonverbal cognition is in literary as well as in ordinary language use. Turner's more recent explorations of the super-concept 'conceptual blending' likewise share the assumption of the central role of nonverbal cognition. I will return to Turner's work again later.

Perceptual readings

Some of the research in cognitive science appears hard-headedly positivist, as in Diane Ackerman's observation that 'the senses feed shards of information to the brain like microscopic pieces of a jigsaw puzzle. When enough "pieces" assemble, the brain says *cow. I see cow*' (Ackerman, 1991: xvii). Surely the mind requires the expectation of what a whole cow looks like before the assembled pieces make sense. Similarly, instead of claiming that 'all smells fall into five categories' it would be more appropriate to say that we are dealing here with a classificatory convention (11). Apart from this kind of criticism, however, Ackerman's *A Natural History of the Senses* (1991) proves a gold mine for a corporeal theory of language. For example, her evidence strongly supports the evolutionary priority of nonverbal readings in comparison with language. She cites research to show that 'the physiological links between the smell and language centres of the brain are pitifully weak', while the connections between smell and memory are both ancient and strong. They form a pathway 'that carries us nimbly across time and distance' (7). How does smell typically work? 'Odour molecules float back into the nasal cavity behind the bridge of the nose, where they are absorbed by the mucosa containing receptor cells bearing microscopic hairs called cilia.' More than 5 million cells of this kind 'fire impulses to the brain's olfactory bulb or smell centre' (10). This is nothing, of course, if we compare this to the 220 million olfactory cells of a sheepdog (31). Unlike other neurons in the brain, eyes and ears, 'the neurons in the nose are replaced every thirty days and, unlike any other neuron in the body, they stick right out and wave in the air current like anemones on a coral reef' (10). As soon as the olfactory bulb picks up an odour molecule it sends a signal to the cerebral cortex, which in turn 'sends a message straight into the limbic system'. This, Ackerman reports, is 'a mysterious, ancient, and intensely emotional section of our brain in which we feel, lust, and invent, long before we embarked on language' (11).

One suspects that some of our other nonverbal sign systems are similarly primordial and yet essential for our daily functioning in the world, including, as I claim here, our linguistic performance. What is difficult is to demonstrate the necessary relation between nonverbal readings and language. Once again, I would like to refer to evidence provided by Helen Keller. In her *Story of My Life* Keller describes the basis of her condition: 'My world is built of touch sensations' (Keller, 1954: 7). All else comes later, and often by way of analogy. In her reflections we find that she is able to give meanings to certain words only by imaginative transfer. A 'venturesome spirit', she says, 'impels me to use words of sight and sound whose meaning I can guess only from analogy and fancy' (Keller, 1909: 46). What is at work here seems to be intersemiotic play, a relation that supports the view that the verbal is dependent at least in certain respects on the perceptual and its imaginative variations. Responding to the pressure of the theories of her day, Keller regarded such mental activities as 'hazardous' games that cheered up her daily routine.

To reiterate one of my basic claims: there is no meaning in language unless something else, something nonlinguistic, is added to sound sequences. Keller certainly felt that there must be meaningful acts outside language, that nonverbal readings were more than mere side-effects or gratuitous extensions of language. She explicitly objected to the assumptions of her time that 'the very sensations we have from the sense of touch are "vicarious", as though our friends felt the sun for us'. We could say with Keller's help that nonverbal readings are essential in two respects. One is their role in providing for us a world as background for all our activities, for our being in the world; the other function is to fill in the empty schemata of language. This has been somewhat cautiously noted for example by Mark Rollins when he says that 'images as representations are essential, in some cases, to establish the *capacity* for reference' (Rollins, 1989: 43). We will return to the question of reference in the next chapter. Here I would like to add three corrections to his view. In the first instance, there is no good reason for the restriction to such referential backdrop to a few isolated cases. If we did not have a coherent and all-embracing background for meanings, they would have to operate largely as do logical terms in an artificial syntax, which is not the case. Natural language is referentially tied to the world not at sporadic points at which we touch down, so to speak, but continuously. If it were not, we would feel disoriented and experience considerable interpretive difficulties in reconnecting with the world when the rare opportunity for touchdown arose. We have arrived at such a grotesque picture because of the assumption that language can be linked to an unmediated world. Now that we have redescribed the relationship as one between two different sign practices, one as linguistic schematization in need of nonverbal activation, the other as nonverbal readings, the difficulty disappears. It is now plausible that we can be in touch with the world and language at the same time, since we have incorporated both as sign complexes under social instructions.

Second, even if Rollins were prepared to accept the ubiquity of nonverbal reference, the argument is still restricted to the referential side of language. This leaves its deictic implications untheorized. In natural language, however, implied deixis, quite apart from its commonly acknowledged explicit relation, carries the totality of cultural modalities. Without these, linguistic expressions would be no more than impoverished abstractions. A third objection has to do with the absence in Rollins's account of other nonverbal practices. Visualization stands alone in this picture, unrelated to such readings of the world as olfactory, gustatory, kinesthetic, aural or haptic significations.

The as-structure of meaning

If such apparently disparate acts are to be associated with one another as perceptual or quasi-perceptual readings of the world and linguistic expressions, then we need to look for a general explanation of how this is possible. I want to avoid adopting Jakobson's *intersemiotic translation* because it merely aligns one autonomous sign system with another. What we are looking for is something else: an explanation that associates two domains of signs in such a way that one is intelligible only by way of the other. Such an explanation can be found in some recent observations made by cognitive linguists as well as in Peirce, Heidegger and Derrida. In *More Than Cool Reason: A Field Guide to Poetic Metaphor* (1989) George Lakoff and Mark Turner add a new perspective to the dynamic of understanding characterized by Heidegger's in terms of a foundational as-structure. Lakoff and Turner refer to it as the principle of 'all reading is reading in'. Their point of departure is cognitive processes and the conviction that 'words are sound sequences that conventionally express concepts that are within conceptual schemas'. But since such schemata are always much more encompassing than the conceptual portion designated by a linguistic expression, there is always a surplus of meaning beyond designation, and hence 'no two speakers speak exactly the same language'. On the one hand, even literary interpretations are constrained by the conventionality of meanings; on the other, interpretations can differ widely because there is no fully shared stock of concepts. Moreover, Lakoff and Turner argue, since metaphor is a fundamental feature of natural-language use, the variation among readings increases. As a result, meaning identity is a highly unlikely event. This is why Lakoff and Turner defend readers accused of 'reading meanings into' poems. 'All reading is reading in' and 'all reading involves construal' (Lakoff and Turner, 1989: 109). All reading, in other words, is a reading of something as something else. Applied to the problematic of activating language schemata by way of nonverbal signs, one could add that since syntax can be fully shared by speakers of a language, any surplus of meaning must be the result of different nonverbal materials being brought to bear on the same signifiers.

In Peirce the interpretive relation takes the form of a sign achieving meaning in yet another sign, called an interpretant sign, or simply interpretant, which in turn becomes a sign to be deciphered by another interpretant and so on, *ad infinitum*. We can derive from Peirce the strong thesis that all semiosis, including that operative in language, rests on this basic dynamic. When Peirce proposed that the meaning of a sign was its transformation into another sign, he anticipated in semiotics what Heidegger, approaching meaning from phenomenology and *Dasein*, was to call the fundamental as-structure of understanding. This deserves special attention. In Peirce's scheme of things the translation of one sign into another introduces two important issues: the infinite chain of signification, recently celebrated by Eco and Derrida, and the intersemiotic relations between signs from different systems. Thus, we can give additional meaning to a tactile reading of a surface by a visual confirmation, to a set of aural signs a confirmation by our olfactory grasp. In short, such transformations along the chain of signs result in the collaborative strengthening of meaning as event. So Peirce provides us with the foundational strategy for a quasi-perceptual theory of meaning. Linguistic meanings are events of linkage between verbal schemas and nonverbal fillings, which too can be regarded as more or less schematic.

In Martin Heidegger's *Being and Time* (1926) the relation between entities of understanding takes a somewhat different form. Whatever we understand is the result of at least a minimal interpretation. In 'The principle of identity', Heidegger pushes this claim as far as to include the very formula for identity relations. Apart from identity, we cannot grasp x as x but only as y. Heidegger calls this fundamental relation the 'as-structure' of understanding. Nor is this relation restricted to predication. It also includes all pre-predicative grasp. Like Peirce, Heidegger notes the dynamics of understanding by insisting that 'the as-structure is grounded ontologically in the temporality of understanding', or the 'ecstatico-horizonal unity of temporality' (Heidegger, 1962: 411):

> that which is explicitly understood – has the structure of something as something. ... The 'as' makes up the structure of the explicitness of something that is understood. It constitutes the interpretation. ... Any mere pre-predicative seeing ... already understands and interprets. (Heidegger, 1962: 189)

What does this imply? First and foremost, all as-structures take place against a holistic background rather than in analytical isolation. For 'in the mere encountering of something, it is understood in terms of a totality of involvements' (189). This totality of involvements is always given as part of our existential condition. And even when the structural 'as' is 'ontically unexpressed, this must not seduce us into overlooking it as a constitutive state for understanding, existential and a priori' (190). The 'as' is always already present in interpretation as well as in its habitual versions of understanding. Now comes an important move. Heidegger notes that whenever we interpret anything we do not simply 'throw a "signification" over some naked thing' (190). For the object of attention is already part and parcel of an 'involvement which is disclosed in our understanding of the world, and this involvement is one which gets laid out by the interpretation' (191). Applied to language this means that when we use a phrase to express something that has been grasped by our visual and tactile readings we do not simply cover it as with a blanket and so block out and replace our nonverbal understanding. According to the notion of 'totality of involvements', we unravel further how we relate to the total of which the object of inquiry is a part. Assuming that Heidegger is right on this point, we could say that by bringing language to bear on our nonverbal relation with the world and its objects we at the same time understand more profoundly what the particular linguistic expression

means. Take the example of a piece of jewellery under our gaze and touch. As
we begin to describe the object before us in words, these very words take on
the significatory potential of our visual and tactile explorations. Why do we
choose the words we do for our description? Because we have been trained to
expect a certain fit between specific expressions and the world, which means
we have already learned how to fill linguistic schemata with quasi-
perceptual signs. Now these very signs are modified by our perceptual grasp
and in turn our language becomes further enriched by nonverbal modifications. We are engaged in a process of tuning. Not every Heideggerian will
agree with this reading but I feel vindicated by Heidegger's assertion that
'language already hides in itself a developed way of conceiving' (199). Given
what he says about the totality of involvements, such a developed manner of
conceiving is possible only if it includes also an epistemic totality, our entire
way of grasping the world. For 'from the fact that words are absent, it may
not be concluded that interpretation is absent' (200).

No doubt this is circular, but, as Heidegger would say, hermeneutically so.
For 'the "circle" in understanding belongs to the structure of meaning' (195).
Usually this hermeneutic circularity is described in terms of interpreting
language. It must be extended to include nonverbal signs, for the fact that we
must already have a certain understanding of the appropriateness of what
we want to say before we say it equally applies to tactile, visual, aural,
olfactory and other significatory acts. 'Only he who already understands can
listen' (208). That this once more is not restricted to the linguistic domain
becomes clear when Heidegger makes the important comment that 'the
person who "cannot hear" and "must feel" may perhaps be one who is able
to hearken very well' (207). The as-structure of interpretation and understanding is a primordial way of coping with the world. It underlies all forms
of signification and so precedes language. As Heidegger rightly claims, 'the
schema "something as something" has already been sketched out before-
hand in the structure of one's pre-predicative understanding' (411). What we
take from Heidegger, then, is that understanding and interpretation are not
restricted to language but underlie both language and nonverbal ways of
grasping the world. Furthermore, the nonverbal corporeal encounter with
the world can now be regarded as the foundation of both our understanding
of the world and our ability to endow linguistic expressions with meaning.

Heidegger's as-structure has been radicalized more recently in Jacques
Derrida's discussion of 'metaphoricity'. Difference and metaphoricity are
two seminal notions in the deconstructive toolkit. If we combine the two
features of Peirce's semiotic transformation in which every sign gives way to
another sign and so a trajectory of infinite regress, then Derrida's notion of
metaphoricity begins to make good sense. Drawing on both Heidegger's

as-structure and Peirce's semiosis, Derrida speaks of the peculiar character of withdrawal of all signification. This he illustrates in 'The *retrait* of metaphor' by pursuing our understanding of metaphor from its figural role in language to its vanishing point beyond the edge of Being. As a result of metaphoricity as a process of retreat, 'Being withdraws into its crypt' (Derrida, 1978: 22). In this sense, metaphoricity replaces presence.

The picture that emerges from our overview of the as-structure from Peirce's transformational chain of signs to Derrida's metaphoricity suggests that whenever something is understood in terms of something else, none of the signifieds so produced is stable. And yet we understand, at least tentatively, what speakers in our semiotic community are on about. This paradox is at the heart of all cultural signification and is crucial for an understanding of language. Furthermore, given our starting-point of the centrality of the body in language, we can now say this: if perceptual and quasi-perceptual readings are employed in linguistic utterances as signs activating empty linguistic schemata, then such activation is never fully identifiable in any logical sense. Rather, we are dealing with a relation of 'more or less', of meaning surplus and semantic scarcity depending on the communicational situation. It is in this sense that we should understand the claim that *nonverbal signs are the deep structure of language*.

The dynamics of the as-structure that exist between linguistic schemata and nonverbal signs are fundamental. As Ackerman illustrates the point, 'when we use words such as smoky, sulfurous, floral, fruity, sweet, we are describing smells in terms of other things (smoke, sulfur, flowers, fruit, sugar)'. Yet without a recognition of those smells as olfactory signs, the language expressions would be meaningless. Often the metaphoricity of the as-structure produces less direct (re)presentations, as in situations in which we try to indicate what effects certain phenomena have on us. Then we might say that 'something smells "disgusting", "intoxicating", "sickening", "pleasurable", "delightful", "pulse-revving", "hypnotic", or "revolting"' (Ackerman, 1991: 7). Yet the same principle holds: without the nonverbal, no meaning.

As I will argue in what follows, the perceptual and quasi-perceptual signs required for both the production and the understanding of linguistic expressions demand a significant shift in our conception of cultural utterance situations and the world a culture projects through language. So the next chapter asks what role the body plays in deixis and reference.

4. The body in deixis and reference

Before we are in a position to rework the traditional notions of deixis and reference, we must briefly rehearse the standard explanations. *Deixis* is derived from the Greek word for 'pointing'. This is why in Peirce's writing deixis is called 'indication'. The concept is regarded as comprising lexical items that make little or no sense without some information about the position of speakers in relation to their world and to what they are saying. Its forms include *personal deixis*, which manifests itself in such words as pronouns and points to the participants in a speech situation. *Spatial deixis* points to the speaker's position *vis-à-vis* other persons and the world of objects. Egocentric particulars such as 'this', 'that'; 'here', 'there'; or verbs such as 'come', 'go'; phrases like 'leave me alone', or 'how disappointing' all refer us back to the speaker and utterance situation. Lastly, *temporal deixis* points to the speaker's temporal locus, the time of speaking in relation to what is said and to the larger temporal matrix of the world to which both speech situation and what is being said belong. Verb tenses as well as such temporal markers as 'tomorrow', 'in two years', 'meanwhile', 'now', 'then', or 'never' fall under the category of temporal deixis. Together, spatial and temporal deixis govern the technical aspects of the point of view from which a text is spoken. Only in realist texts are the two necessarily aligned in a quasi-perceptual way. This chapter introduces an extended version of deixis, *implicit or concealed deixis*.

Implicit deixis

As we spread our examples to the borderlines of the set of obvious candidates for deixis, we sense that we begin to lose definitional control. And if we think hard about what it is that characterizes orthodox deixis, we find that the features that tell us about speakers are neither clear-cut nor all at the linguistic surface. As I will try to show, the vast majority of deictic aspects are concealed or implicit. I want to go as far as to say that this *implicit deixis* is by far the more important, and certainly the more interesting, aspect of this phenomenon of language. Hence neither deixis nor reference as they are traditionally described is suitable for corporeal semantics. When a Liberal Prime Minister in Australia denies that one of his colleagues has any interest in a major shareholding company, what is being denied has a particular semantic field not fully shared by the Leader of the Opposition. What is regarded as giving the appearance of not having followed the relevant guidelines looks somewhat different from the perspectives of the two major parties. At play here is a different implicit deixis, a differing attitude towards what is said and to the nonverbal sign complexes that make up social reality.

Take the abbreviation IMF (International Monetary Fund) as another example. It conceals two entirely different and diametrically opposed kinds of deixis, depending on who utters it and under what conditions the utterance occurs. From the position of the main contributors to the fund – the USA, Germany and Japan – the linguistic schema IMF, beyond its immediate designation, tends to be filled with such nonverbal ingredients as financial responsibility, global order, sound investment, necessary infrastructures and assurance of economic growth. Nor can we separate out what belongs to designation proper and what is additional deictic content. From the perspective of the guarantors of the IMF, this is what it is. Its deixis is largely concealed. It seems that financiers in Thailand and Indonesia do not share this manner of speaking the term. Their deixis hides a number of suspicions which become explicit during economic crises. From their perspective, IMF also means dependency, intrusion into domestic affairs, imperialism by other means, and so on. Again, it is not possible to declare a logical demarcation line where the abbreviation's designative meaning ends and other semantic nuances, such as deictic bias, begin. Meaning construction as a filling of linguistic schemata with nonverbal signs is more like a continuous web without strict boundaries. Certainly, what I have called implied, cultural deixis plays a significant role in language. By way of differing perceptions of the world, the cultural body enters the linguistic scene.

The way a culture supervises language, then, is also embedded in its deixis. Implicit deixis appears as natural knowledge to those who speak the language. But nothing could be more unnatural, since such implicit knowledge is not accessible to the outsider. Implicit deixis is deeply cultural. It is the result of pedagogy from the minute we are born into the community and gradually changes as a culture adjusts along its historical trajectory. In this respect, natural language occupies a position quite different from that of logical variables, for example. Variables are entirely open to redefinition and modal variation. They are mere placeholders. Natural-language terms, by contrast, can be shifted by modalities but not to anything and everything. The approach I suggest is this. Instead of taking what a term is about, its reference, as the starting-point, we should focus on the cultural motivation for discourse as the foundation on which we resolve such questions. Before we can interpret any specific linguistic expression we must construe as best we can a 'totality of involvements'. This means for every linguistic expression that its utterance situation directs us to typical referential relations. Whatever counts as reference is therefore always already coloured by the manner in which a culture views what it is looking at. Such colouring can be minimal or produce a reversal of the very referential content we tend to fasten on. Indeed, the possibility of referential reversal by irony is just such an utterance situation within a culture. However, radical modifications of referential content are only extreme and so obvious cases on a large spectrum of all kinds of possible meaning-shifts. Thus, for the native speaker the Italian *'mama'* has attached to it, as it were, instructions of speaking and meaning, instructions as to what range of nonverbal signs to activate. At any given time in history, these instructions are different from those attached to the English term 'mother', even though both share the same base reference to a biological mother. If this sounds far-fetched, consider the following, seemingly straightforward, example.

The names Gaurisanker and Everest both refer to the highest mountain on earth. But they do so quite differently. In a standard analytical introduction to language philosophy, *Language and Reality* (1990) by Michael Devitt and Kim Sterelny, the expressions 'Everest is Everest' and 'Everest is Gaurisanker' are cited to dismiss the Millean view that meaning is the designation of an object by way of a name. The authors attempt to show that identity statements prove Mill to be mistaken. They point out that the two expressions must have different meanings. The first is a statement of self-identity and so uninformative or trivially true, while the second is informative as well as true. The two statements differ 'epistemically and cognitively' (Devitt and Sterelny, 1990: 26). Hence they have different meanings. If they have different meanings, then their components 'Everest' and 'Gaurisanker' must also have different meanings. So Mill is wrong, for he would have to say that the two statements have the same meaning since they designate the same object.

As I have tried to show elsewhere, I think that both Mill and Devitt and Sterelny are mistaken (Ruthrof, 1997a: 58f.). While their dismissal of Mill seems fairly straightforward, they themselves base their analysis on an unacceptable view of natural language. The main flaw lies in their assumption that language can be uttered neutrally. All we apparently need is syntax and a simple semantic consisting of sense and reference. That language has to be spoken is an additional possibility for Devitt and Sterelny, a pragmatic extension of that basic structure. This is a flawed view of natural language. The speaking of a language by the culture of which it is a part must be an essential feature in our description. If cultural utterance is left out of the picture, we are treating natural language as if it were a formal logical system, which it is not, and our analysis yields results not applicable to linguistic expressions. In other words, Devitt and Sterelny forgot about deixis in both its explicit and implicit forms. If, on the other hand, we acknowledge cultural utterance as an integral part of speech, then we are bound to address not only the fact of implicit deixis but also the way in which it modifies reference.

How does this affect their example? If, as they themselves note, the terms Everest and Gaurisanker play very 'different roles' in 'people's lives' – as well as in 'peoples' lives', one might add – why do they not see that reference is not as clear-cut a case as they make it look? Do 'Everest' and 'Gaurisanker' really have the same reference? Do the Nepalese and the Tibetans actually designate the same object when they use the two different terms? I am inclined to say 'yes' and 'no'. At the level of simple numerical identification, the answer must be in the affirmative. Both cultures refer to what we know to be the highest mountain on earth and not to Anapurna or the Matterhorn. Or to 'that mountain over there, not that one to the left'. But here is the hitch. When the Tibetans use the term 'Gaurisanker', they rarely if ever employ it as a quantifying identification. The cultural deixis that comes into play when the term is typically used, though concealed to the outsider, produces a quite different sort of reference. Implicit cultural deixis includes at the same time a specific geographical perspective, a knowledge that Gaurisanker is not to be climbed (only Everest is), a specific role in Tibetan mythology, profane and sacred aspects, and so on.

Now consider the term 'Gaurisanker' as uttered by a Nepalese tourist guide. Reference is now complicated further. As he explains to his charge how the Tibetans in his view refer to the mountain, he has to feign a subject position not his own, a process I discussed in *Pandora and Occam* under the term 'hypocrisis', or reading as feigning a subject position (Ruthrof, 1992: 165ff.). In this situation, the Nepalese guide imagines the way Tibetans typically speak of and imagine Everest. This is an entirely different perspective, which he has to fantasize in contradiction to his own. Once we take *cultural deixis* in natural language into consideration, identity statements turn out to behave quite differently from those in formal notation. This is where analytical approaches to language are altogether incompatible with descriptions of the kind offered here.

Having pointed to the significance of cultural deixis and especially its concealed or implicit forms, I would like to draw attention to the way it is realized in linguistic practice. A corporeal approach to meaning reveals its force especially in the unstated ways of how we are to see the world through language. We could not possibly produce additional linguistic signifiers in order to rein in our fantasy acts in the construction of the manner in which we grasp the world when we hear someone else speak or in our own utterances. Instead of a linguistic explanation, I suggest it is much more persuasive to invoke nonverbal readings. In our example of Gaurisanker and Everest, different nonverbal sign construals are at work, even though they are roughly directed at the same area of resistance. Nor are the different vistas restricted to the visual and recollected images. Other nonverbal signs come into play when a culture activates sedimented attitudes and beliefs. The argument that such readings are merely additional or supplementary must be rejected. For there is no logical line which would separate the necessary and sufficient nonverbal conditions of meaning from superfluous signs. Depending on the pragmatic constraints, a culture keeps its meaning-chains short or elaborates them at leisure.

Deixis, then, is not primarily a verbal phenomenon but a nonverbal constraint on the manner in which we are to envisage designated objects of thought. Deictic constraints are at the heart of our characterization of a culture. In an increasingly globalized world the dependence of language and nonverbal readings is probably not altered in principle. Rather, culture-specific constraints are gradually replaced by the standardized image chains of international telecommunication. However, *concealed deixis* or, more strictly, deictic entailment is thereby neither abolished nor brought out into the open. The manner of presenting the world via language as activated by nonverbal signs remains a major aspect of communication and should be regarded as a significant level of analysis in the critique of culture.

If this is so, why, one might ask, not call implicit deixis simply *langue*? After all, *langue* is usually described as the implicit system underlying language in use, the sum of paroles in a semiotic community. However, this would stretch the notion of *langue* beyond its precise function. To quote A. Meillett (1919), a follower of the Saussurean principles, '*la langue* exists only if there is a group of grammatical procedures' (Kristeva, 1989: 30). *Langue*, in other words, is a set of abstract rules for the generation of syntactically appropriate texts (*paroles*). Implicit deixis, by contrast, characterizes something less clearly structured, a tendency rather than a grammatical rule. We are dealing here with implications that are shared in a much more fuzzy manner than are noun phrases and participles. We are dealing with an area of meaning where the firm guidelines for syntactic behaviour set by a culture slide off into less and less well demarcated peripheries of semantic negotiation. To describe a culture, one would have to include implicit deixis – which makes Umberto

Eco's idea that by unravelling a single sign to the end one would reveal an entire culture even theoretically impossible. While Eco's holistic perspective is right, the clarity of his notion of 'code' attaches only to *langue* (Eco, 1984). Implicit deixis, on the other hand, is as evasive as it is pervasive. Above all, although we can summarize it only in words, implicit deixis consists largely of nonverbal signs.

Because we can never achieve ultimate clarity in our reconstructions of the nonverbal sign complexes that activate both the deictic and the referential background of language, I have observed three kinds of opacity. *Semiotic opacity* I have called a vagueness resulting from the difficulties of reconstructing the general cultural frame within which language occurs. This is not so immediately obvious in spoken utterances in specific social situations, but strikingly so in written texts and especially in culturally distanced texts. We need to spend a good deal of interpretive labour on the nonverbal, quasi-perceptual reconstruction of appropriate backgrounds for such texts. *Modal opacity* is the kind of vagueness we face when we try to interpret and so (re)construct cultural deixis, especially in its implicit and concealed forms. The better we know a culture – and that includes class and gender cultures – the richer our construals; the more foreign we are to a culture, the greater the difficulties of dealing with modal opacity. Yet no matter how familiar we are with a culture, modal opacity will always play a part in the semantics of its language. On the account offered here, there is no such thing as an entirely transparent natural language. Its relative murkiness reflects its very character. *Propositional opacity* is an indeterminacy that stems from the absence of any strict directionality of the lexicon, the way a language can be described by its own words and what sort of nonverbal material is required to disambiguate linguistic expressions. When we use the phrase 'the current financial crisis in Asia', we know roughly what is meant. We have a rough directionality as to what to imagine. But any further explanations, as well as the nonverbal construals that must be fantasized to embody what is meant, are bound to vary considerably (if not sharply). There is no secure propositional way of controlling linguistic schemata semantically. And the more complex the expression the more obviously is this so. Propositional opacity therefore is an essential ingredient of any construction of reference in natural language. In turn, the very notion of reference requires a redefinition if what we have said so far is at all plausible. But first a glimpse of what has to be so redefined.

Reference

Reference, as much else in modern language theory, has its main origin in Frege's seminal paper 'On sense and reference' (1970) (*'Über Sinn und Bedeutung'*, 1892). In it reference is defined as the relation between a linguistic expression and the object (or referent) it points out to us, its *Bedeutung* (a pointing out). Although the sense of an expression is regarded as a definitional thought, its meaning is considered its truth value; that is, whether the referential relation it established is true or false. Reference, then, is the connection between a word or sentence and what it points to in the actual world, an extralinguistic entity. Because of this link, Frege regarded expressions as meaningful if they had a proper reference and meaningless if they did not. Bertrand Russell in 'On denoting' (1905) distinguishes between referring and nonreferring expressions. The role of all referring expressions is to identify objects in the actual world. If the predicate properly identifies its extralinguistic object, the expression is true; if it fails, the expression is false. If there is no such identification at all, then the expression has neither sense nor meaning. This is where the main difference between Frege's and Russell's semantic theory lies: Russell has no room for Frege's sense. Or, perhaps more accurately, the two are collapsed into a referentially based meaning. The reason for this is that Russell did not accept the possibility of having a thought about something without its identification in the world. Here, positivist reference rules semantics, which it still does to this day in many theories of language as well as folk assumptions about meaning. What Frege and Russell share in their descriptions of reference is the unstated metaphysical assumption that a physical, given world independent of human processes of cognition is directly available as reference. Only if one holds such a hard-headed realist view can one fix reference in the way their theories say we do.

In 'On referring' (1950) Strawson softened the hardness of this position by making reference dynamic. Instead of regarding objects in the actual world as references of language, he speaks of using expressions for the purpose of referring. There is not so much reference as the result of linking linguistic expressions correctly with the world as the option to employ language for referring and ascribing purposes. This goes a long way towards a constructivist view of language and world. The world as humans perceive it is no longer presumed to be a fixed set of prearranged objects but is seen much more as a post-Kantian construct where pregiven stuff and conceptual grasp interact to give us what we see. There are referents, but they are already coloured by the sort of referring use we make of language. In spite of this advance, on the question of fictional statements Strawson very much remains stuck in the tradition he critiques. For he regards fictional sentences as 'spurious' (Strawson, 1950: 336). They are deficient because they do not permit us, even in his more sophisticated description, to employ them for properly referring purposes.

In *The Varieties of Reference* (posthumously 1982) Gareth Evans achieves another significant advance with respect to reference. He suggests that a speaker using an expression for the purpose of referring 'must make it *manifest* which object he intends to be speaking about' and which referent 'an audience must think of' in order to understand what he is talking about. This requires the establishment of the object's '*salience*', which can be brought out by ostensive acts, such as 'shaking it, wobbling it, or causing a searchlight beam to fall on it'. Now we are in a position to grasp the 'speaker's *intended reference*', which, according to Evans, 'is rather like the notion of a *target*' and 'what the speaker thinks about the referent may be irrelevant to what he says' (Evans, 1982: 311–19). We know roughly what he is referring to. At the same time, the world of which that referent is a part is understood in terms of perceptual acts of touching and seeing. We have here the beginnings of a semiotic and corporeal view of reference.

According to a current view of reference in cognitive science advanced by Gilles Fauconnier, what counts 'is the social consensus on objects and properties'. In securing reference, 'all that matters is the assumption that there are objects and that ... they have or do not have the properties we consider'. That said, 'it does not directly matter, either, whether or not this assumption is right as long as its commonsense credibility is sustained'. What counts is that there is a match-up between cognitive constructions and 'real-world situations'. Yet how people achieve social and psychological consensus on such match-ups is another matter. What is important in this picture of reference is that a great many instances of referential 'space constructions' do not function to 'serve in direct matchups with the real world' but rather as a method of inferential reasoning about the actual world (Fauconnier, 1997: 68f.). Different as they may be, the accounts by Evans and Fauconnier are attractive because they have rid themselves of the tight relation between language and world, even though they do not give up certain assumptions about the 'real world' with its 'real objects'. Nevertheless, they permit the inclusion of fictional texts under 'intended reference' and 'cognitive constructions', respectively, and so are much more relevant to language use in its totality than earlier theories. What is not compatible with a corporeal semantics in the shape offered here is a certain naïveté when it comes to assumptions of what the world must be like for reference to work as a link. I do not want to dispute that there is *something* into which our readings of the world bump. Let us call this something 'stuff'. We should not call it objects or world without conceding that when we do so we have already processed stuff by the mechanisms of our perception, by our bodies at the human scale and our scientific instruments at, for instance, the subatomic level of observation. Importantly, we cannot separate out our instruments of perception from the way the world looks to us. It is always perspectival, no matter how we try to gain a position of neutrality. Given that we cannot eliminate ourselves as observers, we can achieve no more than what Humberto Maturana (1988) has called 'objectivity in parentheses'.

If we take seriously the idea that the actual world is a perspectival world and that the perspective is provided by our ways of seeing, including scientific seeing, then reference looks somewhat different. Reference becomes an *intersemiotic* relation between items in distinct systems of signs. Instead of speaking of a link between language and world, we should say that reference is a connection between specific configurations in one sign system, such as aural readings of the world, and specific configurations in another system, such as visual grasp. The more such systems of perceptual configurations interact, the stronger our sense of reference. How does this angle affect reference in a corporeal semantics?

Reference and the body

In a theory of language in which the body plays a central role, what applies to cultural deixis equally applies to reference. Contrary to reference in the analytical tradition from Frege to the kind of naturalist language theory advocated by Devitt and Sterelny, reference in corporeal semantics cannot be a simple relation between language and objects in the world. Reference must be rephrased as an *intersemiotic* relation. Why is this so and what does it amount to?

When we say that the referent of 'the morning star' and 'the evening star' is the planet Venus, we are summing up a process of signification that is a little more complicated than it seems. We are saying that the phrases of a natural language can be linked with physical objects. But this is not what actually happens. At its most innocent, this is a rough summary which ends up combining things that cannot be combined, namely signs and physical objects. What is missing here is a common level of comparison that would allow the apples and pears of reference to be aligned. There seem to be two ways of providing such a *tertium comparationis*. We could treat linguistic expressions as physical objects, which in one sense they are, and so make reference a relation between them and the object of the planet. If we do this, however, we have eliminated an essential ingredient of language, its semantic values. For as far as language consists of material entities, such as sounds or print, it does not mean anything. It is no more than something that occupies space. The second option is to go the other way, to making the level of comparison the domain of signs. In this case the physical planet Venus turns into 'Venus', a linguistic expression and those nonverbal signs of shape, colour and trajectory which we employ to lend the expression content and so meaning. Or we take 'Venus' to be the readings of a telescope; that is, perceptual, nonverbal signs without language. Now we can speak of reference as a relation between signs. *Reference has become intersemiotic.* The question of how this intersemiotic reference relates to the actual 'stuff' that allows us to construe the planet Venus is a metaphysical problem which we must postpone until Chapter 13. Here it is important to stress that intersemiotic reference is the only kind of reference we have always had and always will have. The empiricist and naturalist phrasing of reference as a relation between language as a sign system and physical objects as given is untenable. Both parties of the comparison must become elements in a significatory practice.

If this is so, what is the difference in an explanation of language based on the body between meaning and reference? Are they not now identical? The short answer is that meaning always has a referential character but is always general. Reference, in contrast, is always a specific relation. For further clarification we must briefly return to some basic distinctions that inform not only analytical philosophy but a good deal of folk mythology about meaning. There is a belief that natural-language terms have a sense or meaning and a reference. In its Fregean form this sense is a thought governed by a definition, or, in its folk version, at least an unambiguous description. This makes the sense of 'dole bludger' a close cousin of the sense of a geometrical entity such as a triangle. From a body-oriented language theory, nothing could be more misguided. What precisely is the mistake here? There is no dispute that a Euclidian, non-spheric triangle is defined by the rule that it must have three intersecting lines and that the sum of its angles must amount to 180 degrees. All the elements that make up this definition are likewise controlled by strict definition. Importantly, any image or representation of the triangle is merely an unnecessary supplement which we may or may not entertain. And most importantly, the definition is a priori. The definition comes first, then we can do geometry. Not so in the case of 'dole bludger'. Both elements of the expression have indefinite descriptions, depending on the kind of dictionary we wish to consult. This means first of all that natural language is not governed by definitions at all. Second, in language the invention of the expression and its use come first, then we can write a dictionary. In other words, dictionary descriptions are a posteriori; they come after the fact of language. Third, without being able to imagine the general social back-ground within which both the dole and those who are said to exploit it function, we could not construe the specific reference of 'student X is a dole bludger'. Although in the geometrical example our nonverbal readings are spurious, they are absolutely essential in the construction of meaning in natural language. While in formal sign systems the body has largely been made redundant, in natural language its presence guarantees meaning.

We are dealing here with two entirely different kinds of sense which should be strictly separated in analysis. Indeed, I suggest that they are so distinct from one another that they should not bear the same name. That they both keep reappearing in technical accounts as well as in folk theories about language is one of the consequences of a confusion in a philosophical tradition that used natural-language examples for logical purposes, with disastrous results (Ruthrof, 1993; 1997a: 59–76). Having separated the two kinds of sense, we will find that this way of viewing things also affects reference. In formal sign systems, reference is a 'can' rule rather than a 'must' rule. We may add references to variables such as z or y, but we do not have to do so. In natural languages we have no such choice in the matter. Here we always have two kinds of reference, a general referential background and the kind of reference that points to a specific set of signs. To understand the expressions 'morning star' and 'evening star' we first need the general intersemiotic background of typical mornings, typical evenings and planets. Without this referential background knowledge we would not know what is being talked about. In addition, there is the specific reference of 'Venus'. A purely logical syntax has no such general referential background as a requirement. Its definitions are the only equipment needed to construe sense.

But what about fictional uses of language? Are not fictional statements without reference? Only if we believe that very same tradition that collapsed two incompatible kinds of sense. One could take the opposite view: *fictions multiply reference*. There is reference of the kind that allows us to imagine a fictional world in relation to the actual social lifeworld. There is intertextual reference to all other possibly relevant fictions. There are specific references within the fictional world. And to top this line of thinking, they are just as intersemiotically structured as the references we employ to find our way about in the actual world. But surely, you will say, there must be a difference between fictions and actuality. There certainly is, but it cannot be decided at the level of reference. To make such a distinction, we need to address the question of constraints that frame our constructions, fictional and otherwise. Again, this is a problem to be returned to in Chapter 13.

Both deixis and reference, then, take on a new character if viewed from the perspective of a body-oriented theory of language. At the same time, all reference turns out to be coloured by implicit deixis, which provides an additional, even if concealed, cultural perspective. The very 'same' item in two cultures, the 'same' reference in analytical terms, has a different meaning by virtue of a different cultural speech stance, a culture's implicit deixis or hidden cultural modalities. In part the argument here has relied on the concept of intersemiotic relations without having paid much attention to what this implies. The next chapter addresses the question of how meaning can be regarded as intersemiotic.

5. Sign rapport: meaning as intersemiotic

> My fingers cannot, of course, get the impression of a large whole at a glance; but I feel the parts, and my mind puts them together ... my mind is full of associations, sensations, theories, and with them it constructs the house.
>
> (Helen Keller, *The World I Live In*, 12f.)

The term 'comprehension', to grasp together, still exhibits the nonverbal activities that are summed up by that word. So do a large number of other words. The frequency of the prefixes con- and com- in the Latin languages is testimony to this memory of the nonverbal, pre-predicative and extra-linguistic. In a much more general sense, we can say that the realization of objects as objects rather than as separate aspects has to do with the *inter-semiotic* character of cognition (Ruthrof, 1995). Yet not all readings of the world are intersemiotic in the sense of being harmoniously aligned with one another. Intersemiotic grasp stands in an uneasy relationship with *hetero-semiotic* readings, a phenomenon to be looked at in the next chapter. Here we want to consolidate the fact of intersemiotic relations and ask what such a picture has to say about language and meaning. If the intersemiotic thesis holds, not just between various perceptual interpretations of the world but also between such readings and the empty schemata of language, then we would have further arguments in support of the claim that the body plays a substantive role in linguistic meaning.

In Western thought the interaction between our various perceptual readings of the world has been a topic at least since Aristotle. In *De Anima* (Aristotle, 1968) we find a fairly comprehensive analysis of how our different senses contribute to our understanding of our surroundings and ourselves as bodies within an environment (Ruthrof, 1997a: 38, 267f.). However, in spite of such early comments and a substantial philosophical tradition since, there is no better source of evidence in favour of intersemiotic relations than the story and documentation of Helen Keller's life. From losing both sight and hearing when a young child as a consequence of an illness she grew to adult womanhood able to compensate for her dual handicap and participate fully in public life. Both her own account and the letters of her dedicated teacher Anne Sullivan are a gold mine for the thesis of intersemiotic corroboration. Consider this observation:

> Even in the days before my teacher came, I used to feel along the square stiff boxwood hedges, and, guided by the sense of smell, would find the first violets and lilies ... coming suddenly upon a beautiful vine, I recognized it by its leaves and blossoms, and knew it was the vine which covered the tumble-down summer-house at the farther end of the garden! (Keller, 1954: 24f.)

This is a forceful reminder that we do not live in an undifferentiated world even if we do not have access to a sophisticated language. Keller remembers that her wordless world was indeed highly differentiated. Tactile and olfactory signs allow Helen to recognize flowers as distinct long before she knows their names. They are distinct entities in terms of nonverbal readings. And these very readings later fill the frames of linguistic expressions such as 'violets' and 'lilies'. At the same time these nonverbal realizations are possible because of intersemiotic confirmation or corroboration. Touch and smell applied to the 'same' phenomenon she bumps into produce a cognizable and recognizable object. Helen's objects, 'violet' or 'vine' or 'stiff boxwood hedge', are literally forms that object to or resist her body and so become counterbodies in her universe. Everything apart from herself is made up of other bodies.

As Helen appeared much more sensitive to touch and smell than other people, Ms Sullivan was right to work with her protégée's nonverbal readings. She assured her pupil that the way she understood the world by way of her body was a good thing and did not conflict with her gradual acquisition of language. As Helen remembers:

> Long before I learned to do a sum in arithmetic or describe the shape of the earth, Miss Sullivan had taught me to find beauty in the fragrant woods, in every blade of grass, and in the curves and dimples of my baby sister's hand. She linked my earliest thoughts with nature, and made me feel that 'birds and flowers and I were happy peers'. (Keller, 1954: 37)

When it comes to learning terms and sentences, Helen is well equipped to fill their sounds with her nonverbal grasp of the world. Her own perceptual and quasi-perceptual body is able to make language meaningful not only in social terms, as to what everybody says about things, but in terms of her own, very special construals. However, this intersemiotic linkage does not occur immediately. I am avoiding the term 'intersemiotic translation' for reasons that will become clear further along. What matters here is that language signs can be learned first as a mere syntactic game:

> When I had played with it a little while, Miss Sullivan slowly spelled into my hand the word 'doll'. I was at once interested in this finger play and tried to imitate it. When I finally succeeded in making the letters correctly I was flushed with childish pleasure and pride. Running downstairs to my mother I held up my hand and made the letters for doll; I was simply making my fingers go in monkey-like imitation. In the days that followed I learned to spell in this uncomprehending way a great many words, among them *pin*, *hat*, *cup*, and a few verbs like *sit*, *stand* and *walk*. But my teacher had been with me several weeks before I understood that everything has a name. (1954: 35)

We are dealing here with non-iconic, symbolic writing without phonetics. The imitation of syntax is 'uncomprehending'. Only later is a simple naming stage of understanding achieved. However, we cannot take these comments at face value. They reflect as much her teaching as her actual experience. Above all, 'what's *in* a name'? Both the naming theory of language and its various critiques can be bypassed by emphasizing the 'in' of the phrase. If there is nothing *in* a name then it does not mean. If we can fill it with nonverbal content, such as what a pin, a hat, or a cup *feel* like, a violet or lily *smell* like, what kinetic, proximic and 'motor' readings are as *corporeal realizations*, then a word has become a *name*. Without the prior perceptual realization of where we are in relation to other bodies, in the broadest possible sense, language could not kick in. As Helen remembers, 'She brought me my hat, and I knew I was going out into the warm sunshine. This thought, if a wordless sensation may be called a thought, made me hop and skip with pleasure' (1954: 36). Helen knows her way around in her wordless world, even if this world is limited. Certainly, what Keller describes as 'thought' cannot be the Fregean thought, which is governed by strict definition. It is a nonverbal but nevertheless specific realization of the world. Given the general thrust of our corporeal semantics, this realization too should count as a thought. For in this scenario, both linguistic thought and such instances of comprehending the world have the same basis: nonverbal signs in interaction. On the other hand, the digital computer program in Searle's experiment does not 'comprehend' in the way Helen does. However, remember the extension of his argument via robotics in Chapter 3.

As an adult person Helen Keller tries to remember what life was *like* for her before her entry into fully socialized language. She insists that this is what happened before her training by Anne Sullivan:

> The delicate tremble of a butterfly's wings in my hand, the soft petals of violets curling in the cool folds of their leaves or lifting sweetly out of the meadow-grass, the clear, firm outline of face and limb, the smooth arch of a horse's neck and the velvety touch of his nose – all these, and a thousand resulting combinations, which take shape in my mind, constitute my world. (1909: 6f.)

Notice the emphasis on 'a thousand resulting combinations'. It would seem that even within one and the same semiotic system, here that of touch, a myriad cross-references suggest themselves. In combination, they result in a highly differentiated, intersemiotic world. 'The coolness of a water-lily rounding into bloom is different from the coolness of the rain that soaks into the hearts of growing things,' says Keller. 'The velvet of the rose is not that of a ripe peach or of a baby's dimpled cheek' (1909: 8). In her mind, everything is associated with 'tactual qualities which, combined in countless ways', afford her 'a sense of power' (1909: 7). Without such interpretive mastery Helen Keller would have felt helpless, as we all would. Remarkable here is her emphasis on the multiplicity of tactile readings, her high degree of differential grasp. This is so important to her that she speaks of 'the organ of apprehension' as a source of 'ecstasies' (1909: 33, 29). Even before we speak of an intersemiotic relation between verbal and nonverbal signs, we are always already characterized as intersemiotic beings. What happens, then, when nonverbal signs and the sounds of language are joined with one another?

Few documented examples of how nonverbal grasp and language interact are as persuasive as Helen's eureka experience in the following example. By way of pedagogic, tactile ostension Helen is led to realize at the same time a specific instance of language and a general principle. Importantly, though, first come the tactile signs, to which a summary linguistic sign is then added. In the intersemiotic combination of the two, linguistic meaning emerges:

> Someone was drawing water and my teacher placed my hand under the spout. As the cool stream gushed over one hand she spelled into the other the word water, first slowly, then rapidly. I stood still, my whole attention fixed upon the motions of her fingers. Suddenly I felt a misty consciousness as of something forgotten – a thrill of returning thought;

and somehow the mystery of language was revealed to me. I knew then
that 'w-a-t-e-r' meant the wonderful cool something that was flowing
over my hand. (1909: 36)

Meaning, then, is the activation of the otherwise empty grid 'water', or *'aqua'*,
or *'Wasser'*, by the feeling of a cool liquid running over skin, a tactile, haptic
reading of the world combined with a written, not yet spoken word. It does
not seem to matter in which form of materiality the signifier is fixed, whether
in drawing, writing or speaking. What matters is the transition from a mere
materially fixed and so empty signifier to the meaningful word 'water'. What
counts is that the nonverbal sensation of 'cool', 'stream', 'gushing' and 'hand'
are being consistently linked with a specific word sound. Once the intersemiotic relation between Helen's perceptual readings and the vibrations of
word sounds have been stabilized in her mind, she 'understands'. Helen has
understood one specific linguistic meaning and at the same time its intersemiotic principle. We should not think, though, that two meaningful
semiotic systems have thus been translated into one another. Crucially, one
of the two, language, did not mean at all. This forces us to believe that there
is an asymmetrical relation between nonverbal and verbal signs: *language is
parasitic on nonverbal signs*.

Helen's account is nicely complemented by her teacher's. Anne Sullivan's
attentive observation and record of the same event is as telling as Helen's
autobiographical statement. At first Ms Sullivan fails to teach Helen the
distinction between 'mug', 'milk' and 'drinking'. She fails, I suggest, because
the intersemiotic association between nonverbal practice and word sounds is
offered too superficially. Only after Helen's experience at the water spout
does Ms Sullivan succeed in making her pupil realize the conventional link
between nonverbal construal and linguistic signifier:

We went out to the pump-house, and I made Helen hold her mug under
the spout while I pumped. As the cold water gushed forth, filling the
mug, I spelled 'w-a-t-e-r' in Helen's free hand. *The word coming so close
upon the sensation of cold water rushing over her hand seemed to startle her.*
She dropped the mug and stood as one transfixed. A new light came
into her face. (Letter, 5 April 1887; 1909: 257)

What we have here is a kind of doubling of pathways of the imagination, a
kind of *Nachempfindung* (a re-pathetic realization). Such a doubling is possible only because Helen and her teacher suddenly share two systems of signs.
For us the substantial point is that Ms Sullivan is aware of the tactile reading
that is going on at this moment. Sense interpretation and word are so closely

and consistently linked that meaning occurs. The systemic nonverbal readings of the world, Helen's reading of 'the cool stream gushed over one hand', is aligned by the social act of ostension with the system of linguistic signifiers. This is the proof of the pudding. *Only as an intersemiotic event can language mean.* No sooner has this semantic event occurred than Helen understands the principle of word meanings as a generalized consequence. She immediately adds some thirty new words to her lexicon. 'She drops the signs she used before, as soon she has words to supply their place,' writes Anne Sullivan, and she adds that 'a new word affords her the liveliest pleasure' (10 April 1887; 1909: 257).

There is no doubt as to the attractiveness of the symbolic economy of linguistic signs. Helen is quick to notice the enormous advantages that language offers her in summing up, surveying and manipulating her nonverbal readings of her environment. This realization is accelerated when she begins to work with increasingly complex combinations of words to form conventional English syntax. Once more we have reached a pivotal point in our discussion. Contrary to structuralist linguistic and other 'intragrammatical' assumptions about syntax, the following example demonstrates the close intersemiotic link between nonverbal sign complexes and syntactic order.

Anne Sullivan records how Helen battles with syntax in her attempt to reflect appropriately her nonverbal understanding of a specific situation, her realization that her baby sister cannot eat certain things because she has no teeth. 'Helen shook her head and spelled "Baby teeth – no, baby eat – no", meaning, of course, "Baby cannot eat because she has no teeth"' (24 April 1887; 1909: 259). Neither the individual items addressed nor the temporal sequence of events, indeed the causal relationships established here, is a consequence of syntax. The converse is the case. Helen has already understood the situation by nonverbal semiosis. Now she is looking for a syntax that would match that nonverbal state of affairs. Since her syntax is not yet fully socialized, it appears garbled yet not unintelligible. Her teacher has no problem, and nor would anybody else, understanding what Helen is trying to express in language. Some kind of formal pattern can be discovered in both systems of signs, constructed world and language: no teeth – not eating; baby no teeth – baby not eating. If soon after this incident Helen is able to replace her rudimentary syntax by standard English we should not say that her grasp of the world is now the right one. Again it is the other way round. The more complex our nonverbal construals, the more intricate will our syntactic structures have to be to cope with that complexity.

I am not saying that all syntactic formations in natural languages are iconic reflections of networks of nonverbal signs. A certain syntactic independence cannot be denied, when new syntactic structures are used that draw on and extend some previous syntax rather than primarily reflecting nonverbal signs. The point is that the intersyntactic structuralist thesis as well as its philosophical parallel of 'intergrammaticality', according to which language works as an independent system of syntactic and semantic relations, are not tenable as a general rule. Temporal, causal and other relations between signs are not invented by language. All we can claim is that language is an effective medium for their multiplication and increase in speed as well as combinatorial range. In spite of all this, there is always also the more primitive yet still important intersemiotic relation which surfaces not only at the level of the signified but also at the level of the signifier as an ordered sequence, that is, syntax.

Although Helen Keller's personal account flies in the face of a good deal of linguistic theory, it is not without support from the scientific community. Empirical research in cognitive science has since confirmed a number of her intersemiotic observations. We now know that 'smells stimulate learning and retention' (Ackerman, 1991: 11). Quoting Edwin T. Morris from his book *Fragrance*, Diane Ackerman writes that when children were provided with 'olfactory information' and a list of words, they were able to memorize the list much better than without olfactory stimulation. In the same context, she refers to perfume as 'liquid memory' (11). Likewise, touch 'frequently combines with other senses' (77). If the kind of corporeal semantics I am advocating is highly speculative, no such accusation can be levelled at the experimental evidence for intersemiotic relations cited by Ackerman under the heading 'Tactile vocoders':

> Touch is being used successfully as a substitute for hearing. Varying numbers of gold-plated electrodes are attached to a stimulator belt, which is usually worn on the abdomen, arm, forehead, or legs. A deaf child is taught that particular sounds have particular skin patterns. Then the teacher asks the child to create sounds that will produce the same pattern on the skin. (Ackerman, 1991: 94, footnote)

So far, intersemiotic relations appear to follow a can-rule. We are able experimentally to substitute one sense reading for another. The next step is seeing intersemiotic association as mandatory. As Ackerman claims, 'a mirror would mean nothing without touch' (95). This indicates a progression from semiotic corroboration to 'cross-modal' compulsion. We cannot construe our world as meaningful without employing different semiotic systems. In this picture, language once more is the odd category. We have already seen that we are able to differentiate a complex network of objects and actions without verbal coding. Now we can draw the distinction between mandatory nonverbal signs and their additional linguistic codification.

Of course, this does not mean that all forms of 'sensory blending' are mandatory. On the one hand, we are told by science that newborn babies 'ride on intermingling waves of sight, sound, touch, taste, and, especially, smells' beyond their control (Ackerman, 1991: 289). On the other hand, we are free to play with intersemiotic relations, as artistic synaesthesia has demonstrated through the ages. To call music the perfume of hearing or to speak of the soft scent of the mango moon suggests a palette of synaesthesia of infinite variations. But even here there seem to be biological processes at work that permit such combinations. There is clinical evidence that 'a certain amount of synesthesia is built into our senses' (290). These neural connections between our various sensory centres can be tested, subdued or strengthened by drugs. In support of these claims Ackerman quotes Richard Cytowic, who has traced the synaesthetic phenomenon to the 'limbic system, the most primitive part of the brain'. Hence he calls natural synaesthetes 'living cognitive fossils' (290). Now we have cognitive evidence for the central role in cognition of intersemiotic relations. We also have Helen Keller's as well as her teacher's evidence for the way language is activated by perceptual and quasi-perceptual signs. As a result, the intersemiotic relation between language and body confirms the description of meaning as an activation of empty linguistic schemata, coded in the form of spoken or written linguistic expressions by nonverbal signs such as tactile, olfactory, gustatory and other readings. Significantly, language acquires meaning only when it is correlated with the nonverbal. Language, once more, is parasitic on nonverbal signs.

We are now in a position to demonstrate how this understanding of language and its intersemiotic relation with nonlinguistic systems differs from its most influential competitor, Roman Jakobson's *intersemiotic translation*. In 'On linguistic aspects of translation' (Jakobson, 1971a) he defines intersemiotic translation by distinguishing three ways of interpreting a verbal sign: it may be translated into other signs of the same language, into another language, or into another, nonverbal system of symbols. These three kinds of translation are to be differently labelled:

1) Intralingual translation or *rewording* is an interpretation of verbal signs by means of other signs of the same language.
2) Interlingual translation or *translation* proper is an interpretation of verbal signs by means of some other language.
3) Intersemiotic translation or *transmutation* is an interpretation of

verbal signs by means of signs of nonverbal sign systems. (1971a: 261)

In 'Linguistic types of aphasia' (Jakobson, 1971b) Jakobson speaks of 'various types of intersemiotic relations, such as the transition from gestures to words, from words to gestures, from words to pictures, etc.' (1971b: 330), whereby there is no indication that such transmutations are required to endow language with meaning. For Jakobson, intersemiotic relations are transmutations of signs from one meaningful system to another. In our picture of meaning and nonverbal signs, intersemiotic relations share with Jakobson's the transmutational process as long as we are dealing with nonverbal signs. Where we differ is that in corporeal semantics language does not mean at all unless nonverbal signs are employed to fill the empty grids of linguistic expressions. Where Jakobson allows for linguistic meaning-independence, corporeal semantics does not.

This difference appears also in what Jakobson has to say about intersemiotic relations in art. Here translation does not appear to be possible, but only 'intersemiotic transposition – from one sign into another, e.g., from verbal art into music, dance, cinema, or painting' (266). Linguistic meaning-independence in Jakobson's work appears likewise in his comments on Saussure's view of the sign:

> The word 'tree' and the pictorial representation of a tree ... are correlated signs: each of them has a different *signans* [signifier], but the two signs can replace each other because they have a similar *signatum* [signified]. The first is a 'symbol' and the second an 'icon', according to Peirce's classification of signs. (268)

Jakobson is not interested here in acts of fantasy and the variations on iconic representations we achieve in our imagination. He is talking strictly about concrete iconic representations. And these cannot, of course, as he rightly stresses, be in any way identical. 'A symbol may be translated into an icon and vice versa, but of course only with a certain approximation.' The specificity of the icon sets it apart from the generality of the symbol. In Jakobson's scheme, 'any symbol is endowed with general meaning and the general meaning of any symbol, and of any verbal symbol in particular, has a generic character' (268). What he does not consider is the possibility of various degrees of generalization of nonverbal signs, especially those high-level transformations of perception in our mental world which allow us to make sense of the actual world at lightning speed. But Jakobson does agree that the relationship between verbal and nonverbal signs is by no means clarified when he notes that 'the pertinent role played in language by iconic and indexical symbols still awaits a thorough examination' (335).

Two different kinds of intersemiotic relations emerge from this picture: one between perceptual readings and a second, quite different relation between nonverbal readings and verbal articulations. As a result, we are always dealing with two kinds of constructions of our world: our perceptual world, which we share to a greater or lesser extent with other animals, and a linguistically organized world, which appears to mark a significant difference between humans and other sentient beings. It would be wrong, however, to use this difference as one between verbal and nonverbal beings. This must strike us as no more than a theological prejudice. After all, our linguistically constructed world, as we have seen, relies entirely on our nonverbal grasp. Linguistic expressions, then, are no more than conventional markers which stand in for perceptual readings. This sets the intersemiotic picture sketched here apart from various traditions. The Jakobsonian explanation differs, because there the words and expressions of a natural language themselves have semantic values capable of interacting with nonverbal meanings. But if language itself receives semantic values only from the nonverbal, then Jakobson's position is incompatible. Likewise with analytical assumptions about meaning as definitional thought. As we have seen, a related form of criticism applies to the structuralist assumption that semantic values arise from the differential relations of expressions within a network of other expressions. By the same token, the idea of 'intergrammaticality', according to which meaning emerges from within the grammatical order of a language, appears untenable. Such views cut the body out of language, at their own cost. Intergrammaticality works in formal logical systems where syntax suffices. Language is more than syntax. Without the body in its perceptual and quasi-perceptual functions language has no meaning.

Conclusion

By way of conclusion, I would like to add two minor observations, one on Wittgenstein, the other on Derrida. Why Wittgenstein? Because there are a number of issues which in my view block our full appreciation of the implications of the later Wittgenstein's comments on nonverbal signification. For example, there seems to me a certain tension in the *Philosophical Investigations* between Wittgenstein's use of imagined situations and his rejection of 'ostensive definition' or 'demonstrative teaching' (1953: paragraphs 27–36). To be sure, he does not discard the fact of 'ostension' but rather its role as a necessary part in the mechanisms of meaning. Specifically, Wittgenstein's objections rest on the claim of 'misinterpretability'. He seems to be saying three things: that ostensions do not connect language and reality, that ostensions presuppose an understanding of what is to be defined, and that to regard ostensions as foundational is to confuse meaning with extraneous, additional realizations.

From the perspective of corporeal semantics, in which 'use' is the socially guided act of activating empty language schemata by nonverbal readings and fantasies, a certain kind of 'ostension' always appears to be part of the meaning event. Moreover, ostension appears necessary rather than spurious. In answer to the objections raised by Wittgenstein one could say that misinterpretability is not restricted to ostension. Much in natural language shares this characteristic. More on this point in Chapter 11. However, just as we can, to a certain degree, disambiguate the murkiness that attaches to certain natural-language texts, so too can we clarify ostensive processes. What is required is a more elaborate process of nonverbal negotiation within systemic social activities. It is astonishing to see how much can be communicated even about abstract matters in the absence of a shared language. Efficiency is, of course, another matter. The economy of language is not in doubt. What interests us at the moment is only the principle of ostension.

Wittgenstein's point that ostension does not 'link language and reality' is well taken. Indeed, from the corporeal angle chosen here, such a link must be regarded as an empiricist superstition. Ostension is not a gestural link between language and the world as physically given, as a naïve realist would have it, but rather a necessary, intersemiotic relation. Whether any ostensive gesture actually occurs or not, whenever we mean by language we ostensibly activate meaningless syntax by nonverbal readings. From this point of view, ostensive definition is an actualized form of habitual, nonconscious semantic performance. And as to the fact that ostension presupposes some form of grasp of what we are trying to define, this applies to everything we can possibly understand in terms of natural language. The a priori procedures of formal logic are of course a different matter. The attempt to explain something to us of which we are entirely ignorant, and for which we have no relevant clue whatsoever, must fail. In this respect, it is instructive to remind ourselves of Heidegger's explanation of understanding and interpretation in *Being and Time*. According to Heidegger, all understanding is a reduced form of interpretation which always presupposes a tripartite forestructure: a forehaving, a foregrasp and a foreseeing. A certain tacit knowledge precedes all more precise understanding. Hence meaning events always occur within hermeneutic spirals of increasing acquaintance rather than *ex nihilo*. If this is so, then this cannot be regarded as a special drawback of ostension (Heidegger, 1962: 188–213).

On the question of mental (re)presentations or *Vorstellungen*, Wittgenstein appears to be in agreement with Frege. They are to be regarded as inessential to meaning, for they are merely subjective. Where the later Wittgenstein and Frege are not in agreement is on the point that for Frege meaning is to be resolved inside language, as indeed it is in formal logic, while for the author of the *Philosophical Investigations*, to look at language alone does not allow us to describe meaning. Instead, meaning is 'use' within the frame of a 'form of life'. But suppose that 'use' were best described as precisely the linking procedures between linguistic schemata and such nonverbal readings as olfactory, tactile and other significations. Then some systemic account of mental (re)presentations would be legitimate components of meaning. This is compatible, for example, with findings in cognitive linguistics and cognitive rhetoric. And it is precisely the way corporeal semantics redefines 'use'.

The second aside I would like to make to round off this chapter concerns Derrida's view on perception. Since he has said that he does not believe in 'perception', it would seem that our intersemiotic account also stands in contradiction to deconstruction. However, caution may be advisable here because Derrida's leaning to Peirce and his intersemiotic arguments are not in dispute. So I suspect that 'perception' is being rejected by Derrida only in its naturalistic version and not as a set of signs. The same caution applies to Derrida's position on the question of 'representation', a topic I will be able to touch on towards the end of this book.

In this chapter I have sketched a picture of nonverbal signs as the deep structure of language. The emphasis here has been on intersemiotic corroboration among nonverbal readings and between nonverbal signs and language as a necessary condition for meaning. On its own, this provides too harmonious a scenario. In actual social discourse no such harmony can be observed. I suggest that there are deep reasons for the relative heterogeneity of semiosis at large. Semiotic discrepancies not only may be the result of circumstances extraneous to specific communicative situations but may lie close to the very heart of sign production itself. If this is so, we need to complement our intersemiotic narrative by an account of meaning as heterosemiotic. That is the aim of the following chapter.

6. Sign conflict: meaning as heterosemiotic

Each of us has an exaggerated mental picture of our body, with a big
head, hands, mouth, and genitals, and a small trunk; children often
draw people with big heads and hands, because this is the way their
body feels to them.

(Ackerman, 1991: 95)

Much of the theoretical literature of the late twentieth century has been
affected in one way or another by writers who have explored questions
concerning differentiation. Arguably the most influential authors in this
respect have been the French theorists Jacques Derrida and Jean-François
Lyotard. In Derrida, differentiation finds its deep ground in *différance*, a
principle which operates at all levels of signification. It is at work in the
spatial and temporal aspects of linguistic meaning, as differentiation and
deferral. At the level of the metaphysical question of Being, *différance* offers
an alternative explanation. Instead of building a hierarchy of the positivities
of 'presence' from specifics, or beings, with Being as apex, *différance* tops the
nonpositive pyramid of differential relations, or nonbeings. Any argument
concerning the presence of beings, including their emptiest possibility of
Being, requires differential relations to be thinkable at all. This is why
différance is able to claim a kind of logical priority. As a result, the illusion of
the cohesive, harmonious object-world rests on the empty and more profound principle of difference or otherness. In this way, *différance* could be said
to bring to the fore the fundamental heterogeneity underlying all signification (Derrida, 1973).

In Lyotard, signification, and indeed the world at large, is reduced to
'sentences'. At the same time, sentences are part of the agonistic deep
structure of all discourse. Different discursive regimes are at war with one
another. Religious discourse is incompatible with economic discourse, the
language of philosophy cannot be reconciled with the narratives of history,

while the speech of art criticism is fundamentally alienated from the signs of science and technology. In this nonanthropomorphic perspective of a world of competing sentences, injustice is the necessary consequence of all discursive encounters. Discursive power is always asymmetrically distributed and so there is always a speech participant who will suffer some form of inequity, some version of the 'differend'. Hence, a conflictual heterogeneity of signs could be said to be at the centre of Lyotard's view of the world (Lyotard, 1988). However, the heterogeneity that results from Lyotard's differend can also be employed for critical purposes, when artists, theorists and philosophers state things that need to be put but have not been said as yet. When the unpresentable is presented in this way, Lyotard speaks of a political form of the Kantian sublime (Lyotard, 1986: 10; 1994). Derrida's and Lyotard's contributions to the topic of heterogeneity are foundational in a metaphysical sense. Our aim here is much more modest. What I want to show is that it makes sense to say that the intersemiotic relations between signs is not the whole story and that a certain heterogeneity between signs plays an important role in the overall picture of semiosis. The double perspective of *différance* as the deep principle of differentiation among signs and agonistics as the fundamentally conflictual character of signs in discourse genres provides a frame for the exploration of specific instances of the heterogeneity of signs.

Perhaps the picture of the grotesque body that emerges from our nonvisual and nonverbal signs about ourselves is one of the more powerful pieces of evidence for the fact that standard images of what we are like, and what therefore all 'objects' are like, are only specific versions of less homely possibilities. The 'big head, hands, mouth, and genitals' combined with 'a small trunk' appears to us distorted and frightening, certainly *unheimlich*. We do not feel at home in this body. And yet, it is our body produced by our own tactile, haptic and other perceptual readings. To say that this grotesque body is the wrong one would require a plane of metajudgement which is denied us. All we can say is that ordinary perceptions of ourselves and the haptic body are in conflict. The signs responsible for the two Gestalten are heterogeneous.

Not all sign conflict is that dramatic, of course. Think of the hole in the tooth felt with the tip of your tongue, seen in the mirror, represented by the dentist's X-ray photograph, or felt when the dentist scrapes the hole with his or her instruments. We say that our impressions of the hole in our tooth vary, while the hole itself does not. Or, there must be 'something' that permits our various significations to occur in the way they do. Here we glimpse an instance of the reasons that made Kant stipulate an a-perspectival necessity, the thing-without-signification, *das Ding an sich*. Yet we tend to assume that one of our measurements, namely the visual sign complex, is the correct one, relegating other significations to the level of distortion. The point, though, is that each sign system produces a different picture of the world. For Helen Keller, 'the hardness of the rock is to the hardness of wood what a man's deep bass is to a woman's voice when it is low' (Keller, 1909: 8). In her case the differences are produced by her tactile reading of people's larynxes. While our sense readings can address themselves to the 'same' portion of the world they by no means generate identical impressions. Although my touching of a surface may suggest a fairly uneven object, to the eye the same phenomenon may look smooth and fair. However, neither tactile nor olfactory, nor any other nonverbal reading is a natural, biologically automated process. All such readings are complex interpretations, significations made up of a large number of bits of text. As Helen Keller observed from the double perspective of both pupil and researcher,

> when a blind man recovers his sight, he does not recognize the com-
> monest thing that has been familiar to his touch, the dearest face
> intimate to his fingers, and it does not help him at all that things and
> people have been described to him again and again. (Keller, 1909: 23)

To express this semiotically, we can say that different nonverbal signs not only co-operate with one another in producing a coherent and meaningful world, but also are in conflict with one another. This suggests that sign cohesion is achieved at the cost of suppressing their fundamental hetero-geneity.

How can we get a grip on the specifics of the conflictual side of signs? Let us turn to phenomenological method and play with different perspectives. From the *ontic* viewpoint, the heterogeneity of signs results in different 'worlds'. A surface may appear rough as a result of touch, while the 'same' surface can appear smooth to the eye. A berry that looks attractive is different as an object from the same berry that tastes acrid. The aircraft as a fast object is ontically different from the same aircraft as a loud object. The fact that we reconcile these different ontic features in one and the same multifaceted item does not cancel those differences. Our world is to a significant degree heterogeneous. When we emphasize the *epistemic* perspective a similar picture emerges. When we observe our own perceptual interpretations of the world, the cognitive processes that go with smelling, touching, tasting, sensing changes in gravity, becoming aware of variations in temperature or air pressure, and seeing, we note differences. Though we may direct our various sense readings towards the same portion of the world, let us say a friend's dark wine cellar, we become acutely aware of a shift from sense interpretations that normally deliver the goods but now suddenly fail or turn out to be unreliable. Sight is quickly abandoned as useless, though for a while we may strain our eyes in vain. Tactile, olfactory, aural, proximic and other signs take over. We trust different perceptual signs under different conditions.

Arguably one of the most instructive applications of the ontic–epistemic perspective in this respect is the Polish philosopher Roman Ingarden's attempt at demonstrating the structure of an ontically heteronomous object, the literary work. In *The Literary Work of Art* (1930; English translation 1973) and *The Cognition of the Literary Work of Art* (1957; 1973) he describes in detail the typical acts we perform when we read literature. Proceeding in phenomenological manner, he abstracted from our specific reading acts of specific works the eidetic features that our performances have in common. What evolves is first the base structure of the reading performance, an epistemic schema, and, as a result, what he regarded as the fundamental structure of the object of inquiry, the ontic structure of verbal art.

In these writings Ingarden showed how the heterogeneous elements that make up a literary work are put together by the reader into a harmonious 'polyphony of aesthetic value qualities'. What interests us here is not this classical notion of harmony but the semiotic heterogeneity which the reader must process. It is often forgotten in the commentaries on Ingarden that he was not primarily a literary theorist but a philosopher who wanted to demonstrate how phenomenology talks about ontic complexity, the manifold ways in which an object is constituted by acts of consciousness within realist constraints. He chose the literary work of art because when we perform verbal art we engage of necessity in different processes of cognition. Ingarden demonstrated that we do very different things when we deal cognitively with a material object, such as a rock, compared with how we cognize an ideal object, such as a triangle. Both are what he calls ontically homogeneous and so require only one sort of epistemic performance: the cognitive processes that go with materiality, i.e. the readings of size, gravitational forces, hardness, etc. on the one hand, and, on the other, ideality, i.e. the definition circumscribing a geometrical figure.

By contrast, when we perform verbal art in the act of reading, we cannot help but reconcile heterogeneous ontic principles. We process the materiality of sound and/or print, the ideality of syntactic sequences, the purely intentional objects of mental imagery in order to be able to imagine a fictional world, both as schema and in the portrayal of detail. In addition, according to Ingarden, we may also engage in the construal of metaphysical qualities. This we do at any point in the reading process as well as from the retrospective view, when we have finished reading and are in a position to survey the work as a whole. What emerges for Ingarden is what he called an *ontically heteronomous* object. In semiotic terms, when we read literary works, we confront one set of signifiers, sentences, out of which we construe various kinds of signs. Following Peirce's rule that any sign may be translated into another, more explicit sign and when this occurs meaning is 'more fully developed', we engage in a compound translation process. We appreciate the iconic features of print shape and sound of a poem, its typographic and euphonic aspects. We translate verbal signs semantically into meaning units, which means that we activate verbal schemata by nonverbal signs of a quasi-material nature. This allows us to imagine a three-dimensional world, which in turn we use as a more complex set of signs on which we can construct more abstract signs. It is at this level that we speak of a work's ideational content, its ideology, its message, its ideological motivation, and perhaps its metaphysics. All these signs are different in kind and in terms of level of abstraction, in terms of materiality, ideality and intentionality. In other words, they are *heterosemiotic*.

At a much simpler level of argument, we are able to note a certain heterogeneity among perceptual readings themselves. This is brought out by the fact that our various perceptual centres are not equally important for survival. Persons who are both deaf and blind demonstrate that it is 'possible to get on predominantly by touch, but to be without touch is to move through a blurred, deadened world, in which you could lose a leg and not know, burn your hand without feeling' (Ackerman, 1991: 82). Some senses provide rich information in certain respects, others provide none at all. Apparently, we taste only four flavours: sweet, sour, salty and bitter. The fine differentiations we think we are capable of making beyond these are actually produced by odours. Different sense readings tell a different story about the world. Apparently, complex organisms such as humans have learned to jackboot these differences into cohesion.

Science tells us that 'before something can be tasted, it has to be dissolved in liquid (... hard candy has to melt in saliva); and before something can be smelled, it has to be airborne' (Ackerman, 1991: 13). Ackerman quotes the stereochemical theory of J.E. Amoore, which maps the connections between the geometrical shapes of molecules and the odour sensations they produce. When a molecule of the right shape happens along, it fits into its neuron niche and then triggers a nerve impulse to the brain. Different odours have different molecular shapes and so we can speak of different locks requiring different keys (14). There also appears to be evidence for the claim that unlike our other sense readings, 'smell needs no interpreter'. That olfactory interpretation is more immediate than other nonverbal significations supports the view that we are dealing here with a fundamental kind of incompatibility.

However, Ackerman's extended claim that the effect of smell is 'immediate and undiluted by language, thought, or translation' suggests that one of our nonverbal sign systems escapes the as-structure (11). This is not persuasive. We still construe a world that is not identical with a particular olfactory sign complex. We identify a specific smell as indicating some object or event as a result of corroborating and conflicting sensory readings.

It has been observed that a radical difference exists between tactile readings and other signs. While experiments can be conducted to study vision by researching blind people, no such study has been able to be made as to touch. There appears to exist a deep incompatibility between some of the senses, almost violently reconciled at the level of interpretive grasp of the world and language. 'Every other sense has a key organ to study,' says Ackerman; 'for touch this organ is the skin, and it stretches over the whole body. Every sense has at least one key research centre, except touch' (77). Perhaps it is a mistake, then, to regard touch as stemming from one single sense organ. Perhaps 'touch' or 'the tactile' are no more than crude summary terms for a large range of organs and interpretations. After all, reading different kinds of moisture, from superfluid to highly viscous, different temperatures, different degrees of roughness and smoothness, forms of resistance, gravitational readings, the dynamics of fast and slow motion along the skin, degrees of sexual arousal, and so on, appear to be entirely different interpretive processes. While some tactile readings produce a cohesive picture, some others 'irritate and delight us simultaneously' (82). Heterogeneity may even be built into one and the same nerve receptor. As Ackerman reports,

> we assumed that each sensation had its own receptor and that that receptor had its own pathway to the brain, but it looks now as if the body's grassland of neurons relate any sensation according to electrical codes. Pain produces irregular bleats from nerves at jagged intervals. Itching produces a fast, regular pattern. Heat produces a crescendo as the area heats up. A little pressure produces a flurry of excitement, then fades, and a stronger pressure just extends the burst of activity. (81)

Studies of the tongue have shown that different sensors are grouped together to produce incompatible readings. Registering the sensation 'sweet' is the task of the tip of the tongue, 'bitter' is produced at the back, 'sour' at both sides, and 'salty' can be read by the overall surface, although best at the front. This suggests once more that a good deal of reconstructive interpretive labour is required to put together the various heterogeneous perceptual readings into our overall impression of a coherent world. Here we have *constructivism* at its most basic. There are also other discrepancies between our perceptual readings, as for instance the 'Doppler effect'. Our eyes record a symmetrical relation between a fast car coming towards us, passing by, and speeding away from us. This visual symmetry is contradicted by what our ears tell us. Aurally perceived, the two phases of the car approaching our position and speeding away from it are registered asymmetrically. In this case the visual and aural information appear as two entirely different sets of signs. The scientific explanation why this is so notwithstanding, as far as the human observer is concerned, the visual and aural readings are hetero-semiotic.

With reference to G.E. Lessing's distinction between the 'spatial side-by-side' of pictorial art and sculpture (*räumliches Nebeneinander*) and 'temporal sequentiality' (*zeitliches Nacheinander*), Roman Jakobson notes that

> there exists a profound dissimilarity between ... spatial and temporal systems of signs in general. When the observer arrives at the simultaneous synthesis of a contemplated painting, the painting as a whole remains before his eyes, it is still present; but when the listener reaches a synthesis of what he has heard, the phonemes have in fact already vanished. They survive as mere afterimages, somewhat abridged reminiscences, and this creates an essential difference between the two types of perception and percepts. (Jakobson, 1971c: 344)

In another paper, 'The statue in Pushkin's poetic mythology' (1979), Jakobson speaks of semiotic *antinomies*, 'internal conflicts ... which are the necessary, indispensable basis of any semiotic world'. Generalizing from his reading of Pushkin, he says that

> a statue – in contrast to a painting – so approximates its model in its three-dimensionality that the inorganic world is nearly cancelled out of its themes: a sculptural still life would not suitably provide the distinct antinomy between the representation and the represented object that every artistic sign includes and cancels. Only the opposition of the *dead, immobile matter* from which a statue is shaped and the *mobile, animate being* which a statue represents provides a sufficient distance. (Jakobson, 1979: 267f.)

Herder rejected this kind of classification almost two centuries ago, suggesting instead that mere temporal sequence (*Zeitfolge*) does not occur in art at all; here, we are dealing with *energeia*, a simultaneous synthesis of the entirety of verbal art. Herder finds support for his view in the poetry of T.S. Eliot, who in 'Burnt

Norton' (Eliot, 1963) likewise transcends the orthodox classification. For him language can achieve the tranquil voice of a Chinese jar only via patterned form. Only then is the word able to move 'perpetually in its stillness'.

That more complex reasons for semiotic heteronomy operate at the level of art is perhaps not surprising. Yet it is very difficult to find convincing arguments for why it is impossible to translate radically different musical traditions. Ackerman asks, for example, why 'we cannot translate one musical idiom into another, as for instance Western Romantic music into Chinese music' (Ackerman, 1991: 213). The two traditions are heterosemiotic in a very strong sense.

Given the conflictual base conditions of a variety of sense interpretations, it should not come as a surprise that the interaction between perceptual readings and verbal signs should likewise exhibit a certain degree of heterogeneity. As Paul Kay and Willett Kempton have shown, we see the same colours even if we categorize differently linguistically (Kay and Kempton, 1984). When Diane Ackerman says that 'not all languages name all colours', we note a series of problems (Ackerman, 1991: 253). What does 'all colours' refer to? Wavelengths, the range of colour terms in English, or the data of the prism? None of these produces identical readings. What we call orange-red as against red could be designated by a variety of wavelengths in the same band. Ackerman's brief remark highlights the fact that there is a discrepancy between nonverbal ways of describing colour, nonverbal human responses to colour, and the way different languages conceptualize whatever colour evidence they have, the way different semantic grids are laid over nonverbal realizations.

Likewise intriguing is Ackerman's observation that the 'Japanese only recently included a word for "blue" in their vocabulary' (253). Does this mean that until then the Japanese were unable to experience blue? Most unlikely. The fact of linguistic coarse-grain coverage of nonverbal experience does not allow the conclusion that the experience itself is also coarse-grained. In Japanese the older, broader term *aoi* certainly distinguished shades from green to blue to violet. Likewise, the fact that the Welsh word *glas*, which describes the colour of a mountain lake, could refer to blue, grey or green does not mean that Welsh people do not make such visual distinctions. The fact that *nyakundu* in Swahili covers brown, yellow and red must not lead us to assume that the culture does not have these distinctions. It has them nonverbally. To say otherwise suggests that once we have certain words but not others, the visual messages to our brain are censored by language. The more likely interpretation is that cultures function quite happily in spite (or because) of a certain heterogeneity between nonverbal signs and language.

The Maori have a large range of words for red. For Ackerman there is a connection between 'all the reds that surge and pale as fruits and flowers develop, as blood flows and dries' on the one hand and, on the other, the size of their colour vocabulary (253). Although we observe here a certain relationship between nonverbal and verbal signs, there is no identity. The heterogeneity that separates nonverbal from linguistic signs is also well illustrated by the fact that the experience of smell and our ability to describe its myriad nuances are at odds. In Ackerman's words, 'smell is the mute sense'. Since we lack an adequate lexicon 'we are tongue-tied, groping for words in a sea of inarticulate pleasure and exaltation' (6). As new social practices evolve, such as surfing inside a breaking wave, a new vocabulary emerges to cover the new nonverbal visual, tactile, aural, gravitational and other readings that make up our grasp of surfing in a barrel. Just like colour readings, such new signs are culture-specific and to a certain degree heterogeneous constructions (Kendon, 1981).

A special kind of semiotic heterogeneity appears to characterize what is summarily described under the term 'autism'. I am marking this term in this way because I sense that in the absence of any precise knowledge of the neural mechanisms responsible for autistic behaviour, we should be extremely cautious when we apply a classification of this kind. The more I read about the phenomenon, the more I discover autistic features in myself, though most of them are under the hood, so to speak, and well integrated in the way I present myself as a social being. It seems to me, however, that there may be only a tiny difference between those who have successfully negotiated their 'autism' and those who have not. In other words, and leaving extreme autism aside, we may all have of necessity a certain degree of autistic resistance to being socially tamed.

A fascinating case study of autism is the autobiography of Donna Williams, *Nobody Nowhere* (1992), in which she recalls the terrible struggle of learning to establish herself as an independent and yet socially accepted personality. As unusual, wilful and compulsive as Donna's behaviour may seem during her childhood, there is little that surprises in her specific tactile, visual, aural and other readings. True, the sensation of feeling burned when she is in physical contact with other people and some of her memories of visual idiosyncrasies appear to be highly heterosemiotic. Importantly, however, the majority of her sense readings are intersemiotic rather than heterosemiotic. This is especially so when Donna remembers her bravado acts of balancing. She is particularly happy on swings, on trees and on bicycles. Indeed, her sense of balance and gravitational nuance may have been well above average. What appears to make it so difficult for Donna to relate to the social world around her is, as Todd Oakley observed in a recent e-mail message, the 'intrasemiotic' intensity of the experiences of the autistic person. In this sense, Donna can be regarded as a 'structuralist par excellence'.

With this proviso we turn to the central question that concerns us here. How does her semantic grasp of language (English) relate to her nonverbal grasp of her world? For a very long time, until she is nearly 4 years old, Donna is unable to proceed beyond a phonetic and syntactic grasp of English. Here we have a case of someone who during this early time of her life has indeed no more than signifiers. She is without signifieds, however underdetermined. Instead of answering questions and requests, she repeats the given phrase. No wonder she makes little semantic progress when she is slapped by her mother for her syntactic stubbornness. What Donna is unable to do is to establish the standard links between the sounds of the words and her nonverbal readings of the world. And even later, she likes to mimic rather than to participate in discourse (Williams, 1992: 21), loves echoing the sound of Italian phrases (34), and enjoys the syntactic repetitions in the phone book (44). And although her 'reading was very good', she had 'merely found a more socially acceptable way of listening to the sound of [her] own voice' (25).

The turning-point in Donna's linguistic development is crucial. It occurs at a moment when something very personal and hurtful is said about her and she is suddenly able to make the connection between signifiers and signifieds, words and her body. Donna recalls:

> I have a vague recollection that there were other children there, for the topic of discussion in the living room had disturbed and embarrassed me. A question was asked about my toilet training. My mother replied that I was still wetting myself. (Williams, 1992: 4)

What Donna Williams remembers as traumatic is in principle something we all must go through to a certain, if usually mild, degree. This applies not only to being able to link our nonverbal readings of the world with the sounds of language, but to those nonlinguistic readings themselves. As Oliver Sacks remarks, 'when we open our eyes each morning, it is upon a world we have spent a lifetime *learning* to see' (Sacks, 1998: 108).

Semiotic heterogeneity appears to be something that is present to a small and necessary extent in most of us and to a higher degree in a broad spectrum from Asperger's and Tourette's syndrome to 'classical infantile autism' (Sacks, 1998: 236). Perhaps what is termed normal behaviour is the result of socially reinforced, intersemiotic control over heterosemiotic semiosis. Take 'The case of the colour-blind painter', who was at first devastated by his sudden loss of colour vision, but gradually adjusted to his new condition. So much so that when a possible cure was suggested to him he refused. Sacks concludes:

> Now that he conceived the world in different terms, and again found it coherent and complete, he thought the suggestion unintelligible, and repugnant. Now that colour had lost its former associations, its sense, he could no longer imagine what its restoration would be like. (Sacks, 1998: 36)

Now he was happy in a new, intersemiotically constituted 'world of achromatopsia'.

In spite of a certain heterogeneity among perceptual readings as well as between perceptual grasp and verbal coding, the basic claim of language being activated by nonverbal readings still stands. What we can now add is the observation that this is so no matter whether language schemata are coarse-grained and so cover a large number of nonverbal phenomena (cf. *aoi*) or whether terms are highly specific (the Maori example).

Another way of looking at the heterogeneity of signs is to remind ourselves of the logical arbitrariness of taking human-scale realizations of the world as the norm. It is the norm for us, but only so because we find it difficult to bracket our species-oriented perspective. This becomes clearer when we compare familiar objects of daily life with the way they look under the electron microscope. On the human scale, a table top appears as a solid, continuous surface. By contrast, the picture generated by the electron microscope looks full of holes, so that we wonder how something as loose as the molecular structure before us can cohere at all. The point is that different sign systems produce perspectives that can differ quite radically from one another without destroying the human expectation of a coherent world.

Conclusion

By way of conclusion let me offer a speculative explanation why such therapies as 'eye movement desensitization and reprocessing' (EMDR) have a certain success (Shapiro, 1995, 1997; Parnell, 1997). Certain post-traumatic stress disorders can manifest themselves in a fixation on specific mental images which can cause continuous anxiety and pain. Rapid eye movement treatment makes the patient focus typically on an object in repetitive movement. At the same time, the patient is asked to recall as clearly and forcefully as possible the image or image sequence that causes the pain. Evidence suggests that patients do indeed experience partial or complete relief from anxiety after treatment. Psychology is now in the process of refining present techniques as well as trying to discover the mechanisms at work here. From the perspective of corporeal meaning the following explanation offers itself.

I suggest that we are dealing here with a process which somehow reverses meaning acquisition. We could call this a process of *semantic dissociation*. If it works, one suspects that a more general principle is being instantiated in EMDR, which suggests that we should place rapid eye movement in a broader context. Perhaps EMDR is the visual variant of a general pattern. If this is the case, we need to look for tactile, olfactory, gustatory and aural parallels. As to tactile equivalents, worry beads, prayer drums, Chinese knead balls and rosaries come to mind. At the level of olfactory repetition, incense may play a similar role. In gustatory semiosis, chewing-gum, betel-nuts, cocoa, ginger and tobacco may count as evidence. And as far as the repetition of aural signs is concerned, mantras and ritual chanting appear to qualify. At a more abstract level, transcendental meditation could be viewed as an intersemiotic technique of meaning disassociation. How do these phenomena stack up in a theory of meaning in which nonverbal signs are the deep structure of language?

Let us return to Helen Keller's experience of associating for the first time the cool stream of water gushing over her hand with the word w-a-t-e-r which her teacher was writing into her other hand at the same time. Meaning occurred as an event of intersemiotic association. Could it be that when old people handle worry beads for hours on end while their thoughts gradually disengage from reality, culture is preparing them for the more significant event of death? Could it be that the meanings which they have accumulated since childhood by the poignant association of signs with signs into the powerful image complex of their lifeworld need to be gradually dismantled? Could it be that the secret of handling rosaries lies in its force of diminishing the significance of worldly *Vorstellungen* to give way to the sacred? Could incense likewise function as a pathway of semantic disassociation? And would it not make sense to see transcendental meditation as a well-designed, all-encompassing counter-method to the way meanings are typically acquired over a lifetime?

If this explanation is plausible, we can see why repetitive eye movement therapy should be as successful as it is claimed to be. Traumatic meanings could be regarded as intersemiotic bonds of a very high degree of intensity. They are hurtful because they destroy the meanings of an acceptable or even happily embraced world of *Vorstellungen*, while replacing them with images of fear or dread. Like all meanings, they have been acquired in a process of bonding of different signs to form a sign complex relevant to the mental world of the patient. By forcing the patient to hold in consciousness the feared image chain while focusing on an irrelevant and so semantically empty object in repetitive movement, the customary process of intersemiotic association is nullified by a heterosemiotic alternative. Moving object and fearful image are unrelated thematically and so neutralize, as it were, the intersemiotic bonding that was established too forcefully. It would seem, then, that the painful meanings have been eroded or eradicated and the patient feels relieved.

High-intensity intersemiotic associations are, of course, not restricted to pathological cases. They are at the heart of the notion of culture. The more intense a culture, the deeper the meaning bonds we observe among its members. If too harmonious, a culture's meanings may have disastrous effects. Perhaps one could say that the force of intersemiotic bonds in culture can be such that they become instruments for atrocities. In this sense, the phrase 'culture kills' is no exaggeration. In a culture in which heterosemiotic relations balance intersemiotic intensity, we have a less frightening picture. Multicultural societies could be said to work because of an equilibrium of intersemiotic and heterosemiotic relations.

So far we have pursued the idea of the body in language as a necessary principle. I argued that language is unable to mean without corporeality. The body has been discussed as perceptual and quasi-perceptual agent. Deixis and reference have been redefined in terms of the body; and I have tried to show how intersemiotic and heterosemiotic relations shape meaning. Now we are in a position to ask what role the signifier and the signified play in this account. The next chapter attempts an answer to the first part of the question by tracing the gradual disembodiment of the signifier from icon to symbol.

7. The disembodiment of the signifier

Having committed himself to structuralist principles, in particular to the principle of synchronic intragrammaticality, Claude Lévi-Strauss felt forced to proclaim that

> no matter what the moment and the circumstances of its appearance in the animal scale were, *language could only have been born in a single stroke.* Objects couldn't just start to signify progressively. After a transformation whose study is a matter not for the social sciences, but for biology and physiology as well, a passage was effected from the stage where nothing made sense to another where everything did. (quoted in Kristeva, 1989: 46; my emphasis)

If we look at any language synchronically, this is what one would want to say. But as a remark on the evolution of sign practices, this is an unlikely story. It reads more like a theo-ontological decree than an anthropological description. After all, everything we care to look at appears as a part in some evolutionary network. Why should language be such an extraordinary exception? It is much more probable that all human signification gradually emerged from a close relationship between body and other bodies, as well as between bodies and the environment. And why could the signification of objects not have evolved gradually towards increasing differentiation and complexity? Which law of nature would we have to invent to suggest a line between zero and everything, between no signs at all and sign systems in their totality? Biological need and social usefulness appear to be perfectly plausible candidates for stimulating a gradual increase in human semiosis.

An alternative route for speculation would be to suggest that language evolves progressively out of the gesturing body into an increasingly complex system of conventional signs. In this case we could speak of a trajectory from iconicity to symbolicity. We can imagine that the development of signs occurred again and again under similar circumstances and with principally similar results. Whether we focus on the long history of oral communication or on the more recent evolution of written signs, the signifiers of language appear to be ruled by an inexorable law, *the principle of gradual disembodiment*. Accordingly, the signifiers of natural languages carry with them a history from iconic, embodied sign to disembodied symbols. At the same time, the signifieds of natural languages, one could say, retain their iconic character. At the level of the signified we are iconic beings. Moreover, one could extend this claim by tying the history of the signifier to that of the signified. One could say that the gradual disembodiment of the signifier is matched by a parallel movement in which the abandoned iconicity is gradually absorbed by the signified. *As the signifier lets go of the body, it is incorporated by the signified*. This is why we can imagine portions of the world in the most vivid manner in response to the most abstract terms.

In this chapter I want to focus on the gradual disembodiment of the signifier, leaving the corporeality of the signified to Chapter 8. Before we can address how this evolution shows itself in written signs, we must briefly turn to the question of the primacy of language sounds over graphic characters (Harris, 1986). A foremost proponent of the thesis that languages are primarily phonetic structures is John DeFrancis, who has presented this view in his well-known studies of Chinese as well as in more general books on the relationship between sound and writing systems. In *Visible Speech* (1989) he refers the reader to written expression in a range of ancient and contemporary languages and passionately defends sound systems as the sole foundation of any language. Written signs, be they pictograms, ideographs or logographs, are mere side-effects of linguistic sounds. DeFrancis finds plenty of support for his emphasis among past and present linguists, as for instance Wilhelm von Humboldt, whom he quotes in his *The Chinese Language: Fact and Fantasy*:

> I think that the scholars who have almost let themselves be drawn into forgetting that Chinese is a spoken language have so exaggerated the influence of Chinese writing that they have, so to say, put the writing in place of the language. (DeFrancis, 1986: 35)

DeFrancis most strongly opposes the view that because we can decipher a certain number of Chinese characters without recourse to sound, such a procedure could ever form a basis for learning and performing the language:

The concept of ideographic writing is a most seductive notion. There is a great appeal in the concept of written symbols conveying their message directly to our minds, thus bypassing the restrictive intermediary of speech. And it seems so plausible. Surely ideas immediately pop into our minds when we see a road sign, a death's head label on a bottle of medicine, a number on a clock. Aren't Chinese characters a sophisticated system of symbols that similarly convey meaning without regard to sound? Aren't they an ideographic system of writing?

The answer to these questions is no. Chinese characters are a phonetic, not an ideographic, system of writing, as I have attempted to show in the preceding pages. Here I would go further: There never has been, and never can be, such a thing as an ideographic system of writing. (DeFrancis, 1986: 133)

As a broad-brush observation, backed up by heaps of evidence, the DeFrancis thesis is hard to dispute. However, if he and a massive literature in his support are right, what we want to ask is, what is the role of written symbols in relation to sound? What function does 'writing' fulfil, from pictogram to ideograph and on to their highly stylized forms? While DeFrancis gives highly specific answers to this question as far as Chinese is concerned, the general problematic of the relation between sound and written sign, especially iconic signs, needs an additional perspective.

There does not appear to be too much doubt that languages have evolved as sound systems over a very long time and certainly long before written symbols make their appearance on stone and ceramic products. Sound certainly precedes writing in any form. From the angle of a theory of meaning in which the body plays a prominent role I suggest that a speculative picture emerges in which both sounds and written signs are there to fix something else, namely *nonverbal maps of the world*. Let us call them *mental presentations* rather than representations. We will have to return to this topic in detail in the following chapter. If someone said '*mu*' in Old Egyptian, members of the speech community were all trained to imagine water. Whenever someone uttered the (reconstructed) sound '*ki*' among the Sumerians about 3000 BC, the Sumerians shared typical, even if not necessarily identical, mental presentations of 'earth'.

From this point of view, sounds do not form an independent matrix of differential relations that 'mean' on their own. Rather, they mean because they form the material, phonemic matrix that is systemically related to a second, nonverbal matrix of mental 'maps'. And meaningful utterances are the result of relating the two according to social rules. Assuming that this process occurred in an increasingly sophisticated manner over tens of thousands of years, we can envisage a period of time in which the technical ability of scratching hard materials and colouring surfaces was gradually combined with an already highly developed system of meaningful sounds. Not surprisingly, the literature finds it hard to decide at what structural point in the evolution of painted and engraved narratives artistic presentations are to be called writing systems. We are speaking here of a time scale between at least some 80,000 years ago up to so-called historical times. The assumption here is that, since at least that time, cultural expressions by sound, dance, ritual, incantation, sand drawing, painting, engraving are systemically aligned with mental presentations. When pictograms appear on the scene, then, they form a stage in the development of languages during which the material basis of sound is not only conventionally associated with typical mental presentations but further strengthened by externalized icons that reflected in some way those mental maps. Throughout this chapter I rely heavily on archaeological and other research and acknowledge the original findings with gratitude. I have selected and adapted illustrations to assist my argument.

In *The Civilization of the Goddess* (1991) Marija Gimbutas presents the exciting picture of a Neolithic writing system in use between roughly 5300 and 4300 BC, with earliest findings dated at around 6000 BC, almost 3000 years before Sumerian scripts. Controversy still surrounds her claims, but she is supported by a considerable number of archaeologists as well as carbon dating. This 'Old European' writing system is said to have been primarily for sacred use and appears to be entirely symbolic. Its signs (Figure 1) are inscribed on such religious objects as altars, libation vessels, plaques, figurines and pendants and are argued to correspond to much older phonetic values. About thirty signs make up the core body of the script, with around a hundred additional modified characters. According to Gimbutas, the script disappeared towards the fifth millennium BC when the Danubian areas were overrun by the first waves of Indo-European tribes. The author believes, however, that remnants of this Neolithic writing system survived for a long time on Cyprus and Crete.

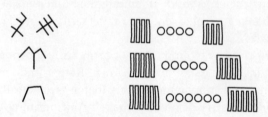

Figure 1 Old European script (adapted from Gimbutas, 1991: 231, 308)

The claims made by Gimbutas find support in studies such as 'The origin of writing and of language' (1981) by Imanol Agire, who suggests that Palaeolithic Basque cave paintings hold the key to even earlier pictographic as well as symbolic, written signs. Recent DNA mapping certainly confirms the likelihood that the present Basques are the descendants of Palaeolithic people in the Western Mediterranean region. This would suggest a long history of continuous language use of which the Old European script could be a highly symbolized form (Schmand-Besserat, 1978).

The evolution of symbolic forms out of iconic representations is much more easily demonstrated when there is evidence of various stages of reduction of signifiers (Figures 2 to 5). We should not be surprised to find that cultures separated by space and time could produce similar icons. As Frutiger rightly points out, comparisons suggesting some kind of influence,

Figure 2 Snake, iguana – Mayan (Davoust, 1995: 29)

Figure 3 Man and falcon – Egyptian (King, 1977: 52); woman and man – Egyptian (Frutiger, 1991: 120); man, walking, and head – Minoan (Evans, 1909: 276); head – Mayan (Baudez, 1992: 103); priest – Mayan (Weaver, 1981: 177)

Figure 4 Icons representing actions: hitting – Egyptian (Jensen, 1970: 58); breathing – Mayan (Frutiger, 1991: 141)

Figure 5 Abstract ideas: death, mourning – Mayan (Jensen, 1970: 231); fasting – Mayan (Förstemann, 1902: 16)

as in Figure 6, are misleading (Frutiger, 1991: 130). Instead of looking for some possible influence, it is just as likely that iconic resemblance has to do with the fact that humans tend to imagine their surroundings in typical and often similar ways.

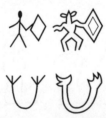

Figure 6 Iconic resemblance: comparison of Easter Island script and signs from the Indus Valley culture (Frutiger, 1991: 130; Diringer, 1968: 66)

This is why we find it relatively easy to understand how signifier and signified are related when generalized or stylized icons are combined to form compound representations. In the example from Sumerian writing shown in Figure 7, the combination of pudendum for woman and cloth to indicate social status produces the icon for 'lady'. In the Egyptian example, the stylized jug in conjunction with the sign for water results in the icon for 'cool'.

Icons are often combined to form narratives. In the Brazilian example (Figure 8) the story is told of three men crossing the mountain in three days and nights, while the Mayan narrative about two gods is compressed into a single icon. In some cases we can only assume that we are dealing with a

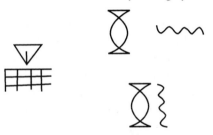

Figure 7 Woman of status – Sumerian (Frutiger, 1991: 121); coolness, cool – Egyptian (Frutiger, 1991: 116)

Figure 8 Brazilian Indians (Rubinger, 1979: 25); Mayan gods of maize and sun (Davoust, 1995: 5)

narrative, as in an example of Easter Island script that has remained undeciphered (Figure 9).

Figure 9 Easter Island signs (Frutiger, 1991: 131)

As the process of disembodiment becomes visible, the variations of how the world can be represented become also apparent. With an increase in abstraction the arbitrariness of the signifier begins to show itself. Abstraction can take the form of generalization, when an icon stands in for a large number of things; it can emphasize formalization, when the contours of the icon are idealized towards geometrical shapes; or it can be the result of stylization, when a certain technology of inscription produces signs more akin to a style of writing than to iconic mimesis. We can also observe combinations of these three kinds of abstraction. In Figure 10, we have generalized icons which already point the way towards symbolicity. At the same time, they remind us that there are many ways of (re)presenting water. The three signifiers not only display what they mean, but also demonstrate a certain degree of arbitrariness within iconic constraints.

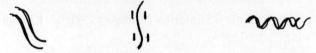

Figure 10 Water – Sumerian, Chinese, Egyptian (Frutiger, 1991: 115)

The attraction of increasingly formal representation can be observed in scripts from very different cultures. Obvious advantages of approaching formal idealization are clarity, iterability and reproducibility, longevity, learnability and aesthetic appeal. In the illustrations shown in Figure 11 the cultural will to formal expression has produced highly effective signifiers.

Figure 11 Hittite signs (Jensen, 1970: 150)

The Chinese script could be used on its own to make all the points to be made in this chapter. Figure 12 shows a selection of three signifiers that illustrate formal reduction and communicatory efficiency.

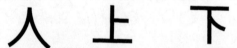

Figure 12 Chinese (person, up, down)

The trajectory of the disembodiment of the signifier is nicely documented in the examples of Brazilian Indian writing shown in Figure 13. From the stylized iconic representation of 'crocodile' we proceed in a number of steps towards a radically reduced formal signifier. Much the same process is at work in numerous other signs, such as the signifier for scorpion (Figure 14).In the signs' fully reduced formalization, this Brazilian Indian script stands out by its aesthetic design, clarity and economy. As Denise Pahl Schaan explains,

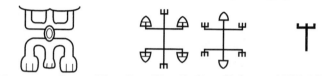

Figure 13 Crocodile – Brazilian Indian (Schaan, 1997: 181)

Figure 14 Scorpion – Brazilian Indian (Schaan, 1997: 182)

Brazilian Indian ceramic art evolved over a time period from about AD 400 to 1300, during which time highly iconic signs were gradually anonymized and formalized to an extent that immediate recognition is no longer possible (Figure 15). We could say that the reading instructions that attach, as it were, to the early highly (re)presentational signs are now part of the specialized, cultural pedagogy that must go hand in hand with the learning and usage of the formalized script.

Figure 15 Fully formalized script – Brazilian Indian (Schaan, 1997: 182)

A somewhat different style of formalization can be found in Hopi signs. Some of its signifiers retain sufficient iconic content to make reading by the outsider possible. The majority of the signs, however, exhibit a degree of arbitrariness which bars direct translation. Once we are given the respective signifieds, however, we can recognize their iconic origins (Figure 16).

Figure 16 Hopi script (Fundación Santillana, Museo de América, 1980)

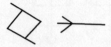

Figure 17 Movement, speed – Mesopotamian (Frutiger, 1991: 116)

Such abstract concepts as movement and speed pose no difficulty for iconic (re)presentation, as the Mesopotamian examples shown in Figure 17 demonstrate.

Stylization could be called the process in which the gradual disembodiment of the signifier is brought about by a certain technique of writing rather than formal design. The best-documented examples come from Cretan and Chinese writing (Figure 18). But there are also other scripts in support of stylization as a slow historical form of adaptation.

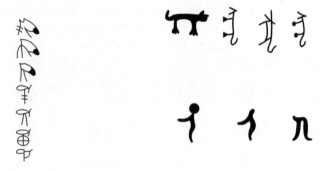

Figure 18 Horse – Minoan (Haas, 1976: 54); dog – Chinese (Norman, 1988: 59); person – Chinese (Straits Times, 1995)

Sumerian cuneiforms provide clear evidence of the technological influence on the evolution of a script. Figure 19 sums up the stroke techniques employed during the classical period in the production of cuneiform writing on clay tablets. A spectrum from highly mimetic icons to full stylization in Sumerian writing shows that pictographic representation reflects not only typical contours of objects but also their position in the world. In early (re)presentations the head is portrayed as upright (Figure 20). Efficient writing, however, dictates a horizontal depiction, while the use of stencils results in the straightening of lines and a preference for lines in a minimum of directions. Disembodiment by reduction, then, is at work here in various ways: imaginative variation, elimination of intricate contour, direction of lines, elimination of contour, full stylization. The umbilical cord between icon and signifier has been cut, but there remain traces of the stylized body.

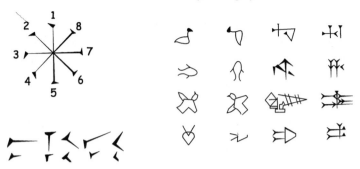

Figure 19 Standardized stencil moves in cuneiform writing (Gaur, 1984: 49); applic.._.ion (Coulmas, 1989: 74; Gelb, 1965: 70)

Figure 20 Person – Sumerian (Driver, 1976: 36)

We should not assume that only pictographic scripts have undergone this kind of transformation. Our alphabet too can be traced to its iconic forebears. However, very little in the alphabet would permit tracing of iconic residues. But we do know that individual letters have gradually evolved from pictorial (re)presentation. The letter 'A', for example, traces its ancestry back to the head of a bull (*aleph*). Various stylizations of earlier icons in Egyptian, Sumerian, Babylonian, Cretan and other scripts can be shown to have had an influence on a Phoenician sign which in turn reappears transformed in the early Greek letter alpha, whence it entered Latin. Now the signifier is fully disembodied and arbitrary.

The story of arbitrariness, however, is not as straightforward as it may seem. Leaving Plato aside, the claim of the arbitrariness of signs is most readily associated with Saussure. However, its modern roots are to be found some thirty years earlier in the work of the Yale linguist Dwight Whitney (1827–1894), who, in the 1860s and 1870s, insisted on the conventionality and so arbitrariness of language. Both Peirce and Saussure took their cues from Whitney's writings. Saussure's strong emphasis on the arbitrary link between signifier and signified should be read, of course, against the histor- ical background of philology and its liking for natural explanations of word meanings. This applies in particular to explanations via onomatopeia, which sought to demonstrate a natural relation between word sound and meaning. Although every language has a considerable number of terms to support this kind of linkage, it cannot be used as a general explanation for how word sounds and meanings are to be associated with one another. What is problematic in Saussure is that he extended the arbitrariness of the signifier to include the signified. From the perspective of corporeal semantics, this was a mistake.

Peirce was more cautious when he proposed a certain significatory impurity. Neither icon (picture of *x*), nor index (something that suggests an inference about *x*), nor symbol (an artificial and so unrelated sign about *x*) occur in their purity in actual sign processes. The likeness of icon and perceptual reality is assisted by certain conventional ways of drawing, painting or taking photographs. An index is always partly iconic, to the extent that we can tie it to a specific portion of the perceptual world, and partly symbolic, to the extent that the object itself is no longer imitated but only indirectly implied. And symbols in natural language retain a certain indexicality in the sense that linguistic expressions still carry evolutionary traces of social situations out of which they emerged. I will address this question later on (Chapter 9). Suffice it here to point out that this claim looks less outrageous when we consider artificial symbols, such as variables in a formal language. *X* and *y* in formal logic are pure symbols in that no social traces contaminate their 'lexicon'. The social frames of 'doing logic' are an entirely different matter. Peirce, then, was extraordinarily sensitive to the implications of his semiotics for the description of natural language, and we should be careful not to fall behind his insights a hundred years later when we talk of the arbitrariness of signs.

If we overemphasize the conventionality of the sign, what is overlooked is that 'if all uses of signs are taken as arbitrary, then multiple uses of the same sign must also be seen as arbitrary' (Sweetser, 1990: 5). In this case, we cannot analyse metaphoric and other extensions of base meanings other than by returning to their signifiers. Yet it is precisely such extended meanings which point to a systemic relationship between ways of speaking and perceiving; that is, ways of reading the world by nonverbal signs. If Sweetser is right, and I think she is, we must conclude that though signifiers may be arbitrary, the sign as a whole is not. There remains a nonarbitrary relation between signifier and signified in the sense that signifiers mean only when they are related to signifieds. In turn, signifieds are what they are only by virtue of our perceptual and quasi-perceptual grasp of the world.

This leads me to conclude that arbitrariness is an aspect of a broader principle. If we view signification, including language, on an idealized scale between the poles of iconicity and arbitrariness, the following law can be observed. The higher the degree of iconicity, the more conspicuously are the semantic instructions a part of the sign itself. The more arbitrary a sign, the more intricate are the supplementary semantic rules that have to be provided via pedagogy. Thus, as language sheds its acoustic and pictorial iconicity, the community elaborates its indirect controls over the association of sounds and quasi-perceptual fantasy acts; that is, the event of meaning.

If this is so, then the question of what happens to the iconic content of signifiers once they are fully disembodied, and so symbolized and arbitrary, can be answered. The quasi-conceptual content of the disembodied signifier lives on in the corporeality of the signified. How it functions there is the topic of the next chapter.

8. The corporeality of the signified

The sense which could invert things is basically *touch*, our body as *tactile tool* for apprehending and manipulating the world, ourselves, the other.

(Luce Irigaray, 'The three genres', in *The Irigaray Reader*, p. 141)

Let me ask again: why does Wittgenstein in his later work so often use expressions like 'Imagine a case ...'? Why does he not always say 'Take a sentence like ...'? When we inhabit the Wittgenstein text and ask what motivates his rhetoric we arrive, I believe, at a picture that is at variance with dominant readings (Baker and Hacker, 1983). I think the reason Wittgenstein returns again and again to this phrase is because he needed a second level of significations to show how language works in actual social situations. This second level of signs is the domain of nonverbal readings of the world, the way we use tactile, olfactory, gustatory, thermal, gravitational, aural, kinetic and other nonlinguistic signs to make sense of our surroundings. On this issue, corporeal semantics takes its main cue from Peirce's insistence on the indispensable role of icons, signs related to referents in a relation of at least partial resemblance. We can communicate an idea directly only if we share an icon, and even

> any indirect method of communicating an idea must depend for its establishment upon use of an icon. ... Hence every assertion must contain an icon or a set of icons, or else must contain signs whose meaning is only explicable by icons. (Peirce, 1.158)

Theories of language and meaning readily accept that speech is typically accompanied by nonverbal signs such as body stance, facial expression and gestures. But Peirce's insight goes much further. He is saying that nonverbal signs, such as mental images, are an essential part of language if it is to be meaningful communication. This is the emphasis that corporeal semantics wishes to elaborate. Later semioticians writing in the tradition of Saussure have also offered two-track semiotic explanations, without, however, making the secondary system an essential ingredient of linguistic meaning. In Louis Hjelmslev's scheme in his *Prolegomena to a Theory of Language* (1953), denotative signifiers and signifieds constitute the denotative sign. This in turn acts as a connotative signifier that in conjunction with a connotative signified creates a higher-level, connotative sign. Although the two systems interact with each other, this is a 'can' rule and not a 'must' rule. For meaning can be resolved independently in the denotative system before we proceed to further, connotative signs. According to Hjelmslev (1953), first we perform a denotative semiotic, followed by a separate analysis for connotations, with a logical break between the two. Similarly, Yuri Lotman distinguishes between first-order and second-order semiotic systems, the latter of which is parasitic on the former. And Roland Barthes in *Mythologies* (1972) adapts the Hjelmslev scheme to his purpose of a political reading of signs. Interestingly, in Barthes, although we begin our reading with denotative signs, it is the secondary, connotative sign that in the end gives the denotation its place value in the overall social system of signification and so Barthes appears to destroy the idea that language could ever return to a primary or natural form of language (Barthes, 1973: 109–59). However, even in this version of the Saussurean semiotic we find no deep challenge to the single-track, differential and intralinguistic definition of meaning. Without stepping outside the single-track view of language as a network of linguistic elements that signify only in relation to each other, we can do no more than play a kind of chess. Yet neither chess nor syntax produces meanings. We must step outside syntax to mean. And when we do so, we step into the sign systems of the body.

To return to our examples from Wittgenstein, 'anyone who is unable to imagine a case in which one might say ...' (Wittgenstein, 1972: paragraph 412) suggests that we could not talk about the role language plays or describe language itself if we were not able to fantasize certain relevant, nonverbal scenarios in which language is embedded. This is crucial. We certainly cannot write off this recourse to the nonverbal domain of signification by calling it a merely heuristic strategy. Without it, Wittgenstein could not proceed. Nor is he alone in this situation. All theorists of language come up against the problem of 'exteriority', as Michel Foucault calls it – frames that have a bearing on what language is and how it functions.

The nonverbal exteriority of language has a number of important consequences. It rules out the popular idea that we are only ever dealing with signifiers. It also undermines any attempt at arriving at a pure description, any project centred on the 'ideality' of linguistic meaning. Third – and this concerns Wittgenstein's problem – the necessary condition of nonverbal signs for language also qualifies the emphasis on 'intragrammaticality', the view that language use is determined alone by syntactic rules. I believe this is mistaken. Instead, I propose that 'use' always has a dual set of constraints: intragrammatical relations and our nonverbal grasp of the world. 'The wounded surgeon plies the steel' demonstrates both at the same time. Without a compound nonverbal realization, we would not know what we are saying at the most elementary level. Yet without its specific syntactic order, it could be the steel that is 'plying', which would be the sort of rule-breaking that generically belongs to experimental language use.

In the last chapter, the claim was made that the evolution of the signifier is characterized by a trajectory of 'disembodiment', from gestural cry to conventional sound, from pictogram via stylization to symbol. Yet this corporeality did not altogether vanish in the process towards anonymization. The disappearing corporeality of the signifier was matched, I suggested, by a process of conceptual interiorization. As a result, corporeality, it seems, lives on in the signified. To express this in Peircean terms, the iconicity of early signs in the evolution of language gives way to indexical and eventually merely symbolic representamens. However, at the level of the interpretant, iconicity remains a vital ingredient. We are speaking here of the *corporeality of the signified*.

In what way can linguistic signifieds be regarded as corporeal? Have we not embarked on a high-speed train of signifiers as soon as we enter language? Do we not merely move from signifier to signifier when we speak and listen? Yes and no. We do move from word to word, explain phrases by other phrases, and so engage in a network of linguistic substitutions. However, as I have argued before, if we did not know at every step in this process what we are talking *about*, we might as well exchange the phrases in a foreign tongue according to instructions given by a native speaker. Intragrammaticality does not by itself facilitate meaning. We must get off the train of signifiers. To stay with this metaphor, we must run on a double track. And this is what semantics requires: two systems which are conventionally aligned to facilitate meaning. What has to be avoided here is what one could call the positivist or naturalist trap: to assume that what we exit to is the world as univocally given. A constructivist and perspectival picture is needed here, a topic to be addressed in Chapter 13.

If we consider a linguistic text as a set of signifiers, where is the parallel track of the corporeal signifieds? The answer that has emerged so far is 'nonverbal readings'. Without a nonverbal imaginative realization of 'acrid', the word by itself would mean no more than 'x'. Fantasy constructions of possible appropriate scenarios, then, provide the corporeality we are looking for. Cognitive semantics speaks of 'mapping' and 'schemata'. I mention this again here to show that corporeal semantics is not a solitary, lunatic undertaking. What distinguishes cognitive linguistics from corporeal semantics is dealt with elsewhere in this book (Chapter 12). If meaning is the event of activating empty linguistic schemata via nonverbal signs to produce corporeal signifieds, then the question arises how such a semantic relates to the problematic of *(re)presentation*. (See Chapter 13.) To prepare for a discussion of representation, the remainder of this chapter attempts to shore up the notion of the corporeality of signifieds.

It will come as no surprise when I say that we fantasize a mental picture sequence when we read the lines 'An aged man is but a paltry thing,/A tattered coat upon a stick ...'. We imagine a portion of a possible world, not just in addition to the words, but in order to make sense of the text. At the same time, we construct an implicit speech situation, with appropriate, inferable deictic features. Leaving intertextual complexities aside, literary language games by convention invite the reader to enrich linguistic expressions with a multitude of nonverbal realizations, starting from the frame of community-sanctioned use. Contrary to the assertions of literary grammarians, there is no logical limit either to the amount of such realizations or to their detail and depth. There is no inbuilt rule as to where denotative and associative nonverbal responses begin or end. There is only a politics of reading that imposes such rules from the outside. What matters here is that without the fantasy performance of quasi-corporeal or, in short, corporeal signifieds reading could not even begin.

This process is less obvious when we read a historical report. Nevertheless, here too corporeal signification is indispensable if we wish to proceed from syntactic mumble to meanings. We have to be able to *imagine* Gibbons's Roman world as well as the world of its speaker, at least schematically, to be able to understand how one empire legitimates itself by reference to another. In an earlier study I tried to show that one can envisage a ladder of discourse from literary to digital signs according to a gradual reduction in the referential and deictic content that is required on the part of the reader (Ruthrof, 1992). Expressed in terms of corporeality, this means that the signifieds of the literary, both those referring to the fictive world and those referring to the fictive utterance situation, conventionally demand a maximum of fantasy work varying nonverbal material. As we go down the ladder towards juridical discourse and finally formal logic, the corporeality of the signifieds is reduced until neither reference nor deixis can be construed at all.

We must postpone the nagging question of how subjectivism and mentalism are controlled in this account. (See Chapter 10.) Suffice it to remark

here that nonverbal fantasy acts are no more or less subjective than are
'incorporated' lexicons and so-called dictionary definitions. They all are part
of the way in which a semiotic community trains its speakers to speak a
natural language and 'see' the world. Another way of demonstrating the role
of the perceptual body in the signified is to unravel the typically compound
clusters of nonverbal sign complexes that (in)form language. As Jakobson
teaches us in 'Quest for the essence of language', a linguistic expression is
always a *general rule*, one that 'specifies only through the different instances
of its application, namely the pronounced or written – thinglike – *replica*'
(Jakobson, 1971d: 358). While Jakobson's explanation supports what I want
to say here, the question of how verbal signs are able to function precisely in
this manner remains open. Rules for what? we should ask. From the perspective of a body-oriented theory of language the answer is: *rules for selecting
appropriate nonverbal signs*.

Let us look at how our olfactory readings activate language. Smell, science
tells us, is our most ancient interpretive contact with the world. What
happens when we read the expressions 'acrid', 'pungent', 'putrid', or the
metaphor 'he lives on the smell of an oil rag'? Without a nonverbal, qual-
itative identification of the differences between actual olfactory memories,
we would be hard pressed to make sense of such words. As to the metaphor,
we distinguish a habitual reading which jumps across the iconic reference
and imagine a situational schema of frugality or poverty. In this case, both
figurative and 'literal' readings can be performed. In this case they reinforce
one another. Both require a certain quasi-perceptual grasp to activate the
signifieds. That we tend to relegate olfactory readings to the less important
rungs of interpretation seems unwarranted. As Ackerman explains,

> Smell was the first of our senses, and it was so successful that in time the
> small lump of olfactory tissue atop the nerve cord grew into a brain.
> Our cerebral hemispheres were originally buds from the olfactory
> stalks. We *think* because we smelled. (Ackerman, 1991: 20)

Note the nonvisual emphasis. Our olfactory mapping of the world comes
first. All else follows: first the other senses, then their increasing interaction
and intersemiotic governance. Linguistic signifieds act as a metasystem and
yet depend on nonverbal signs for their existence. Ackerman traces our
olfactory readings to early stages in 'our' evolution 'when we thrived in the
oceans'. We have the ocean inside us, she says, 'our blood is mainly salt
water' (21). Only later, when we left the ocean, did the sense of smell lose its
interpretive primacy. 'Vision and hearing became more important for survival' (30). Assuming this broad-brush picture is more or less right, how can

we persuasively theorize the link between anatomical structures and linguistic signifieds? Summing up the relevant cognitive research, Ackerman tells us that

> odour molecules float back into the nasal cavity behind the bridge of the nose, where they are absorbed by the mucosa containing receptor cells bearing microscopic hairs called cilia. Five million of these cells fire impulses to the brain's olfactory bulb or smell centre ... the neurons in the nose are replaced every thirty days and, unlike any other neuron in the body, they stick right out and wave in the air current like anemones on a coral reef ... When the olfactory bulb detects something ... it signals the cerebral cortex and sends a message straight into the limbic system, a mysterious, ancient, and intensely emotional section of our brain in which we feel, lust, and invent. (10f.)

These are the kinds of processes that we must acknowledge as the biological base of our olfactory interpretations. When it comes to deciphering linguistic texts in which olfactory readings are called upon to bestow corporeality on empty signifiers, we should not invent a radical break between biological processes and sign production. An explanation acknowledging some kind of continuity seems advisable.

How can we use Jakobson's concept of linguistic expressions as 'rules'? How do expressions govern those 'intensely emotional' realizations in our limbic system? How is the sensation of 'lust' reined in by language? Once we have learned how to use the term 'musty' in accordance with community expectations it could be said to set boundaries around a certain range of odours which we must be able to imagine for the word to be meaningful. However, the metaphor 'boundaries' shows its limitations because it suggests that certain odours are included, whereas others are excluded from the range of the term. While this is so with clearly distinct odours, the reality of mixes and nuances is not captured. A structuralist linguist would say that certain signifiers such as 'lemon scented' are excluded and it is this differential exclusion that determines the semantic value of 'musty'. This begs the question of the meaning of 'musty' as well as the meaning of all 'nonmusty' terms. For meaning to occur we cannot rely on difference within one and the same set of signs; we must exit the linguistic system and activate it by something other: the nonverbal. In this case, the nonverbal is made up of perceptual or quasi-perceptual, fantasized instances of musty odours.

The corporeal signified of language, then, is a linguistic signifier activated by nonverbal signs. In this explanation, the signifier acts as a rule agreed upon by a community that sets 'boundaries' for what sort of nonverbal readings are to be selected in each instance as activating signs. This applies to entire discourses as well as to its subordinate expressions. Nor does it matter whether the signifiers still display traces of iconicity or whether they are fully symbolized. What matters is that the partially disembodied as well as the empty signifier have handed over their iconicity to the signified. In the signified iconicity has been interiorized. And because iconicity is a memory of the body, we can say that *in the signified iconicity is incorporated*. The signified is corporeal.

This appears to apply even to sign systems that aspire to the semantic emptiness of music. Diane Ackerman cites the fascinating case of the Guanches in the Canaries, who

> use an ancient whistling language to communicate across the sprawling valleys. They trill and warble a little like quails and other birds, but more elaborately, and, from as far away as nine miles, they hear one another and converse as their ancestors did. *Silbo Gomero* the idiom is called. (1991: 215)

Do these sounds function just like Jakobson's 'rules' rephrased in corporeal terms? It would seem so. The community teaches its young what nonverbal signs to activate for each sound and their specific combinations. A related case is the iconic bond between land, culture and music in Australian Aboriginal culture, which suggests that a community's entire semantic system could be coded in musical notation. This supports the view that no matter how disembodied the signifier, as long as the signifieds are governed by principles that ensure systemic and consistent associations with tactile, olfactory, visual, gustatory and other perceptual readings of the world as well as their fantasy variants, semantic values are guaranteed. As long as signifieds are corporeal we have meaning.

The bottom-up approach of cognitive science is instructive not only by providing striking examples, but also because it offers an evolutionary, materialist explanation that can deal with high-level semantic questions. In Mark Turner's 'cognitive rhetoric', cognitive insights are applied to the reading of literature. Take, for example, his focus on the body's gravitational readings in *Reading Minds: The Study of English in the Age of Cognitive Science*:

> We are subject to gravity and we are self-propelled. Our bodies there-fore differ up to down and forward to back. But in general, the world on our left is the same as the world on our right. What we can do on the

right can be done on the left. ... We say of such a body that it is bilaterally symmetrical. (1991: 69)

Turner argues that we cannot separate our gravitational orientation and its physiological consequences from our higher-level performances such as language and even literature. He shows that the bilateral symmetry of the body frequently reappears in literary constructions, as for instance in the way Shakespeare arranged Hamlet's famous soliloquy:

The soliloquy begins with a bare opposition, 'to be or not to be', which we understand metaphorically as symmetrically opposed forces. This defines a stasis of action and decision. The question is repeated and defined. The first 'To die: to sleep' introduces one force, the argument for one side. The second 'To die: to sleep', occurring at exactly that point in the line where its predecessor occurred, introduces the symmetrically opposed force, namely the argument for the opposing side. But Hamlet never decides. Instead, he remains at the point of equilibrium. The question abides unresolved while the remainder of the speech elaborates the case for acrasia and indecision. (82)

This is the argument from below, from the body upwards to metaphors and speculative thought. In this way Turner evolves a method of demonstrating the continuity between our biological selves and our most elaborate fantasies. If the body is so fundamentally embedded in all our mental processes, it follows that we need to return to the body to cash in the semantic values of language. A top-down approach starting with the observation of the complexities of interacting nonverbal and verbal signs arrives at very similar insights. What it adds, however, is an explanation of how precisely the body is able to be aligned with linguistic expressions or, more accurately, is able to inform otherwise empty verbal schemata.

As to visual signs, I have mentioned the problem of the asymmetrical relation between colour terms and the actual differential experience of colours. I showed that it is a mistake to think that linguistic organization entirely rules nonverbal grasp. There is evidence that languages tend to follow a certain list of priorities in the evolution of colour terms. First come black and white, followed by red, yellow and green. Sometimes green and blue remain undistinguished. Nor is the 'full' spectrum developed in any language. It does not seem to matter much, to fine-grain nonverbal distinctions, whether or not language actually codifies the distinctions. The point is that nonverbal colour grasp can be measured by means other than language and the results appear to be beyond doubt (Ackerman, 1991: 253).

The opposite scenario is equally fascinating. People faced with an entirely new environment find it hard to register its fine-grain colour gradations. Early European settlers to Australia, for example, were unable to distinguish the very subtle greens of the more than four hundred eucalypts and hundreds of other species, describing them all in terms of a uniform olive green. Painters worked very hard for generations to develop techniques which they felt would do justice to how they saw the light and colours of Australian landscapes. In this case, both nonverbal readings and verbal expressions had to be evolved gradually as a cultural task.

In habitual meaning acts we are in an altogether different situation. Here, high-speed imaginative variations rule our schematic nonverbal grasp of the world. It is no accident that Wittgenstein so frequently employs the phrase 'imagine . . .' throughout his later writings. 'Anyone who is unable to imagine a case (*Wer nicht im Stande ist, sich einen Fall vorzustellen*) in which one might say "I know that this is my hand" (and such cases are certainly rare) might say that these words were nonsense' (Wittgenstein, 1972: paragraph 412). To make meaning of linguistic expressions we must fill empty verbal schemata with appropriate nonverbal fantasies. The result is a process of signifieds which, though never stable, nevertheless allow us to identify persons, objects and actions that make up our environment. What counts as appropriate fantasies is guided by two principles: the rules of language (a kind of *langue*) and the systemic nature of our nonverbal readings of the world, both of which are grounded in culture. Structuralist linguistics acknowledges only the first of those principles and hence finds itself in a vicious syntactic rather than a hermeneutic, semantic circle.

How do we imagine a case? We fantasize variants of a typical social situation. Usually, our quasi-visual fantasies dominate in such acts. This is why cognitive science, including cognitive linguistics, is almost exclusively focused on the notion of visual mapping. Mark Turner, who has persuasively adapted the principal findings of cognitive science to his own research in cognitive rhetoric, has also inherited this emphasis. When he discusses the conceptual metaphor *understanding is seeing* he points out that it 'provides us with an appropriate domain, vision, for the comprehension of understanding itself'. He then goes on to say that 'there is a reason why understanding is conventionally understood in terms of seeing and not scratching or bathing or flexing one's muscles or feeling the wind against one's follicles' (Turner, 1987: 17). True enough. However, the majority of metaphors for understanding are indeed tactile and not visual. Comprehending, grasping, *begreifen*, *comprendre*, etc., as well as a host of non-Indo-European tactile metaphors for 'understanding', can be listed in support of this claim (Ruthrof, 1997a: 170f.). 'Understanding' itself is a proximic and tactile metaphor rather than a visual trope. We need to try to redress this imbalance in thinking about meaning. Our world is more than a visual field. We live in a 'sense-luscious world' (Ackerman, 1991: xv).

At the level of the signified we are iconic beings. This implies that we understand the largely arbitrary and symbolized signifiers of natural languages by cashing them in at the level of meaning via the body. The imaginary routines which we typically perform when we understand verbal texts provide the necessary link between sounds and world. I have called those links 'routines' in the sense that imagining a portion of the world in response to the sounds of linguistic expressions is not merely subjective but, in significant measure, socially steered. Recent philosophies have struggled with this tension between the symbolic side of language and our corporeal presence in the world. Formal and perceptual signification seemed difficult to reconcile. Nowhere is this paradox more obvious than in the writings of Gilles Deleuze. We cannot help but observe a deep tension between the formalism of his earlier works and the corporeal leanings in the writings co-authored with Felix Guattari (Deleuze and Guattari, 1987, 1994). Such antistructuralist notions as 'rhizome', 'becoming-animal', 'desiring machine', 'nomadism', 'deterritorialization', 'conceptual personae' and 'body without organs' contrast sharply with Deleuze's earlier 'logic of sense', in spite of the conceptual rigour that informs *A Thousand Plateaus* and *What Is Philosophy?* (Ruthrof, 1997b).

In Deleuze's work we witness a biographical trajectory of thought prefigured in Husserl's struggle towards a 'geometry of experiences'. Starting from his own mathematical and later Fregean convictions of formal purity in the description of language, Husserl, by the time he theorized the lifeworld (*Lebenswelt*), found himself trapped by his early eidetic convictions. What is grasped in perception (a noetically evolving noema or meaning unit) has, just as does language, an eidetic or formal core. It is this formal essence at the heart of our readings of the world and our grasp of words in syntactic order that allows us to communicate. It seems that Husserl was thus misled by his formal training to transfer eidos from definitional systems, such as formal logic and mathematics, to sense interpretations and natural language. In the formal domain of symbolic logic, eidos and noema are indistinguishable. In perceptions as in verbal meanings there simply is no eidos at all. Communication is possible for other reasons, as I shall argue in Chapter 11, 'Sufficient semiosis'. Once logos has taken hold of a philosophical project it is difficult to dislodge, even in phenomenology. As we saw in Chapter 1, Merleau-Ponty is a perfect case in point. It was left to Alfred Schutz and his successors in ethnomethodology to complete the transition to a nonformal description of our typified grasp of the world by language and nonverbal signs. Both

Husserl's and Deleuze's shifts mark the realization that in natural language, even in its abstracted philosophical forms, the body cannot be eliminated. This is neatly illustrated by the paradoxical term 'conceptual persona' created by Deleuze and Guattari to highlight the corporeality inherent in philosophical, speculative reason. It is one thing to note that we cannot but grasp 'things' and the universe as ordered, quite another to jump to the conclusion that a universal logos makes it so. There may be other reasons why this is so, and logos may very well be yet another effect of such a cause. Instead of saying that logos underlies everything, let us say that logos is a historical achievement and a typical feature of all cultures at certain stages of evolution. Let us say there is a discursive development from concrete representations to their abstract alternatives and to fully fledged formalization. As a consequence we would have to say that natural language within which this sequence can be observed remains fundamentally tied to the concrete. Both in its ontic relation to world, to what language refers, and in its epistemic relation to speech situations and ways of knowing, language is deeply anchored in the body.

The touching body is of particular interest to this study. This is so partly because tactile signification tends to be undermined by the dominance of visual signs both in social practice and in its theorization. We should return to the tactile also because it is a pervasive sign in language, as the examples of our metaphors for comprehending show. Something that 'touches' us has special significance even though the tactile origins of the expression are not realized in habitual discourse. In Helen Keller's world of touch sensations, 'paradise is attained by touch' (Keller, 1909: 3). The necessity of touch in early childhood development and the phenomenon of psychosocial dwarfism is worth mentioning at this point (Ackerman, 1991: 71ff.). As Ackerman observes,

> Some children who live in emotionally destructive homes just stop growing. ... If the mother's touch is removed (for as little as forty-five minutes in rats), the infant lowers its need for food to keep itself alive until the mother returns ... if she never comes back, then the slower metabolism results in stunted growth. (75)

Similar results have been recorded in primate research, where touch deprivation has been linked to brain damage (77). 'Touch', says Ackerman, 'seems to be as essential as sunlight' (80). But like everything else, this relation too undergoes evolutionary change. Ackerman cites the case of the Kung! to make this point. 'Kung! infants are in touch with others about 90 percent of the time, whereas our culture believes in exiling babies to cribs, baby carriages, or travel seats, keeping them at arm's length and out of the way' (78). If we see human evolution as a process from sense-based communication towards more and more symbolic exchange, from strongly intersemiotic to increasingly heterosemiotic, from inclusive cultural discourse to exclusive specialized languages, including chemical codes and computer languages, then a change of the species can be predicted in the long run, from beings in touch with the body to beings framed by syntactic codes. Yet even robots must be in *touch* with the world to have immediate effects in the world. And they are in touch by a variety of nonverbal sensors.

Tactile signification is of interest here for one more important reason. It has been used as a basis for a number of sustained attacks on dominant theories of language. In this respect, the writings of Luce Irigaray, Hélène Cixous, Julia Kristeva and Pamela Banting are highly relevant. How do corporeality and meaning relate in some of their work? In Irigaray's *Speculum of the Other Woman* the tactile is theorized as a challenge to our visual, representational bias (1985a). In *This Sex Which Is Not One* (1985b) Irigaray offers a radically new account of female experience and of *'parler-femme'*, what it means to speak as a woman. Writing against the Freudian tradition in which woman is conceived as a kind of 'atrophy' (Irigaray, 1985b: 23), Irigaray attempts no less than to reclaim woman as a ground for a radically different view of the world and of language. It is the tentative relation between Irigaray's female corporeality and language that is of particular interest to a semantics based on the body. At the heart of her book is a view of female sexuality that is always auto-erotically in touch with itself, a perspective from 'self-affection'. In this account, the tactile plays a central role. *Parler-femme*, 'speaking (as) woman', disrupts the orthodox 'syntax of discursive logic' (1985b: 222) and its concomitant preoccupation with truth, by diminishing the distance between body and language. 'Your body remembers,' Irigaray tells us, and 'truth is necessary [only] for those who are so distanced from their body that they have forgotten it' (1985b: 214).

From this emphasis Irigaray makes the important point, too tentatively it seems to me, that woman threatens dominant discursive modes by her presence 'as a sort of "prediscursive reality"' (1985b: 89). This flies in the face of assumptions in the wake of the linguistic turn that there is no such thing as an extralinguistic or prediscursive reality and everything we can think and imagine is somehow already language. Irigaray locates the point of departure from male-regulated discourse in a description of female sexuality in contrast to Freudian and post-Freudian descriptions. Contrary to sexual desire and pleasure focused on a theorization of penis and clitoris, Irigaray assures us that 'woman has sex organs more or less everywhere' (28). Since the time of ancient Greek philosophy and its visually oriented logic, female desire has been denied and replaced by descriptions 'foreign to female eroticism' (26). Significantly, 'woman takes pleasure more from touching than from looking' (26). This preference for the tactile over the visual and its propositional abstractions leads Irigaray to an entirely different approach to language. Instead of foregrounding truth, reference, coherence of meaning, she wants to allow for contradiction, fragmentation and unfettered creativity. Instead of well-formed or grammatical propositions, Irigaray favours 'an "other meaning"', one that is 'always in the process of weaving itself, of embracing itself with words, but also of getting rid of words in order not to become fixed, congealed in them' (29). Woman's 'silent, multiple, diffuse touch' eschews identity, for it is primarily 'contiguous. *It touches (upon)*' (29):

> This 'style' [of women] does not privilege sight; instead, it takes each figure back to its source, which is among other things *tactile*. It comes back in touch with itself in that origin without ever constituting in it, constituting itself in, as some sort of unity ... Its 'style' resists and explodes every firmly established form, figure, idea or concept. (Irigaray, 1991: 126)

What Irigaray aims at is no less than a radical transformation of discourse and its 'sexuation' on the basis of the haptic body. She projects this reinterpretation to occur at two levels: the level of formal analysis, and the level of 'style, the subjective involvement ... of his/her relationship with the body, with the sexuate body'. The former is seen as formalizable, the latter as resisting formalization (1991: 142). Irigaray's aim is

> to reveal who is speaking, to whom, about what, with what means. In technical terms, this means that it is a matter of uncovering the dynamic of the utterance [*énonciation*] underlying the statements [*énoncés*] produced. Beneath what is being said, it is possible to discover the subject, the subject's economy, potential energy, relations with the other and the world. The subject may be masked, bogged down, buried, covered up, paralysed, or may be engendered, generated, may become, and grow through speech [*en parlant*]. (1991: 147)

But there is also a broader goal in Irigaray's reorientation of the study of language from the perspective of sexual corporeality. For 'the issue is not simply a matter of justice for one sex, but of responsibility for the preservation, organization, consciousness and creation of life, of the world' (143). What would language have to look like at the level of basic ingredients to accommodate Irigaray's *parler-femme*? What would the relation between linguistic expressions and the way we view the world, the relation between syntax and meaning, have to be to permit the 'presence' of corporeality inside the linguistic? And why is it so difficult for feminist thought to find an appropriate place for the body *in* language? As the literature shows, there is no lack of attempts at achieving a feminist theory of language in which the body plays a significant role, the sort of role to allow for all the features of female difference and maternal biomateriality. Kristeva's presymbolic 'semiotic' and Irigaray's celebration of the tactile perhaps have achieved what can be accomplished given the constraints of their linguistic presuppositions.

A reading from the perspective of corporeal semantics of Hélène Cixous's 'The laugh of the Medusa' and its spirited defence by Pamela Banting will show the reasons why the body remains supplementary even in feminist writing dedicated to the restoration of the body to the centre of language. To anticipate my conclusion in summary, it is a commitment to a largely Saussurean and Jakobsonian conception of language in which signification is governed by intrasyntactic, differential relations that in the end undermines a corporeal feminist theory of meaning. In 'The laugh of the Medusa' Hélène Cixous insists that woman's body 'vitally supports the "logic" of her speech'. Woman signifies 'with her body' (Cixous, 1997: 351). But Cixous also speaks more broadly when she warns that to 'censor the body' is to 'censor breath and speech at the same time' (350). This applies centrally to our conception of language, and a good deal of language philosophy and linguistics has been guilty precisely of this charge. When Cixous writes, 'women must write with their bodies, they must invent the impregnable language that will wreck partitions, classes, end rhetorics, regulations and codes', she is primarily attacking the historical facts of patriarchally controlled discourses (355). Yet to achieve the revitalization of language from the perspective of woman as a signifying body, we also need a revitalization of the dominant theorization of speech. For woman to be able to 'put herself into the text' effectively we need a suitable explanation of how precisely linguistics allows for such an insertion (347). There seem to be two issues here. The one concerns the specific history of patriarchal discourse, the other, a form of theorization of language which argues the signified in terms of corporeality. That we must be wary of 'the signifier that would take you back to the authority of the signified' is spoken with an empiricist and definitional theory of language in mind that would result in the dictate of a Lacanian 'symbolic order' (360). If, however, signifieds are redefined as fantasy constructs necessary for the transformation of syntax into meaning, the discussion shifts. But to go this way, Cixous would have to jettison her Saussurean heritage.

Pamela Banting, in 'The body as pictogram: rethinking Hélène Cixous's écriture feminine', mounts a persuasive defence of Cixous against charges of

'essentialism', a debate I will leave aside, where its confusions largely belong
(1992). Regarding the body as a Freudian pictogram, Cixous is shown to
propose a discursive practice which takes its cue from the hysteric's way of
relating language to the body. This relation is interpreted by Banting as a
kind of translation in Jakobson's intersemiotic sense. At this point it is crucial
to understand the difference between Jakobson's widely used notion,
summed up in Chapter 5, and the manner in which 'intersemiotic' is defined
in corporeal semantics. For Jakobson the various semiotic practices, language, painting, music, cinema, all have their own semantic structures which
an intersemiotic translation negotiates. Language means in itself as a system
of signs. By contrast, in corporeal semantics, language on its own does not
mean at all. Here, nonverbal signs are indispensable for linguistic meaning.

Having adopted a Jakobsonian notion of intersemiotic translation, Banting
has also assumed a series of semantic presuppositions which, I suggest, are at
war with her political goal. So her call to us to change language can yield only
limited results. How can we 'trespass between different discourses, languages and semiotic systems' (Banting, 1992: 240) when that trespass is
already constrained by the intrasyntactic relations that govern it? What both
Banting and Cixous need, it seems, is a view of language that allows
nonverbal signs not merely to trespass but to form part of the foundation of
meaning in language itself. It is not quite right to say that 'intersemiotic
translation provides a process by which the body can *insert* its signs *into*
language'. For Jakobson does not allow an insertion as much as a supple-
mentation of one semantic system, language, by another, a set of
nonlinguistic signs. This means that language does not really *need* the body,
it merely allows its additional signs to be added as a supplement. But if
Jakobson's intersemiotic rule merely allows the body to be attached to
language in a supplementary capacity, then his theory is not conducive to
Cixous's or Banting's much more radical goal, which is to get the body *into*
language. What must language be like to allow for an insertion of this
kind?

Banting is sensitive to 'the problem how bodies get into and mark written
texts' (226). She describes Cixous's view as to how a woman's body relates to
her words as a 'fluctuating process', once more a Jakobsonian intersemiotic
translation rather than an incorporation. As Banting explains, 'For Cixous,
translation between and among different signifying systems, both verbal and
nonverbal – speech, writing, image, song, gesture, caress, and flesh – is not
only possible but provides a way out of the problematics of representation'
(237). Representation here I take to refer to some form of realist mimesis
naturally not conducive to the kind of fluid interaction Cixous and Banting
have in mind. As we shall see towards the end of this book, in a section on

Derrida's comments on representation, the all-too-quick dismissal of what could be covered beneath the term 'representation' is definitely not in the interest of any corporeally oriented linguistic agenda. At the same time, the very fluidity and freedom of interrelation sought seems to me stymied by a trust in structuralist linguistics, especially since 'the body retains its ability to sign for itself' and in situations where 'linguistic sign-making breaks down' (231). In that case, how does the body come to the fore? For Cixous, hysteria points the way. But it is not only in hysteria that corporeality 'returns with a graphic insurgence' (231). Nor are the nonverbal signs that constitute the body welded to linguistic signs. Nor indeed is 'translation' a concept strong enough to carry Cixous's corporeal grammatology. This surfaces again when Banting stresses the role communicating bodies continue to play in the transition from the 'ideolect' shared between mother and child to 'communo-lect', when, in the language of Kristeva, semiotic creativity is overruled by discourse as symbolic order:

> signification has always already been constituted in the sonorous envelope, the eye contact and the gestural hieroglyphs of the relation between child and mother. Just as the word 'mother' needs to be reinterpreted in order to break the monopoly that patriarchy has over the practices of mothering, so too, in the phrase 'mother tongue', the word 'tongue' becomes inadequate, as this domestic vernacular pervades the entire body and in fact simultaneously marks, and blurs, the boundaries between two bodies. Furthermore, this bond with the mother (and, within the present shifting economy of signs, with the 'feminine') or intimate bonds between any bodies need not and in fact cannot be irretrievably forfeited or signed away in negotiating the social contract – unless, of course, the body is signed away at the same time. (Banting, 1992: 235)

Why is it then that 'Cixous does not advocate the development of a language with its source in the body' nor indeed thinks of natural language as always already functioning in a fundamentally corporeal way? And why is it that Banting does not transcend the 'master' discourse she is defending as a disciple in this crucial respect? The answer, it would seem, is provided by Banting's attack on empiricist or perhaps also naturalist conceptions of representation: 'Theories of the body which are based, consciously or unconsciously, on representation cannot escape from the premise that the body exists outside of signification, prior to language, only susceptible to meaning through representation in language' (239). This strikes me as extraordinarily misguided. Here we must have either a metaphysical realist and naïvely representational view of bodies on the one hand and language on the other or a structuralist semiotic view in which everything that has meaning, including bodies, does so only because it is already signified in language. Crucially, for both Cixous and Banting 'outside signification' is identical with 'outside of language'. This is, I believe, precisely what vitiates the feminist search for a corporeal signified. There is another way, one that avoids the naturalist trap of the world as given and the linguistic fallacy according to which sentient beings, such as humans and other animals, live in a differentiated world only if they have language in the linguistic sense. As cognitive science is demonstrating with painful clarity, 'mapping' is the primary link between mind and world; language comes second. A semiotic that does not take note of such research does so at its own peril. Fortunately, a long time ago Peirce initiated a semiotic theory compatible with an emphasis on nonverbal grasp. That is the direction, I believe, we should take if corporeality is to be granted its rightful place in language. Cixous's contribution to 'poststructuralist feminist' writing as a 'project to sign the body back into semiosis, from which it has been exiled by dualist, metaphysical philosophies and theories of representation', goes only halfway because it remains anchored in a structuralist view of language as syntactically self-sufficient. Language allows translation by nonverbal signs, but does not need them. This is a mistake. If the body is to be put in the text, there must be an argument to show what features of language make such a move not only possible but necessary. Leaning on a structuralist view of meaning neither furnishes the required theory nor promotes the desired political goal. Cixous's corporeal grammatology in the end does not amount to a theory of language based on the body. To be sure, the body is retrieved, but as no more than a supplement aligned with language via a restrictive intersemiotic translation.

Other feminist theorists who share with Kristeva, Irigaray and Cixous the conviction that the body must be reinstated as central not only at the general level of gender politics, but also at the level of signification, and especially language, face similar problems. Moira Gatens's Spinozist, nondualist account of the body is an exception (Gatens, 1988). In 'Notes towards a corporeal feminism' Elizabeth Grosz takes her point of departure from the position that 'the body can be seen as the primary object of social production and inscription' and suggests that 'the relations between the socially distinguished forms of body, and the positions occupied by each, may help to provide the bases for a non-essentialist, non-humanist conception of sexual/personal identity' (1986: 1, 2). For Grosz, 'corporeal feminism' primarily has a political goal, namely to create 'an understanding of corporeality that is compatible with feminist struggles to undermine patriarchal structures and to form self-defined terms and representations' (3). Part of such a struggle

includes a challenge to the very systems of signification that act as foundations of patriarchal society. Consistent with such a challenge, Grosz explicitly
aims for

> not only the creation of new words, syntactical and grammatical rules
> and formal structures, but the creation of different representational
> structures, different ways of using language, different contexts in
> which discourses can function. It implies re-appropriating language by
> speakers who have been disqualified as such from enunciation. It is
> thus not a new language that is required, but, more feasibly, the
> construction of new knowledges. This seems necessary insofar as
> bodies themselves are never brute objects external to discourses and
> representations; it is relevant, then, that the activity of *making meaning*
> be reordered so that the bodies it conditions and the social subjectivities
> it makes possible can be changed. (Grosz, 1986: 12f.)

What is required in Grosz's own terms, it would seem, is a new way of
theorizing natural language, among other things. This is not offered here, nor
in her more recent book *Volatile Bodies* (1994). Yet without an analysis of what
enables language in certain social practices to exclude specific elements, such
as a (re)presentation of the body congenial to feminist goals, such aims
cannot be realized. Unless we confront the deep ground on which language
has been theorized from Saussure to Lacan, a basis hardly deconstructed in
the most important feminist writing, the body remains barred from entering
meaning as a *sine qua non*.

Lacan is right, it seems, to reject the idea that language is a code since we
cannot align signifiers and signifieds in any strict sense. However, this
should not lead us to give up on a description of signifieds and focus our
energies on 'floating' or even 'flickering' signifiers. In fact, if we did so, it
would not be possible to debate signifiers either. Pedantically, any sort of
claim cannot be run on signifiers alone without signifieds. This is the
performative paradox at the heart of much of such theorizing. So let us look
for a more promising avenue. It offers itself if we concede that words help us
to 'corral how we feel and think', as Ackerman puts it (1991: 213). By the same
token, our words would mean nothing without the corporeality of feeling, or
any other form in which the perceptual body activates language. That the
relation between linguistic signifiers and their embodied signifieds should
escape strict codification is no obstacle to either their practical success or their
persuasive theorization. Speakers more or less successfully negotiate the way
they activate linguistic expressions by nonverbal signs within cultural
frames.

Meaning occurs when we are able to match signifiers with corporeal signifieds. The corporeal signified, then, is a vital element in a performance theory of language in which meaning is understood as an event in a chain of intersemiotic and heterosemiotic realizations. Meaning events are fantasy acts, whereby quasi-visual realizations are merely a dominant form and not the general rule. Such acts are more or less controlled by culture. They are controlled to the degree that we have learned to respond to the sounds of linguistic expressions in such a way that we produce typical and largely shared fantasies about the world. Meaning events as acts of the imagination also always display a certain loss as well as surplus of meaning. That is, the deviance from the social norms of fantasizing our world goes both ways, beyond the semantic recipes provided by culture as well as falling short of their scope. Meaning as events within networks of potential meanings are more or less schematic, from fairly precise 'realist' fantasies to highly abstract grids.

Perhaps even the sceptical reader may now concede that there is something to the claim that certain kinds of signifieds could be said to be embodied by nonverbal signs. But there remains the nagging doubt whether corporeality could ever be shown to be a factor in abstract expressions, let alone in function words. This is the topic of the next chapter.

9. Social traces in abstract expressions

All the metaphors conveyed by likenesses taken from bodies to signify the operations of abstract minds must date back from times when philosophies were taking shape. The proof of this is that in every language the terms needed for the refined arts and recondite sciences are of rustic origin.

(Vico, The New Science, [404], 129)

Perhaps it is not too hard to accept the idea of a corporeal semantics as long as it involves concrete expressions. But what about abstract terms, such as justice, freedom or democracy? And what about prepositions, function words or syncategorematic expressions such as 'and', 'if', 'although', 'or' and 'even'? In Anne Sullivan's 'Second report' on the progress of her charge Helen Keller, we find the following passage worth quoting in full:

> I am constantly asked the question, 'How did you teach her the meaning of words expressive of intellectual and moral qualities?' I believe it was more through association and repetition than through any explanation of mine. This is especially true of her earlier lessons, when her knowledge of language was so slight as to make explanation impossible.
>
> I have always made it a practice to use the words descriptive of emotions, of intellectual or moral qualities and actions, in connection with the circumstance which required these words. (Keller, 1954: 299f.)

When Helen breaks her new doll and cries, Miss Sullivan says 'Teacher is sorry', repeating the phrase under similar circumstances. Not surprisingly, 'after a few repetitions', the report notes, 'she came to associate the word with the feeling'. And likewise with words such as 'happy', 'right', 'wrong', 'good', 'bad', as well as the function word 'also' (1954: 299f.). What is especially remarkable in this passage from our point of view is the teacher's realization that pedagogy by linguistic analogy works well only once a fairly rich vocabulary and a basic syntax have been established. During this early stage of Helen's development a more direct association between sense readings about the world and abstract language proves to be a necessity. What this cloaks, though, is the very strong possibility that the later stages in the child's learning process, when generalizations and other abstractions can be transmitted more quickly, are likewise operating on the background of nonverbal sensations. This is what corporeal semantics emphasizes. Far from being now absent, nonverbal signification has gone underground and fulfils its necessary base function without being visible at the behavioural surface.

When we talk of abstraction we must distinguish two kinds, generalization and formalization. To generalize is to find superterms for subordinated ones, such as 'furniture' for 'chair', 'table', 'cupboard', 'couch', and so on, or 'fruit' for 'apple', 'mango', 'lime', etc. To formalize is to empty a term of its material content and so turn it into a mere 'placeholder' in a certain syntactic relation. Thus, replacing 'chair' by 'x' and 'table' by 'y' allows us to repeat the form of statements without repeating their specific content. In this way a general principle can be formulated as a template for specific contents. For example, the principles of mechanics, initially derived from observations of actual relations in the world, can be provided as a formula, an empty schema of relations ready for application. Formulae for speed, acceleration, leverage, relations of temperatures, weights and volume measurements all belong to the domain of formalization. We can also be specific as well as general in a formal system, such as Euclidean geometry, when we distinguish specific figures from their ruling, formal principles. By the same token we can formalize both specifics and their generalizations. Generalization and formalization, then, are distinct discursive operations.

The point of insisting on the distinction between generalization and formalization is this. In certain artificial signification systems, such as formal logic, mathematics or geometry, the distinction is demonstrable. By contrast, in natural language we are able to generalize but we never arrive at full formalization. Natural-language terms are themselves not formal. This does not, of course, mean that we cannot insert formal phrases, such as mathematical equations, chess moves, or the formulations of physics into a natural-language text. Yet when we do so, we are dealing with two fundamentally different kinds of signs, the heterosemiotic signs of socially saturated language and the homosemiotic and definitional signs of a formal system. The result of this argument is that even the most abstract terms in natural languages are never mere placeholders but always retain some traces of their social origins. I want to test this claim against two groups of abstract terms, abstract nouns and function words.

When we use the word 'democracy' in an English-speaking environment we tend to say that we understand the term because we hold a definition or a kind of lexicon entry in our memory. This would mean that we understand language by yet more language, which begs the question of how we understand this additional text. Or we say that we have learned to link the word 'democracy' with the relevant realities in the world, which begs another question: how do we know that world if not via signification, including language? On the theory advanced in this book the mechanisms of understanding linguistic expressions are quite different. When someone says 'democracy' I am able to fantasize at very high speeds a series of more or less schematic images that characterize 'democracy' in a given culture. My ability to do so is partly a biocognitive process, partly and more importantly the result of a cultural pedagogy which makes an entire community imagine similar portions of the world when word sounds are uttered in a specific order, in specific nonverbal, social contexts.

However, we should not merely replace standard linguistic solutions by a visual alternative. Words like 'image' and 'phenomenon' carry with them as part of their semantic package a prejudice in favour of seeing, light and ultimately the sun that tends to undermine the intersemiotic relations at work here. The terms 'mental (re)presentation' would be preferable were it not for the unfortunate prefix 're-', which suggests some sort of realist copying. Perhaps 'mental presentation' would be acceptable. Alternatively, there is the German term '*Vorstellung*' which suggests a putting or setting in front of oneself, irrespective of whether the imagined item is a tactile, olfactory, gustatory, aural or some other construct. Given this proviso, 'democracy' is a shared and more or less schematic fantasy or *Vorstellung* rather than a definition or a naturalist link with the world as given. Individual *Vorstellungen* typically overlap to form an intersubjective mental, social world. If this works, then far from being a highly abstracted linguistic construction, the signifier 'democracy' turns into a communicable signified via such concrete *Vorstellungen* as of typical parliamentary behaviour, voting, and other features of the politically organized public sphere. Likewise, we could not understand 'academic freedom' if we could not fantasize actual restrictions and privileges and their critical effects in society at large. 'Oppression' makes no sense as a definition, unless we apply the same fantasy procedure to its explanatory text. The term means something only on condition that we are able to imagine forms of oppression, even if such fantasies must remain sketchy or schematic. It is partly the tendency to underestimate how much mental content humans are able to process in a fraction of a second that has favoured semantic explanation via definitions. And yet, if we test how long it takes for anyone to come up with any definition of 'oppression' or 'democracy', it turns out that our fantasy acts are very much faster than the most well-trained definitional memory.

When we think of 'globalization' we grasp the meaning of the term by flashing before our mental eyes virtual variants of the electronic transformations responsible for the global village effects. We imagine an increasingly digitized world. An abstract noun, like the most concrete term such as 'mango', in principle requires the same procedure to become meaningful. We must be able to imagine something. If we cannot, the signifier remains a signifier. We suspect that it means something, but we do not know what. We do not understand. To proceed from signifier to signified, appropriate acts of fantasy are a prerequisite. The same applies to technical terms, no matter how abstract. Take, for instance, Jean-François Lyotard's term 'differend'. Even in a case like this, where we immediately look for linguistic substitutions – that is, further linguistic descriptions – those 'definitional' texts once more have to be given mental material form to mean anything. To say that 'differend' is well explained by the phrase 'an injustice resulting from the application of discursive power' merely says that we have provided an appropriate verbal alternative which is equally in need of semantic transformation. We have offered no more than an acceptable alternative set of signifiers but not yet a signified, a meaning. 'Differend' becomes meaningful if we are able to match it, as well as its explanations, with an appropriate string of fantasy acts about the world – if we are able to conjure up in our minds typical situations of discursive bullying, for instance. Having done so, we do not have to provide an alternative, explanatory text because the nonverbal text gears into our social world more immediately than does language. The fact that we are always at liberty to find further linguistic alternatives to sum up our understanding is a 'can' rule only. Meaning even of the most abstract terms, then, is the event of matching the sounds of linguistic expressions with appropriate fantasy constructs about the world. No matter how concrete or abstract a term, to proceed from signifiers to signifieds means to imagine the right portion of the world or the appropriate relations between images. The dual character of our quasi-perceptual acts and the nonverbal aspects of what is imagined then 'anchor' all linguistic expressions in the corporeal. We could say that we are able to play with *Vorstellungen* in this way because we have learned the rules of what to imagine under what sort of cultural conditions. Such rules or semantic recipes make the construction of meaning a social event.

If the most abstract terms display their hidden corporeality once we ask how we construct meaning, can the same be said about what are summarily called 'function words'? Are not terms such as 'and', 'or', 'if', 'even', 'not', 'never', 'all', 'some', 'yes' and 'no' formal elements within natural language? At first glance this is precisely what they look like, especially if we have in mind their equivalents in symbolic logic. Indeed, at the surface there does not appear to be a difference between a natural-language 'is' and the copula 'is' in a formal text. We tend to think that the 'or' of English is the same as the 'or' in a binary digital logic gate. It is not. It is precisely in this grey area where natural language *looks* like formal signification that the difference between the two is fundamental. I will argue that all function words in natural language carry the traces of their social origin and must not be equated with their formal cousins. What, then, is the difference?

Take the conjunction 'or'. Formal systems distinguish several kinds of 'or', such as the vel-function 'a ∨ b', the exclusive 'or' or non-function, a seq-function to indicate a sequence of possibilities [→ or ⊂], and an equivalent function [→ or ≡]. By comparison, in English the 'or' has not been dis-ambiguated in this way and so carries a number of possible meanings depending on the situation represented. Above all, 'or' still displays traces of its social origins. Though we can only speculate about such origins, it seems that we cannot conceive of the beginnings of language without a rudiment-ary grid of conjunctions and disjunctions having been used. From this angle, whatever the early equivalents of the English 'or', the Latin *'vel'* or the Chinese *'haischi'*, they marked the realization of specific social situations of separation and/or equivalence of natural phenomena, goods or persons. Such acts of alignment and distinction were probably taken over from nonverbal communication, which lacked the degree of syntactic differ-entiation made increasingly available during the evolution of languages. That the natural-language 'or' still carries opposite semantic values – exclu-sion and equivalence – reminds us of studies in the early twentieth century in search of an Ur-language as well as Sigmund Freud's fascination with words indicative of a less differentiated vocabulary. Freud draws our attention to such words as Latin *succus* and *siccus* suggestive of an earlier single signifier which carried the opposite meanings of juicy and dry, or the German *Stimme* (voice) and *stumm* (dumb, speechless), which likewise invites the reconstruc-tion of an early nondifferentiated form referring to speaking/not speaking. A further difference between the natural-language 'or' and its related logical operators is the fact of intonation. While this makes no difference in logic, considerable modal shifts can be achieved by variation in intonation in ordinary speech. The discursive 'or' is able to take on threatening, ironic, sarcastic and other modalities which add further, differentiating semantic values to segregation, equivocation, listing and so on.

It is tempting for logicians to say that natural language is deficient because multiple meanings are often contained in one single word such as 'or'. Indeed, a good deal of the work in search of a perfect language, sketched recently by Umberto Eco in *The Search for a Perfect Language* (1997), reflects this dissatisfaction with ambiguity. However, logical disambiguation is a *tour de force* approach to language unable to rival the speed and efficiency of intuitive interpretation in complex social situations. Furthermore, the very process of meaning negotiation which typically marks the discursive equivalent of logical clarification is a crucial characteristic of the social dynamics of meaning as event.

As straightforward a word as 'and' similarly reveals hidden complexities once we subject it to interpretation. The 'and' still carries with it the social traces of aligning things and persons spatially, of assembling people and gathering tools and food, of close associations and looser alignment. The 'and' also still contains for us its primeval content of temporal ordering. First one thing, then another, one person and one to follow, one event succeeded by another. We can imagine that the 'and' in this sense played a fundamental structuring role in the emergence of narrative. Both the spatial and the temporal sides of 'and' are familiar to those who closely observe the speech patterns of children. What a delight for the child when she first realizes what power the 'and' affords her in her world of toys and the members of her family! And how annoying the temporal use of the 'and then' is to the parent tired of having to retell the same story another ten times. Both in its evolutionary emergence and in its realization in early childhood the 'and' is far removed from a mere formal conjunction. It is rich with the promise of holding things together and tying past and future into a wished-for stability.

Take a preposition such as 'on'. Not only does it require our imagination to conjure up scenarios in which things are put on surfaces, the 'on' also demands a deictic fantasy. We must be able to imagine from which position the 'on' is spoken – from below, from above, from far away, from very close up – and from which temporal frame. It matters whether it is part of a prophecy or part of a retrospective view. All these possibilities require fantasy acts to be realized as potential frames for how we are to position our 'on' in an imagined world. This kind of argument is more forceful if we imagine what it would be like to shoot a video or a movie. Then suddenly both the referential and deictic sides of the 'on' spring to life. What sort of 'on' do we need? The 'on' can be tentative or assertive. From where is the camera viewing the 'on'? Is the camera looking down at the person 'on' the chair or is the sitting figure viewed from below? In each case the 'on' changes its modalities and hence its meaning. Only in a propositional theory of language is such doubling disallowed; it is pertinent to a theory of language in which the body holds centre stage. Fortunately, what is being asserted here is not entirely without support.

That certain function words in natural language differ from logical operators is by no means a novel claim. Such discrepancies have been noted in the literature, in particular with reference to conditionals like 'if-then' (Austin, 1961; Comrie, 1986; Sweetser, 1990). What is more attractive is Eve Sweetser's general claim that syncategorematic terms or function words in natural language 'partake of a much broader set of functions than the logical joining of propositions'. I will present a few of her observations on the topic and attempt to radicalize some of her insights in the light of the corporeality of language. Starting from the position that 'human perception and understanding of the world' is the 'basis for the structure of human language', Sweetser goes on to include abstract terms in her theory (Sweetser, 1990: 2). She presents a strong argument for the claim that 'not merely lexical items, but the conjunction process itself' is affected in natural language by 'ambiguity between uses in the content, epistemic, and speech-act domains' (87). She shows that 'and' can be symmetrical and asymmetrical, a situation ruled out in its formal use. In 'John eats apples and pears' and in the sentence 'King Tsin has great mu shu pork and China First has good dim sum' the reversal of text left and right of the conjunction 'and' would not seriously affect our meaning constructions. Yet in the case of 'John took off his shoes and jumped in the pool' the case is different. Here 'and' functions as a temporal operator or as 'and then', and so a reversal of the conjoined expressions would radically alter the meaning of the sentence. Likewise, in the case of 'Mary got an MA in basket-weaving, and she joined a religious cult', the sentence is not reversible without semantic change. This time the conjunction stands in for 'and so', with an emphasis, according to Sweetser, on the epistemic side of language suggestive of a certain conclusion to be drawn (87).

The function word 'and', then, can be used symmetrically and asymmetrically depending on what sort of social situation we wish to evoke. No such ambiguity exists in formal logical notation. However, it is not enough simply to point out yet another difference between artificial and natural languages. What is more important is to demonstrate that only by imagining the kind of life situation which we have learned to link with a given set of linguistic signifiers as an appropriate meaning are we able to sort out what kind of 'and' we are dealing with. Without such fantasy acts language remains meaningless, even at the level of function words. Sweetser rightly concludes that 'whatever "putting things side-by-side" may mean in natural language, it only sometimes means something equivalent to $\wedge$. Perhaps the closest we get to stating the relation between AND and $\wedge$ is to say that $\wedge$ is a mathematical crystallization of one of the most salient uses of AND (93). For all practical purposes this will do. Yet there remains the deeper question whether the fact that we can so crystallize a formal sense should lead us to assume that therefore something like a formal 'and' actually operates in natural language. Given the bias of this book, I am inclined to say that formal principles and relations are always derivable but are not there in any sense of situational presence.

'Or', like 'and', can be shown to fulfil functions somewhat different from those of its formal derivative [or]. It can separate two actual alternatives in the world, as in 'left or right'. There are actually two roads leading opposite ways, though only one of them is the proper way to travel. 'Or' can separate alternatives, of which only one is actual, as in 'Bill is reading or has nodded off', suggestive of a situation in which the observer is not in a position to see which one of the two is the right description. In this case, one interpretation excludes the other. Sweetser draws our attention to epistemic uses of 'or', as in 'John is home, *or* someone is picking up his newspaper' (94). Here the speaker draws a conclusion from the observation that the newspaper is not in front of John's house: either he is at home and is picking the newspaper up himself, or somebody else is doing it. This is referred to as an epistemic use of 'or' because it says something about the speaker's reasoning process.

'Or' can also conjoin two speech-acts. Sweetser illustrates this case with 'Have an apple turnover, *or* would you like a strawberry tart?' in which an implied listener is asked to respond to two alternatives. To this I would like to add what I regard as an important rider. Even if speaker and listener were to play the same language game or were to co-operate in a Gricean sense, the listener still enjoys the freedom of taking one of four options rather than the two alternatives offered. He or she can also say, 'Thank you, I'll have a piece of each' or 'No thanks, I am not hungry'. This means that any natural-language exchange is always ready to explode into a larger text. And it is in the nature of social discourse to do this, because natural language is the result of a social world and its complexities and not a cause of syntactic relations or merely specific references. In natural language, terms and syntax serve the mirroring of nonverbal readings about the world.

When the exclusive 'or' function is used in a formal language, we observe a reversal of this set of relations. A priori defined signs are tied together by a syntax which determines the proposition. That such propositions can be used to refer to strictly circumscribed phenomena of the perceptual world must not seduce us into assuming that this is how natural languages work. An indication of the validity of this claim is the fact that when we separate two variables or constants in a formal language (x [or] y; a [or] b) there is no opportunity for any social effect as a result of two 'inappropriate' items being juxtaposed to one another. 'What would you prefer, bread or a beating?' If this is uttered in jest, one sort of community response is guaranteed. The serious alternative of a cruel speaker is likewise imaginable. In the first case, only the first conjunct 'bread' is part of the actual world, while 'beating' belongs to the domain of fantasy. Yet fantasy is a crucial element in language processing. Hence in the second case, both conjuncts belong to a potentially actual situation rather than an impossible one.

This is why Sweetser is not quite right when she compares discursive and formal uses of 'or'. The basic meaning of 'or', she writes,

> seems to be that of conjoining alternatives; these alternatives are nor-
> mally taken as jointly filling all possible options, so that one or another
> of them must be the right alternative. In the content domain, conjoining
> with OR thus indicates that some one of the conjuncts must describe the
> genuine state of affairs in the real world. (94)

This view, I think, is mistaken. There are endless possibilities in natural language of combining items by 'or' that are feasible, actual-world altern-atives:

> You may choose: these spears or those arrows.

> Which text should we read first, *From Etymology to Pragmatics* or *Reading Minds*?

In each example, both alternatives are actual possibilities. Hence we are able to remain at the level of the perceptual world in the construction of meaning for both. There is also the serial 'or' which acts as a disjunctive link in a chain or list of items, all of which can be genuine, actual-world alternatives.

> Dinner has been booked at the Fat Crab. For lunch, we can have fish and chips, or cold chicken, or the rest of the ham, or a tin of pink salmon, if you like.

The exclusive 'or', the either-or and the inclusive 'or' of listing all have their formal counterparts. However, as with 'and' they function differently. This becomes visible once more when we replace the habitual, actual-world examples with fantasy disjunctions. In something like 'now or black, never or green, always or red', the sort of phrasing we would readily accept in experimental speech, meanings are indeed construed, even though the items separated remain fluid fantasy acts waiting to be confirmed in some ways further down the text. The fantasy then may make cohesive sense and provide a functional role for our expression. Here, the 'or' appears to be extended beyond strict disjunctive exclusion to act as a substitute for 'think of the present or think of a colour', and thereby the role of 'or' is shifted closer to that of 'and'. The resulting fluidity is as important in the reading of artistic texts as it is when we wish to get a sense of the subtleties of pragmatic speech. This is especially so when the phrasing is not strictly appropriate to the occasion, a situation which is the rule rather than the exception. This situation does not arise in a formal system, because there is no semantic leeway for interpretive exploration. So even where function words appear to play the same role as their formal relations at the textual surface, their semantic-pragmatic deep reading transcends formal confines.

In her analyses, Sweetser makes use of the distinctions drawn between content reading, epistemic reading and speech-act reading of function words. Although this kind of differentiation is valid and makes for neat, fine-grain analysis, it must not obscure the fact that it depends on our imaginative variations of actual social speech situations. The term 'content' gives the impression that it refers to situations that are more closely associated with the actual world, while 'epistemic' and 'speech-act' conjunctions appear one step removed from it. I want to emphasize that they all occur in our social world, including all those myriad variations that we perform in our minds as things are going on around us. Those virtual texts and their social contents are just as 'real' as are the descriptions of our immediate perceptual reality of shopping malls and freeways. A similar criticism can be made of the use in cognitive linguistics of 'iconicity'. In Sweetser's formulation, 'iconicity may be involved' in sentences in which causal relations and temporal sequences are implied which demand our anchoring of meaning in the actual world. This is where I believe cognitive approaches are too hardheadedly realist for their own good. Having already shown that even function words have their roots in the way humans relate to the world perceptually, that is apart from language, we have no reason to say that any language item could be exempt from some form of iconicity, however indirect. In this sense, most cognitive research does not appear to wish to draw the radical consequences of its own position.

I would like to reinforce this argument with reference to the disjunction 'but'. Sweetser is happy to demonstrate that the epistemic and speech-act uses of 'but' differ from formal disjunction because they involve of necessity the larger text of a speaker's consciousness of his or her intentions and performance and a communicative utterance situation. However, she is hesitant in admitting the 'content' use of 'but': 'The obvious question which I have left unaddressed is whether there is a content usage of *but*.' Unfortunately, Sweetser in the end cannot 'conclude that *but* has a content-domain usage' and accepts that indeed it 'lacks such a usage' (104). Let me take Sweetser's own example for the opposite conclusion. Let us replace 'John is rich but Bill is poor' by a contextualized example:

Romeo and Juliet are in love with one another and want to marry. Juliet is rich but Romeo is poor. Juliet's parents do not approve of the proposed marriage. (103)

In this case it is no longer true that, as Sweetser says, 'there is no bar in the real world to the simultaneous existence of poor and rich people' (103). There certainly can be, and when there is, then we are dealing with a content usage of 'but'. In any case, iconicity in a broad sense informs all usage, be it content, epistemic or speech-act, because without any anchor in our nonverbal readings of the world there would be no such thing as a culturally consistent, or reasonably consistent, meaning.

Lastly, let us look at a radical claim made by Mark Turner in *Reading Minds: The Study of English in the Age of Cognitive Science*. In a chapter entitled 'The poetry of argument' Turner rejects our customary 'default concept of reason' and instead plays with the idea that

our concept of rational argument would appear to be a product of poetic thought ... without metaphor, we would not have the concept of argument we have ... without a body, we could not have the concept of argument we have ... without a symmetrical body, we could not have the concept of argument we have. (Turner, 1991: 100)

This looks like a tall order and yet is entirely consistent if we take corporeality seriously as the ground on which all forms of cognition and all forms of signification rest. Indeed, without the body there would be no perceptual world, and without a perceptual world, language would have nothing to do. In terms of argument, as well as its logical refinements, what is at issue here is to show whether logical relations are the basis for corporeality or vice versa. Turner makes a very persuasive case for the foundational role of the body, arguing that all understanding, including the most abstract reasoning processes, 'is structured by the same force-dynamic image schema' (120). By way of summary, let me quote the following seminal passage by Turner in full:

By virtue of the body, the brain has an understanding of force-dynamic image-schemas. Our bilaterally symmetrical body makes it particularly easy for us to understand oppositional forces, equilibrium between them, and the consequences of strengthening or weakening a force. We can project this knowledge metaphorically onto the domain of propositions, giving us a metaphoric default concept of rational argument as the conflict of bilaterally opposed forces situated in certain ways in the space of propositions ... our default concept of reason ... is not disembodied. ... Rather than opposed to the body and poetic thought, it is their product, and shares this derivation with many of the strongest and most universal parts of our thinking. (120)

The most abstract terms in natural language still carry the social traces of the rudimentary linguistic acts by which our ancestors codified the relations between our bodies and our perceptual world. Such relations may not all have been premised on symmetry. And it is most unlikely that they were driven by some logos underlying everything. Both language and nonverbal readings are likely to avail themselves of a broad range from fairly concrete to highly schematized configurations.

It is probably a linguistic prejudice to assume that only words and expressions can act as general 'rules' in Jakobson's sense. When someone asks a child to draw a horse, the resulting sketch will typically be recognizable as a nonverbal rule. The child does not draw any specific horse, but a schema that sufficiently resembles all kinds of horses, the principal pattern of 'horse' rather than any individual portrait. Nor should we assume that the visual or any other nonverbal patterning can operate only at one level of generality. It is much more likely that all sign systems have a range from the closely mimetic to the highly abstract, from narrowly representational to fantasy variations and distortion. As Diane Ackerman nicely puts it, 'in our mind's eye, that abstract seat of the imagination, we picture the face of a lover, savour a kiss' (1991: 281). If all sign systems allow for a range of more or less realist, immediate and more radical transformational constructions, then one such line of transformation is likely to operate along the trajectory of abstraction and formalization. Think of the emergence in the history of cultures of such geometrical abstractions as circle, mandalas, pentagram, squares, triangles or spheres, all of which appear to be transformations of observations of nature; and likewise such formalizations as, for example, the relevant equations of radius, circumference, angles and diagonals, or stereometrical equations for rotating bodies.

If natural languages evolved, as I assume they did, as economizing grids covering existing rudimentary forms of reading the world and of communication, then it should not be surprising that our languages even today reflect the fundamentally iconic nature of their signs. Why should abstract expressions be an exception? At the moment, cognitive science appears to provide the strongest arguments for such claims. However, there is also an argument from an altogether different way of thinking that we could call upon. This is Heidegger's idea that something as abstract and indeed formal as logical assertion is no more than a shrunken interpretation. In curtailed forms of assertion, such as logical predication, 'The table is round' or '*S* is *p*', Heidegger reminds us that the 'as' of the interpretive 'as-structure' now 'no longer reaches out into the totality of involvements' (Heidegger, 1962: 200). Here the 'as' has dwindled to 'the structure of just letting one see what is present-at-hand', and so conceals the larger picture. The 'existential-hermeneutical "as"' has been reduced to what he calls the 'apophantical "as" of the assertion' (201):

> If the phenomenon of the 'as' remains covered up, and, above all, if its existential source in the hermeneutical 'as' is veiled, then Aristotle's phenomenological approach to the analysis of the logos collapses to a superficial theory of judgment, in which judgment becomes the binding or separating of representations and concepts. (202)

Indeed, Heidegger insists, even in the slightest form of making sense of something 'there lurks the possibility of interpretation – that is, of appropriating what is understood' (203). As a consequence, Heidegger rejects the logos of assertion as the foundation of the 'science of language'. Instead, he suggests a deeper ground:

> there emerges the necessity of re-establishing the science of language on foundations which are ontologically more primordial. The task of liberating grammar from logic requires beforehand a positive understanding of the basic a priori structure of discourse in general as an *existentiale*. (209)

For Heidegger this means that the study of language, like anything else that concerns humans, must be viewed from the tapestry of *Dasein*. From the more modest metaphysics of corporeal semantics we can take Heidegger's reversal of priorities and put the totality of involvements first, relegating logos to its reduced forms of discourse. In other words, we adopt from Heidegger what allows us to give priority to the body as embedded in a culture and leave to the Heideggerians his preoccupation with Being and his nostalgia for a *Heimat* in early Greek thought.

In this chapter I have given at least an indication of how one could argue that even abstract terms in a natural language still show traces of corporeality and so are distinct from their formal logical cousins. I have emphasized once again the role of the imagination in the construction of nonverbal scenarios necessary for meaning, even in abstract expressions. What I have not done as yet is to show how one can defend corporeal semantics against charges of mentalism and subjectivism. That is the objective of Chapter 10.

10. The role of the community

When one emphasizes, as I have done, the prominent role of the imagination in semantic processing of verbal expressions, the charges of subjectivism and mentalism are the foremost objections to confront. If we say that nonverbal signs are the deep structure of language and that these signs are brought into play by quasi-perceptual processes, then we must show that such signs are not merely private mental construals and entirely subjective. We must show that neither the criticism of mentalism nor that of subjectivism applies. For if they do, it would be very difficult to argue our body-oriented theory of language in terms of general principles.

We recognize the fear of subjectivism in Frege's elimination of the quasi-perceptual components of meaning in his influential paper 'On sense and reference' (1970). The idea, *Vorstellung*, or mental projection, which we are able to produce when we entertain a 'thought' should be erased from the description of meaning on the grounds that it is merely subjective and cannot be shared by a speech community. Frege's thought, on the other hand, is objective in the sense that it can be strictly defined. And definitions proper are fully sharable. This emphasis is understandable from Frege's perspective of a purified language of univocal terms. What is often forgotten in this kind of move is that the majority of 'thoughts' do not yield to the definitional purity required by the logician either, as I shall demonstrate in Chapter 11. And in any case, it would seem that natural languages are governed by social practice rather than by a priori rules. Add to this the further complication that dictionary substitutions, often and wrongly called definitions, vary from speaking subject to speaking subject to a very high degree and so are no longer sharply distinguished in this respect from nonverbal fantasies about terms. In short, verbal explanations of meanings display subjective elements just as do nonverbal responses to language and, more importantly, neither is well described as either subjective or objective. They are both performed under cultural regimes and so can best be called intersubjective.

As to the related objection of mentalism, Hilary Putnam's phrase 'meanings ain't in the head' perhaps best sums up what is at issue. This is an observation to be taken seriously in any description of semantics. However, Putnam should not be understood to be saying that nothing occurs in our minds when we mean by language. What he wants to emphasize is the social dimension of meaning. And so should we. The question is how meaning events as described so far can be shown to meet this criterion. Having said this – and I will say more on the question of social control below – I do wish to stress that without individual acts of fantasy, under some form of guidance, meaning events cannot be well explained. Perhaps we could say that meanings are 'in the head' in the sense of necessary instantiations of a community practice. What is a community?

Community can be understood as a shared interpretive attitude in the sense of Kant's *sensus communis* or in the related sense of Peirce's semiotic. In Kant's *Kritik der Urteilskraft* (Critique of judgement) the community is viewed as a control group for judgements that go beyond private maxims and involve a *sensus communis*, or attitudes shared by members of the culture to which we belong (Kant, 1968). Since this frame is not the boundary of a logical set, as are the frames of pure reason, our judgements as well as their guiding principles are subject to reflective reason. Contrary to determining reason, as in deduction and tightly controlled induction, reflective reason is an interpretive procedure in which we invent the rules as we go along. This procedure has two aspects. One is the judgement itself, which is always a tentative negotiation between what is before us to be judged and the larger whole of which we think the particular object of judgement is a part. The other is the stipulation of that larger whole, a purposiveness, which we need for any specific item to make sense. This part–whole dialectic is one of the founding principles of the entire hermeneutic tradition up to Heidegger and Gadamer. Because Kant needed a flexible notion of purposiveness for this kind of reasoning, he redefined 'telos' and replaced its deterministic principle by an open-ended process. Teleological judgements in this revised sense require the background of a *sensus communis*. This applies both to our judgements about nature and to our judgements of art. Neither could be further analysed if they were merely a matter of personal maxims. To form judgements proper in Kant's scheme they have to be communicable within social principles even though such judgements concern the 'harmony' we experience between objects and the imagination. We could say that in interpreting complex phenomena we achieve meanings by successfully associating data with our own imaginative construals and so endow the object of judgement with a certain purposiveness, an open-ended telos. In the face of the popular emphasis on Kant's subjectivism, we should remind ourselves of these two constraints. Kant's 'I' performs nonverbal readings, *Anschauungen*, rather than 'intuitions', via the social rules of concepts and judgements and so is a species 'I' rather than the centre of subjectivity. Humans are such that they cannot but have *Anschauungen* and form judgements. The second constraint is *sensus communis*, public opinion.

In the published works of Charles Sanders Peirce we find a significant improvement on Kant's fairly thin notion of the community. Here, the construction of our world by signs 'essentially involves the notion of a *community*, without definite limits, and capable of a definite increase in knowledge' (Peirce, 1974: 5.311). This idea of the community provides a highly flexible frame for guided and yet not deterministically controlled semiosis. Since in Peirce signs are not restricted to linguistic expressions but most definitely include nonverbal signs, we could say that he puts a powerful constraint on mentalist and subjectivist explanations of signs. This is the way a defence of corporeal semantics should go. In a similar vein, Alec McHoul's recent *Semiotic Investigations* describes the community as the 'space around the sign, its framing' (McHoul, 1996: 52). A community, then, can vary considerably in size and social character, as well as gender stratification, and still be conceived as a rule-providing mechanism for the speaking and fantasizing subject.

How, then, does the community guide individual acts of the imagination? Kant was right in regarding concepts as social rules. But what does this mean? It certainly allows for an explanation whereby the community acts as a kind of control panel for the way groups of speakers conceive the world. In this way, individuals from infancy onwards learn not only the typical pathways along which we imagine the world but also the right way of associating language sounds with certain fantasies, from the most realist reflections of physical reality to their most bizarre transformations. When someone says 'x' (e.g. *'arbre'*), we imagine 'a' (e.g. the generalized image of a tree); when someone says 'y', we imagine 'b'. When someone says 'mama' the baby is being trained to imagine sweet smells, the taste of honey milk, the soft touch of skin, the pneumatic roundness of the breast, a gentle, soothing voice. When someone says 'Aborigine', we imagine a person struggling to be recognized as an equal, someone having to strain against an entire history of prejudice to get even close to the 'level playing-field'. And if someone says 'Aboriginal lawyer', we imagine not only such a person but at the same time the exceptional achievement that lies behind his or her social status. In the communities of the Third Reich, when someone said 'Jew', the sound was typically associated with a member of a race to be eliminated from society, first by expulsion, later by extermination. All of these relations are community-steered acts of the imagination. They are relations defined by semantic rule and their nonverbal instantiations by the individual and, by entailment, the collective imagination. If meanings are events of combining empty linguistic schemata with nonverbal signs, then concepts could be seen in a Kantian way as the social rules that direct the construction of those combinations.

From this perspective we can now revisit two Wittgensteinian favourites, 'use' and 'form of life', and say a few words about Deuleuze and Guattari's 'order words'. Once more, why Wittgenstein yet again? Let me make a stark claim. Without the radical revision of his notion of a 'form of life' as the nonverbal ground for language as 'use', we fail to appreciate the potential of the late Wittgenstein's view of meaning. Wittgenstein's definition of meaning as 'use' in the *Philosophical Investigations* has been highly influential as a bridge between analytical approaches to meaning and what one could call their critical, speculative counter-streams, such as phenomenology, Peircean semiotics, structuralism and poststructuralism. We must be careful, however, not to try to fit Wittgenstein's term into any of these schools of thought without critical adjustment. From a broad-brush perspective, in phenomenology 'use' could be said to refer to typified acts of consciousness sanctioned by the lifeworld; in a semiotics informed by Peirce 'use' would have to be aligned with community-informed 'habit'; structuralist 'use' could be described as *parole* in accordance with *langue*; while for poststructuralism, meaning as 'use' might be regarded as the ephemeral side-effects of speaking subjects temporarily entering infinite chains of signifiers. Since for postmodern theorizing, at least in its Baudrillardian guise, meaning has been declared dead, 'use' in a semantic sense would be a kind of necrophilia. All we have to play with is the bare bones of a skeletal syntax.

How would we rephrase Wittgenstein's meaning as use to suit a corporeal semantics? Here we must pay attention to the fact that for Wittgenstein, linguistic expressions acquire meanings when they are uttered within certain generic frames, or language games, embedded in a specific form of life (*Lebensform*), which I shall address below. However, he does not give us any more detail as to what precisely 'use' consists of. From the angle of the perceptual presence of the body in the construction of meaning, 'use' can now be refined. Meaning as use is the activation of linguistic signifiers by nonverbal signs (tactile, haptic, olfactory, gustatory, etc.) in relation to specific forms of life and according to social instructions.

One of the effects of the 'linguistic turn' during the second half of the twentieth century was to write a good deal about meaning as use as a linguistic problem and to neglect the equally important concept of *Lebensform*. And yet one could say that 'form of life' is the rock bottom of the late Wittgensteinian picture of language. Unfortunately, the description given in the *Philosophical Investigations* is sparse. Nevertheless, it provides enough direction to invite conceptual refinement. A form of life is made up of various social practices such as ways of eating, drinking, greeting and so on, and it is within such cultural frames that language games have their function. I would add, it is within the loose boundaries of such frames that meaning processes take place as negotiatory events. What is being negotiated here is what sort of intersemiotic activation of verbal schemata by nonverbal signs is the most appropriate. A combination of forms of life with corporeal semantics has two consequences: a more precise description of *Lebensform* and a better under-standing of the systemic relation between language and culture. Let us have a closer look at what Baker and Hacker have called a 'dark saying' and a 'notorious expression' (Baker and Hacker, 1988: 238; 1983: 47). I take their two-volume commentary on Wittgenstein's *Philosophical Investigations* as my guide.

Wittgenstein uses both the singular 'form of life' and the plural 'forms of life' in his later work. The following are the main references: 1953: para-graphs 19, 23, 241; pp. 174, 226; 1972: paragraph 358:

> To imagine a language is to imagine a form of life. (1953: paragraph 19)

> Commanding, questioning, recounting, chattering, are as much a part of our natural history as walking, eating, drinking, playing. (1953: paragraph 25)

> speaking is a PART of a form of life. (1953: paragraph 23)

> human beings agree in the language they use, not in the opinion but in form of life. (1953: paragraph 241)

> What has to be accepted, the given, is – so one could say – forms of life. (1953: p. 226)

> One might say: 'I know' expresses *comfortable* certainty, not the cer-tainty that is still struggling. (1972: paragraph 357)

> Now I would like to regard this certainty, not as something akin to hastiness or superficiality, but as a form of life [*als (eine) Lebensform*]. (1972: paragraph 358)

Wittgenstein cautions our reading by adding in parentheses, 'That is very badly expressed and probably badly thought as well.' Nevertheless, what he appears to be getting at is, I think, something that Peirce called 'habit'. Our habitual linguistic performance is part and parcel of a form of life. In

Wittgenstein's manuscripts this picture of *Lebensformen* as systemic frames for language is strengthened further, as in the phrase '*Formen unseres Lebens*' (MS 160, 51; in Baker and Hacker, 1988: 242), 'forms of our life' and in the observation 'es ist charakteristisch für unsere Sprache, dass sie auf dem Grund fester Lebensformen, regelmässiger Handlungen, emporwächst [It is characteristic of our language that it grows up from the ground of stable forms of life, rule-governed actions]' (v. 15, 148; in Baker and Hacker, 1988: 242). Baker and Hacker are adamant that Wittgenstein's forms of life refer to culture alone and relegate biological readings as aberrant. I think that they are largely right, except that Wittgenstein perhaps did not wish to draw such a sharp line between nature and culture. Look again at his famous conjecture, 'If a lion were to speak, we could not understand him' (1953: 223) and his clarifying comment on what he means by 'comfortable certainty', which he wants to conceive as 'something beyond being justified or unjustified . . . as something animal' (1972: paragraph 359). Here it seems to me that 'forms of life' may very well be grounded in biological conditions or at least allow for an evolutionary trajectory on which culture gradually emerges from nature. This would be compatible with findings in recent cognitive research and would avoid too ready a wholesale identification of language with culture.

If we can say that culture is made up of all forms of signification, such as tactile, olfactory, aural, gustatory, and other nonverbal readings as well as linguistic schematization, then forms of life can function precisely as the sort of cultural frame for language that I think Wittgenstein was moving towards. By reading Wittgenstein against the background of nonverbal signification, in its interactive as well as its conflictual character, we can redefine forms of life in this way. Forms of life are culture-specific clusters of nonverbal signs.

The circularity of having nonverbal signs appear both in linguistic meaning events under social rules and in forms of life is not a logical error, but a fact to be confronted. The presence of nonverbal interpretations in both language and social life enables us to make sense of the world by means of language as well as enabling us to find our way about in the world without language. I will have a little more to say about this relation later (Chapter 13). Suffice it to add here that our ability to translate between two or more languages is likewise to be grounded in this dual presence of nonverbal signs. We translate referential and fictionally referential texts in a rich way when we are able to imagine to a high degree of specificity what sort of world the reader is supposed to fantasize. For only then are we in a position to ask what linguistic schemata would best reflect this nonverbal scenario. Community-governed clusters of nonverbal signs inform both linguistic meanings and the sort of world to which they refer.

Having introduced community control into a semantic theory in which fantasy plays a prominent role, we have, however, by no means achieved a satisfactory description of what goes on in the process of meaning-making unless we also address the character of control. In other words, we must acknowledge that the relation between community guidance and individual instantiation can go nasty either way. Just as individual acts of imagination can defy and harm the community, so too can the semantic recipes prescribed by the community obliterate individual freedom. Or, in Deleuze and Guattari's words, the community is always in a position to effect subjectification and so impair the emancipatory process of subjectivation. Deleuze and Guattari treat this problematic under the term 'order-words'. The kind of control exerted through 'order-words' is the focus of the rest of this chapter.

A battle line appears to run through the history of language philosophy. It separates philosophers trying to resolve semantic issues via linguistic interiority from writers arguing that what is exterior to language determines questions of meaning. Like Foucault (1978), Deleuze, under the influence of Guattari, in the end opts for exteriority and hence a pragmatics. In these later works, co-authored with Félix Guattari, Gilles Deleuze abandoned his earlier formalist style of inquiry into sense in favour of a broadly politically oriented pragmatics. With this shift also goes a move away from an emphasis on ideality and towards an interest in the corporeal. This pragmatics has two sides, one political, one purely functional. The latter can be summed up under the heading of the 'abstract machine'. What interests us here, however, is the political aspect of Deleuze and Guattari's view of language. At the centre of their semantic politics, understood strictly as a pragmatics, they place what they call *mots d'ordre*, or 'order-words', marking a radical extension of such items as imperatives, slogans or military orders and passwords to cover the entire scope of a language (Deleuze and Guattari, 1987: 106ff.). Order-words, then, are not to be understood as a particular category of words but rather as 'the relation of every word or every statement' and in general 'every act that is linked to statements by a "social obligation"' (1987: 79). As to pedagogy, 'the compulsory education machine does not communicate information,' they say; 'it imposes upon the child... the dual foundations of grammar', the binaries of plural–singular, noun–verb, subject–object, masculine–feminine (1987: 75f.).

From the perspective of the corporeal semantics outlined here, this amounts to viewing the role of the community as largely negative. As the framing space for signs or as the mechanism that tells a speaker how to fill the empty language grid with nonverbal signs, the community appears as the prison guard of meanings. The result is what Deleuze and Guattari call 'subjectification', the formation and fixing of subjectivity from the outside. This is the death sentence for 'subjectivation', the emancipatory process of self-positing of subjectivity. What emerges is a semiotic picture in which not information but the imposition of power is the primary function of language. Hence 'language is not made primarily to be believed but to be obeyed and to compel obedience' (1987: 76). If we read the heading 'nudity' (usually in the vicinity of 'violence') at the beginning of certain TV programmes we cannot but develop a very strange set of semantic values to be associated with nakedness. Moreover, if 'embezzlement' and other antisocial acts are never mentioned in the same slot, viewers cannot help but get used to the idea that nudity is a more heinous crime than theft.

How, I want to ask, is it possible for order-words to do their work? Is it because we learn their definitions like a string of program commands outside of which we cannot think? Or have we learned under what conditions we must link them with the social and the physically given? The first answer suggests an a priori language view based on formal assumptions, while the latter establishes an empiricist divide between signification on the one hand and the world as given on the other. Neither answer is satisfactory. The first fails because it provides no exit from words to world and so is viciously circular. The second fares no better because it offers a nonmediated view of the world and so cannot account for the feedback role of signification in the constitution of the world the way we sense it. I suggest once more that our fantasy acts about the world are crucial in this process. From the perspective of corporeal semantics, order-words appear as community rules for what to fantasize about in response to linguistic sounds.

The imposition of power by the community, then, is so insidious because it has entered the very way we imagine. As a result, we take for subjectivity something that has largely been constructed by the community. If we combine the Deleuze and Guattari picture with Jean-François Lyotard's term 'differend', which indicates an injustice by the application of discursive power, we could say that since the entirety of a language amounts to an imposition of order-words, the differend is everywhere. We can, of course, take a less sinister view of the role of the community as the framing mechanism for meaning events, a view in which the relations described make possible both communication and oppression. On this position, different communities are posited with opposing functions. This would allow for the very nomadic and other minoritarian communities celebrated by Deleuze and Guattari, communities without which there would be no hope of escape from subjectification to subjectivation.

Conclusion

If the community trains its members to imagine the world in similar ways, individual nonverbal readings lose their importance. In a world such as ours in which televisual standardization of images is a powerful formation of how we are to see the world, individual nonverbal deviance is significantly reduced. Nor is there any likelihood that this trend will be reversed. But even in pretelevisual societies, the control over the way people are to fantasize the world is much stronger than is generally acknowledged. In any case, there does not seem to me to be any substantive difference as to subjective variance when we compare language and nonverbal, quasi-perceptual construals. If this is so, then attacks via mentalism and subjectivism lose much of their force.

Having substituted the looser guidance by the community for definitional control, we still need an explanation of how such guidance translates into the mechanisms of linguistic communication. The next chapter suggests that the core principle at work here is *sufficient semiosis*.

11. Sufficient semiosis

In this chapter, I propose to replace the traditional reliance on 'truth' and 'truth conditions' in semantics by 'sufficient semiosis'. In spite of the threatening philosophical package these terms suggest, the issues involved can be simply put. As long as we are dealing only with single terms and their meanings, questions of truth do not arise. We can create a rudimentary semantic theory without recourse to whether what we are saying is true or not. However, as soon as we introduce indicative sentences (such as 'There is a glass of water on the table' or 'You were wrong to imply that Judith Goodall had misrepresented the registrar's legal advice'), we want to be able to check whether what is being said is the case or not. In other words, we are inclined to tie meaning to 'truth' or 'verification', or 'truth conditions'.

This, I believe, has to do with the temptation to explain what is complex by simple analogies. And indeed the procedure seems to work as long as we stay within a range of uncomplicated examples. But even then, any straightforward explication of the relation between linguistic meanings and their effects in the world tends to give us a wrong picture. This is especially the case when a simple truth notion appears to do the trick, as in the case of 'There is a glass of water on the table'. Because the sentence refers to a portion of our world and because this reference can be supported by visual and tactile signification (in short, observation), we feel that it is a good procedure to link language and 'truth'. And yet we have performed a leap of faith from our visual, tactile and other readings to equating them with the facts of a hard kind of reality. We have identified our epistemic procedure with the ontic, the being of the world. Certainly, this has not prevented an entire analytical tradition following in the footsteps of Bertrand Russell and his claim that if an expression has no reference in this narrow sense, then it also has no meaning. Unfortunately, this approach leaves a great deal of very meaningful language in the lurch. Where does this truth-oriented approach come from?

A representative of the classical positivist verification approach to meaning is Moritz Schlick. In his view, to give meaning to a sentence means to transform it into a proposition that we can apply to reality. To decide whether a sentence is meaningful or not requires a listing of the conditions under which a linguistic expression forms a true proposition and the counter-conditions under which its proposition is false. For Schlick and his tradition, 'there is no gradual transition between meaning and nonsense. For either you have given the grammatical rules for verification, or you have not; *tertium non datur'* (Schlick, 1936: 352). Over time it became clear that only a small portion of language could be explained in this way and the verification principle was gradually weakened in the literature and in the end abandoned.

A discussion of the relation of language and truth misses a crucial piece of evidence if it does not at least mention Alfred Tarski's Convention T, an argument by which the Polish logician wrapped up how signification and truth can be presented formally. He writes, '"snow is white" is true, iff snow is white'. The following needs to be added as minimal explanation. We have a *denotation* such that 'snow' denotes actual snow, a *satisfaction* in that 'snow satisfies the condition "x is white"'', and *definitions* which determine 'uniquely' the semantic values of the terms employed. The bi-conditional iff (if and only if) disambiguates the natural-language 'if', so it does not allow for unwanted alternatives. Tarski's formula is an elegant solution to an old problem, the relationship between meaning and the world. However, as Tarski himself insisted, we should not be too hasty in applying his Convention T to natural languages (Tarski, 1956: 153). Tarski's formula seems to work for natural language only if we invent sentences for which we can assume general agreement on the relation between verbal expression (a statement about snow) and the appropriate nonverbal sign complex we bring to bear on the expression (our perceptual readings). As soon as we complicate the linguistic expression so that no easy agreement can be assumed as to the right construal of nonverbal signs, the formula loses its force. In other words, we are dealing here with a sliding scale. The more technical the language, the better the fit of Tarski's solution; the more socially complex the less useful it becomes. Since social discourse tends to be complex rather than technical, Convention T cannot serve as a general rule for deciding on meaning.

A further complication is introduced by the cognitive linguist Eve Sweetser. She suggests that if the Latin *'candidus'* were chosen as sample instead of 'white', with its additional meanings of 'open' and 'honest', the relationship between expression and world no longer holds. The world 'outside human cognitive organization', or 'stuff' as I have called it, 'is not so constructed as to group the white with the honest. Rather, it is our cognitive structuring of the world which can create such an identification.' It follows, then, that if language is functionally related to our cognitive processes, then 'it cannot be described in terms of a pure fit between Word and World: unless we mean our experiential picture of the world' (Sweetser, 1990: 5). In that case, 'truth' has been radically qualified.

When we look at Donald Davidson's papers in *Inquiries into Truth and Interpretation* (1984), we see a gradual shift away from his work on truth, facts and truth-conditions, such as Tarski's Convention T, towards concerns with mood, performance, belief, inscrutability, metaphor and communication. Both the author's own arrangement in this order and the original publication dates seem to indicate a disillusionment with positivist certitude and an increasing acknowledgement of interpretive complexities. Most importantly, Davidson in a later paper makes a compelling observation about how he now sees the relation between meaning and truth: 'Trying to make meaning accessible has made truth inaccessible' (Davidson, 1989: 307–19). Of course, one must not take this observation out of context and exaggerate its relativist ingredients. But we must take note of his emphasis on the problematic relationship between semantic values and truth claims. Another observation compatible with the view on body and corporeality offered here is David-son's Wittgensteinian phrase of having erased 'the boundary between knowing a language and knowing our way around in the world' – except that Davidson does not think in semiotic terms. For us, the reason why one should agree with him on the removal of those boundaries is the claim that language and world rely on nonverbal signs, as far as they have meaning for us.

Readers steeped in postmodern theorizing may be under the impression that talk about truth-conditions is flogging a dead horse. Yet truth-conditions are vigorously defended by David Wiggins in 'Meaning, truth-conditions, propositions' (1992). The author offers an updated formula for truth-conditional semantics designed to silence its critics for good: 'Sentence *s* has as its use to say literally (in the thinnest possible acceptance of "say") that *p* just if whether *s* is true or not depends upon whether or not *p*.' This, Wiggins suggests, is to be embedded in a 'larger theory' which 'will persist in the Fregean explication of the literal meaning of a sentence as consisting in its truth-condition but explain the fuller kind of saying by building upwards from literal meaning' (Wiggins, 1992: 66). This is unsatisfactory at least, for the following reasons. Wittgenstein's notion of use, richly tied to forms of life as it is in the *Philosophical Investigations*, appears sadly reduced. We take the opposite tack and redescribe *use* and *Lebensform* in the richest possible way. Wiggins also feels compelled to ground all meaning in a minimalist literal starting-point, a concept which owes a good deal more to the purity of formal semantics and the idea that meanings are governed by definition than to a careful look at social discourse. And lastly, if the literal meaning of the sentence 'Pass me the cake, would you' amounts to its truth-conditions, the theory is in serious trouble, at least in all cases where there is no cake and the speaker is a nasty host who enjoys tricking his or her visitors. The so-called literal meaning of the sentence pales before its modalities whenever the politics of language becomes foregrounded, a situation typical rather than atypical in social discourse.

Truth-conditional theories, it would seem, have introduced more problems than they have solved. In particular, they are inept at addressing the question of fictional statements, which make up a very large part of the kind of language processing we perform with the assistance of the imagination. As Eve Sweetser writes, 'By viewing meaning as the relationship between words and the world, truth-conditional semantics eliminates cognitive organization from the linguistic system' (1990: 4). Moreover, metaphorical extensions of base terms such as seeing for knowing render truth-conditional explanations suspect. Perception and knowledge are related in a different way and so need a different description, such as the one offered via meaning and corporeality or cognitive semantics along the lines argued by Sweetser (6). Truth-oriented explanations are also less than convincing when it comes to the sort of complexity of interpretation involved in our opening example, 'You were wrong to imply . . .' This is not because formal procedures cannot mirror the semantic relations before us. It is because once such a mirroring has been achieved its complexity is just as baffling as that of the original. So instead of an explanation, we have a competing complexity in need of disentanglement. Furthermore, the range of implied possibilities here is such that their formal trudging out cannot compete with the speed by which the human imagination is able to play them through. Lastly, it is in the nature of truth-oriented theories to emphasize the information content of language while failing to deal with its modalities, especially its politics, on which so much social discourse turns.

Broader notions of truth have been invoked for the theorization of meaning. One such concept is Heidegger's truth as *aletheia* or unconcealment. This looks attractive at first, mainly I think because its holistic emphasis stands in such stark contrast to the interest in literality and self-sufficient sentence meanings in the analytical tradition. Heidegger's truth also promises to open a path towards unravelling the complexities of individual linguistic expressions in relation to a 'totality of involvements', and so initiates an interpretive rather than a definitional approach to meaning. And yet I believe we do not have to invoke the heavy metaphysical artillery of 'truth' in Heidegger's or in any other sense to describe the relations between individual expressions and our overall interpretive horizon. Since Nietzsche at least, truth in its various forms has had an increasingly bad press. And often for good reason. While Nietzsche pointed to the deep and concealed corporeal motivation for various truth claims, the writings of Derrida have more recently had a profound effect on the traditional privilege afforded truth in all kinds of shape. Yet poststructuralist writers on the whole have not pushed meaning beyond the brink. That was left to Jean Baudrillard, who has declared its death, together with the demise of any ground in which signification could be anchored. Now we have nothing but simulations and so we are barred from asking the question, 'Simulations of what?' Now we are dealing with simulations of simulations, a closed (non)significatory circuit, and the most radical application of the structuralist idea of language as a differential system of signifiers without reference (Ruthrof, 1997a: 230–233).

Derrida's and Baudrillard's positions perhaps best mark the significant differences which exist between poststructural critique and rampant post-modern theorizing (Lucy, 1997). A kinder response to Baudrillard's recent writing would be to say that he is speaking metaphorically, of course. In that case what he has to say about the digitized world sounds about right, even at times inspired, but we are still at a loss as to precisely what claims are being made. Yet even if we avoid Baudrillard's performative paradox, Derrida's *tertium datur* position still demands an answer to this question: if we abandon the ground of truth about the world in relation to linguistic meaning, how is communication possible?

This is an important question recently addressed in *Deconstructing Communication: Representation, Subject, and Economies of Exchange*. Its author, Briankle G. Chang, proceeds from a critique of phenomenological subjectivity as the ground of standard presuppositions about communication to a deconstructive investigation of the theoretical obstacles that undermine those assumptions. What Chang proposes is to replace our view of communication as a hermeneutic affair tied to the truth of some historical outside by a perspective which acknowledges that to communicate is to negotiate a conflictual social heteroglossia. If undecidability rather than definitional certitude or externally anchored truth determines meaning, then semantic exchange is better described as rhizomic and so communication shades into miscommunication. At this point, Chang wisely avoids the Baudrillard trap. He concedes that for an utterance to be communicable at all, 'its meaning cannot be infinitely open'. Hence the deconstructive title of the chapter, 'The (im)possibility of communication'. Far from meanings being secured by truth, they appear to function to a certain degree even under the most perilous conditions. Resistance to communication, even noncommunication, 'voluntary mutism', feigning of ignorance and 'counterfactual fabrications', do communicate. One simply 'cannot not communicate' (Chang, 1996). The credit for such insights must, of course, be given to Derrida in the first instance. As Niall Lucy has convincingly argued in *Debating Derrida* (1996), these are precisely the sorts of complications which destroy the basis on which, for example, John R. Searle builds his speach-act theory.

The critical literature concerned with the validity and invalidity of the link between meaning and truth spans an extraordinary range. Indeed, one could take this perspective as an umbrella view of some of the major disagreements on language over the past century. Here a somewhat different response is required. At the poles of the spectrum covered in the literature, we note that under certain conditions of meaning processing, both positions are untenable. On the other hand, there do exist situations in the economy of social signification where each is able to provide appropriate descriptions. This is how I propose to resolve the discrepancies. I suggest that to knock the notion of truth out altogether does not reflect well what communities actually do. Truth does have its place. Yet to insist that it must rule everything can be demonstrated to be no more than a logician's fantasy. Truth works well in formal systems, including mathematics. At this point it is popular to throw in a comment on Kurt Goedel's critique of formal systems as if Goedel had actually rejected the notion of formal truth. This is simply wrong. Goedel addressed two incompleteness theorems, the first of which deals with formal systems which can be shown to be true but are not provable. Goedel's second incompleteness theorem says that 'arithmetic is not sufficient to prove its own consistency'. The solution to the problem requires what is called 'transfinite induction' outside the formal system in question (Crossley *et al.*, 1990: 46, 57). The arguments involved go well beyond the scope of our inquiry and need not concern us here, except in so far as the incompleteness theorems could be regarded as an extension to formal systems of Kant's discussion of the incompleteness of the analysis of concepts. Nevertheless, truth works in arithmetic and other formal systems. On the other hand, it does a lousy job when it comes to dealing with complex sentences, let alone their elaboration in texts. If this is so, what suggests itself is a ladder of usefulness. Truth in relation to linguistic meanings appears to follow the law of diminishing returns. This suggests the following abbreviated scale:

- formal signification (where truth holds, even if it cannot always be proved);
- technical use (where it is indispensable for re-production);
- juridical discourse (where truth is used but turns out to be problematical);

- social communication with a 'technical' emphasis (where truth will do as a short cut);
- meaning exchange in complex social situations (where truth is unattainable, or at least as troublesome to fix as the range of meanings it is supposed to secure).

Unfortunately for truth-oriented theories of meaning, it is the last one of these categories which dominates social discourse. The intricacies of human relations, our elaborate fantasies about them, the network of accrued meanings, the politics of language, the mutability and multitude of exteriorities all conspire to tell us that truth is not a good thermometer of meaning events. In that case we should look elsewhere for an explanation for why it is that what is so complex nevertheless works reasonably well or, more accurately, always works more or less. As Irigaray puts it, 'truth is necessary for those who are so distanced from their body that they have forgotten it' (Irigaray, 1985b: 214).

How does a corporeal semantics resolve the relationship between words and world? Let us recapitulate. Language is a schema by which we can refer to the world if we know which nonverbal signs to use in order to fill in empty linguistic formulae. Our world is given to us perceptually or, more accurately, through a network of nonverbal signs. That nonverbal signs such as tactile, aural, olfactory and other readings turn up under both language and world is the crucial point. Nonverbal grasp is the basis for both language and world, and *nonverbal signs act as the deep structure of language*. Now comes the question of linkage. How can we check whether our nonverbally activated language is an appropriate reflection of our nonverbally constituted world? How can we relate language and world without resorting to disqualified truth-conditions? The procedure I propose is 'sufficient semiosis', a construction out of certain features from Leibniz and Peirce. From Leibniz (1934) comes the distinction between sufficient and insufficient reason. The first is restricted to formal operations – that is, signification systems ruled by definitions. Insufficient reason applies to all reasoning about the world, or all synthetic statements. If we were to pursue them logically, synthetic statements would always form an infinite chain. Leibniz bridged the two domains of reasoning by suggesting that at a certain point in nonformal reasoning we should call it quits and declare that sufficient reason has been given. In this way, we can proceed to further arguments where, strictly speaking, logic would not allow us to do so. Sufficient reason thus is a pragmatic solution.

In Charles Sanders Peirce's works semiosis is a series of transformations of signs, generating meanings along an infinite chain. Combining Leibniz and Peirce allows us to stipulate *sufficient semiosis*. It rests on a community-based assumption that sufficient meanings have been produced for communication to continue, to conclude with agreement, or to be terminated as fruitless. 'Sufficient' means that the kind of nonverbal material used to fill the linguistic schemata counts as equivalent to the appropriate, nonverbal grasp of our world. Sufficient semiosis, then, retains the idea of linking language and world but requires the notion of mediation of world by signs. At the same time, sufficient semiosis abandons any strict equivalence between what is said and what is there. It suffices that we know roughly what our language is about. In formal and technical signification sufficient semiosis can be defined strictly to meet the requirement of the relevant discourse. In fictional language where no immediate deep constraints inform our grasp of the world, sufficient semiosis can be relaxed to whatever our fantasy dictates. In complex social situations sufficient semiosis reveals best its suitability as a replacement for truth. Reconsider our earlier example:

'You were wrong to imply that Judith Goodall had misrepresented the registrar's legal advice.'

Our reading typically relies on the wobbly assumption that the speaker of the sentence has given a fair description of the intentions of the person who spoke or gestured about Judith in a certain manner. Yet even if that person were to deny that any such implication of misrepresentation was ever intended, the sentence utterer and others present would retain a sense of suspicion and certainly could never resolve the 'truth' of the matter. Nevertheless, meaning exchange goes on in the face of a situation that, from the purity of truth notions or truth-conditions, must remain unsatisfactory. By contrast, in ordinary life this situation is typical. Instead of testing truth relations in such situations, we apply the strategies of *sufficient semiosis*; we fantasize at high speed a variety of options and settle for pragmatic solutions.

I have proposed, then, that the mechanism for dealing with interpretive difference is something like sufficient semiosis, based on meaning negotiation rather than the check mechanisms of truth. I have also pointed out that the path to verification and truth-conditions even in weakened forms comes from the logician's starting-point, formally empty and therefore univocal signs. No such univocality can be assumed in natural language, and hence the route via meaning negotiation and sufficient semiosis is more appropriate to the task. But what is it in natural language that introduces polysemy to the degree that warrants this alternative? There are many good explanations, such as by pointing to the strongly metaphorical nature of language, or historical semantic drift, or the differences in language use according to class, race and gender, or differences which occur when a language is imposed on or taken over by a different culture. Informative as such explanations can be, they tend to describe symptoms of language rather than the reasons for the differential potential in language, its deep *différance*, that allows metaphors and drift to occur in the first place. In a previous study, I have proposed three basic forms of opacity responsible for polysemy as an endemic feature of natural language (Ruthrof, 1992: 4f.). I briefly summarize them here.

We can distinguish three kinds of vagueness characteristic of linguistic expressions: *modal opacity*, *propositional opacity* and *semiotic opacity*. *Modal opacity* refers to the manner of speaking of an utterance. Modal opacity is a necessary vagueness arising from the fact that language exists only when it is uttered. The relation between the utterance situation and what is said, however, requires a good deal of interpretive labour. In an actual social situation the reconstruction processes that occur between speakers and hearers are enormously complex and impossible to circumscribe fully. And since the implied and appropriate, inferrable deictic or, more broadly, modal stance of a speaker is never covert, modal vagueness or modal opacity cannot be eliminated. When we are reading a written text, the reconstructive labour required increases considerably. We are now not even in a position to use our perceptual readings. Now we have to rely on our imaginative variations of possible utterance events. As our interpretive fantasies increase to cope with this task, so do our meaning constructions. This is why it is so difficult to find one's feet in a foreign culture, where the web of implicit deixis is as opaque as it is pertinent to interpretation. Stating this situation more radically, we could say that the modal constructions we perform on linguistic expressions override their assumed propositional contents.

I said 'assumed' because when we look at the definitional guidance of words and expression, we note a second fundamental kind of vagueness, which I have termed *propositional opacity*. To run this argument, we have to return to our earlier description of the nature of language as directional schema. As expressions are given in a dictionary they are no more than linguistic substitutions without semantic content. To make them semantic we need to fill these schemata with nonverbal signs, and we do so under the social rules. We have learned to link certain sound sequences with our mental constructions about the world, perceptual, nonverbal readings as well as their fantasy extensions. Semiotic communities, it would seem, do not instruct us to apply fully shared definitions to the pregiven world, but rather tell us to fantasize such and such scenarios. There is a schematic direction-ality at work which becomes more and more concrete as we enrich the empty schema of language with more and more different and increasingly detailed nonverbal materials. In this way, our cognitive grasp of the world and our linguistic competence are matched to produce meaning.

However, the schemata of language are not as thoroughly controlled as it would seem. In workaday life people tend to assume that we share the conceptual grids associated with language. In the classroom, teachers try hard to impose a certain conformity on our ways of using language. And indeed, the conventionality of meanings seems to be achieved to a high degree. However, the final arbiter, the dictionary, lets us down. It cannot provide the much-needed definitions to back up the pedagogue. In fact, it does not contain any definitions at all. The substitutions we find in the dictionary are not really definitions, for two reasons. First, the detail of the so-called definition depends on the size of the dictionary. Gender as a social construct has no entry in the *Shorter Oxford Dictionary*, while it occupies more than half a page in the *Fontana Dictionary of Modern Thought* and fills pages in the relevant literature. This does not satisfy the requirements for a definition in any strict sense. There should be only one description and it should be exhaustive. Second, the so-called definitions always come after the social fact of language. Every so often, dictionaries have to be revised, sometimes quite radically, to cope with historically, technically and socially induced semantic drift. They are, in other words, a posteriori. Meaning comes first, then dictionaries can be written to cope with them as social facts. The opposite is the case in formal languages. Here definitions are a priori. First come the definitions, then we can do mathematics. In short, linguistic expressions are not defined at all. What we have in dictionaries are no more than differing descriptions, or no more than strings of signifiers of varying lengths. As a result, the propositional content which analytical philosophy finds in natural-language expressions is largely the dream of logicians. It is their sublimation for propositional opacity. Only if one denies propositional opacity is one able to substitute the purity of propositional content. Nor is such semantic certitude required for communication to take place, if we replace truth-conditional requirements by the idea of sufficient semiosis. Indeed, the very search for truth-conditions strikes us as a consequence of propositional assumptions about language. It is a certain view of language that produces a certain kind of description. Alter the assumptions, and a different description will ensue.

To make matters even cloudier, we can discover a third kind of vagueness, which I called *semiotic opacity*. Here we take a broad, bird's-eye view of linguistic communication. Neither propositional complexities nor even the inclusion of immediate speech situations is sufficient when it comes to describing meaning. We also need to look at the broad framing conditions of an utterance, a description of how social and cultural frames influence meaning events. We need social context. To reconstruct the multiple semiotic regimes that interact to form such framing conditions is, of course, outside the reach of any language user. So we proceed intuitively, we go by our feel for what sort of meaning construction best fits a specific cultural frame. We accept semiotic opacity as an inevitable fact of meaning. We sacrifice analytical accuracy for the speed of intuition in order to get by, and so find ourselves once more in the realm of sufficient semiosis.

With *sufficient semiosis* as our negotiatory checking mechanism for meaning in place, we have a reasonably cohesive picture of a corporeal semantics and how one could argue the role of the body in language. I now want to show how such a semantics compares with a number of traditional and more recent approaches to meaning by looking at their principal assumptions. This is the aim of the next chapter.

12. Semantic assumptions

The reader should not expect any attempt at an exhaustive survey of semantic theories. An uneven sketch of what I regard as relevant assumptions is all I am able to offer. To make the comparison a little more transparent, let us reconsider the main axioms of our corporeal, pragmatic picture of meaning that have emerged so far.

- Language is an empty syntactic grid.
- Language does not mean by itself.
- Language is parasitic on nonlinguistic signs.
- The dictionary does not contain any meanings, only verbal substitutions.
- Meaning is not governed by definition.
- Meaning is not a relation between language and an unmediated world.
- Meaning is an event.
- Meaning events occur when language grids are activated by nonverbal signs.
- When meaning occurs, linguistic expressions act as directional schemata.
- This activation applies to both utterance situation and to what is said.

- Nonverbal signs are made up of tactile, olfactory, gustatory, aural, visual and other perceptual readings as well as their fantasy variants.
- Nonverbal readings stand in a twin relationship to one another.
- Nonverbal readings are intersemiotic and heterosemiotic.
- Intersemiotic relations characterize the interaction between different signs.
- Heterosemiotic relations refer to the discrepancies between different kinds of sign.

- Only the linguistic signifier is arbitrary.

- The arbitrary signifier is the result of a history of iconic disembodiment.
- Signifieds are not arbitrary.
- At the level of the signified we are iconic beings.
- Signifieds are quasi-perceptual readings and their fantasy extensions.
- All natural-language meanings display traces of concrete social situations.
- Abstract expressions likewise reveal nonverbal imprints.
- There are no purely formal expressions in natural language.

- Communities set the framing conditions for signs.
- Communities largely control the activation of language by nonverbal signs.
- The world is not given directly but mediated for us by nonverbal signs.
- Nonverbal signs are the basis for both world and linguistic meaning.
- Nonverbal signs are the deep structure of language.
- Nonverbal signs reflect deep constraints as filtered by a community.
- Sufficient semiosis checks the relation between language and mediated world.
- Sufficient semiosis occurs under community rules.
- Sufficient semiosis replaces truth-conditions.

This set of axioms does not sit well with those of traditional approaches to meaning. Many of the popular ideas about how meaning works tend to be versions of established positions in linguistics and the philosophy of language. Of such views, arguably the most widespread are those associated with meanings as definitions, meaning as links between language and world, and meaning as determined by the differential relations between terms. The following positions strike me as representative of certain beliefs about meaning: definitional semantics (Frege, Carnap), naturalistic semantics (Devitt and Sterelny), behaviourist semantics (Bloomfield), relativist semantics (Humboldt, Sapir, Whorf), structuralist semantics (Saussure, Hjelmslev, Benveniste), psychoanalytic semantics (Lacan), transformational semantics (Chomsky), functional semantics (Halliday), poststructuralist semantics (Derrida, Foucault, Lyotard, Deleuze and Guattari), postmodern semantics (Baudrillard) and, lastly, cognitive semantics (Johnson, Fauconnier, Sweetser, Turner).

In Western philosophy the question of how language relates to the world is as old as Plato's dialogues. In the *Cratylus*, Socrates and Hermogenes debate whether the content of language is attached to its form as a result of a natural connection or whether this is a result of society's having made it so. This seemingly simple problem has undergone many transformations through time, and every new paradigm has produced new answers based on different assumptions. Corporeal semantics, as we have seen, cuts across the two options offered in the *Cratylus*. In the following, I sketch some of the major reformulations of this old problem. Not all of the schools of thought listed have produced fully fledged theories of meaning. While some offer cohesive semantic models, others provide no more than the bare bones for further theorizing.

Definitional semantics in the Fregean tradition regards the sense of a linguistic expression as a definitionally governed thought. The meaning of a sentence is its truth value, whether what it says about the world is true or false. Reference is the relation between a sense and actual objects in the world. Nonverbal signs are eliminated from Frege's picture of language. From our perspective, the equation between formal sense and natural language violates what happens in social discourse. None of Frege's definitions is compatible with corporeal semantics. Naturalist semantics of the kind advocated by Devitt and Sterelny (1990) views both language and the world physicalistically. Sense is Fregean and reference causal rather than semiotic. Meaning is guaranteed by referentially argued truth. Cultural deixis or any other form of implied deixis is not part of a naturalist picture of meaning. Naturalist semantics contradicts corporeal semantics on most counts.

In the behaviourist semantics of Leonard Bloomfield (1933), meaning is a physical chain of events of speech and action. Jill sees an apple and asks Jack to get it for her. This is presented as a double stimulus–response scheme.

$$S \rightarrow r \ldots s \rightarrow R$$

Stimulus (S) is followed by a verbal response (r) which, in turn, acts as a stimulus (s) for Jack to respond (R). Bloomfield's classical version of a behaviourist semantics was characterized by the strongest possible anti-mentalist stance. This involved the elimination of all nonphysical mental events from the theory of meaning. Feelings, images, and even concepts and thoughts, were banished from semantics. To cope with any necessary background information required as explanatory context, Bloomfield invented what he called 'predisposing factors'. In the later, modified version by the famous Skinner, Bloomfield's predisposing factors are replaced by the notion of 'reinforcement'. Just as a rat learns to press the right food dispenser lever after a while, so too do language learners engage in a process of reinforced stimulation and response (Palmer, 1982: 56ff.). One might expect a corporeal semantics to be able to sympathize with the event emphasis of behaviourism. And indeed, a refocusing on what goes on in the body when we are engaged in meaning-making is of interest to such a semantics. Furthermore, most of the processes relevant to meaning are generated by bodies. But this is where any possible similarity ends. Above all, the role of fantasy, crucial in corporeal semantics, is definitely off the behaviourist menu. Without acts of fantasy, which vary imaginable scenarios at high speed as we communicate, language would be without content.

The relativist semantics associated with the Sapir–Whorf hypothesis regards culture as relative to language. The assumptions underlying the position of linguistic relativity are of special relevance to corporeal semantics. This hypothesis should actually be called the Humboldt–Weissgerber–Sapir–Whorf hypothesis, to do the work of their predecessors justice. In 1929, Edward Sapir proposed the related thesis that the world we inhabit is largely 'built up on the language habits' of the native speakers (1949: 160). Benjamin Lee Whorf added the more specific claim that language cuts up 'nature along lines laid down by our native languages' (1956: 214). With reference to the culture and language of the Hopi Indians, Whorf tried to show how language produces different attitudes to space and time, and hence fundamentally different views of the world. It is not clear how far Whorf wanted to press his claims. At their extreme extension, we would have to say that peoples with strongly contrasting languages should find it very difficult to negotiate between their cultures. Though difficulties cannot be denied, we must ask what it is that allows them to communicate in spite of their linguistic differences. The answer that emerges from a corporeal semantics is that what appears so differently coded at the level of language is much more open to comparison at the level of nonverbal signs. The closer to human physiology, the more readily are our nonverbal signs translated from culture to culture. By contrast, the theoretical possibilities of how languages can reflect similar nonverbal readings of the world are vast and highly divergent. Unfortunately, the linguistic relativity thesis runs into contradictory evidence, as we have seen. If nonverbal colour distinctions are not necessarily matched by the linguistic scale of verbal expressions, as Ackerman has documented, the Sapir–Whorf hypothesis is in trouble. But we should not dismiss this line of thinking altogether. Let us return for a moment to Wilhelm von Humboldt's earlier observations.

In spite of obvious shortcomings, Humboldt's nineteenth-century insights are still intriguing in the way they construct language and culture. In *On the Diversity of the Structure of Human Language and Its Influence on the Mental Development of Mankind* (1836), the author regards language as 'a manner of conception' pertaining to 'our entire way of thinking and feeling' (Humboldt, 1836: 45). Languages, for Humboldt, are so 'inextricably integrated with the innermost nature of humans' that we are entitled to view the 'intellectual character of peoples' as being an effect of language (48). Humboldt sees a relation between the structure of language and the nature of other intellectual activities. It resides in the 'inspiring breath' which a language instils during the 'act of transforming world into thought' (51). This is why intellectual endeavour and language are inseparable. Indeed, for Humboldt this fusion is so intense that 'if only one of them were given, one should be able to derive the other entirely from it' (53). As we have seen with reference to colour distinctions, this extreme view of congruence cannot be maintained. At the same time, the claim that when we try to 'separate intellectual life from language, such a separation does not truly exist' must strike us as cogent (53).

Intriguing also is Humboldt's dual observation of language as activity (*energeia*) and production (*Erzeugung*) rather than as work (*ergon*) and dead product (*totes Erzeugtes*) (55, 57). Language is both 'something constant' and at the same time 'ephemeral at every moment'. As a result, we cannot look at linguistic items in isolation but must address language 'only as the totality of speaking' (57). What, in Humboldt's view, then, is the relation between language and world? On the one hand, he says, 'the real material of language is above all the sound'; on the other, the totality of the sense impressions and independent mental processes which precede the formation of concepts with the help of language (61). In other words, we have linguistic sounds expressing nonverbal readings. In this process, 'the entire manner of subjective perception enters the use of language of necessity'. Linguistic expressions evolve from perception, although we are not dealing here with 'a copy of the object as such, but a picture of it produced in the mind' (74). For Humboldt, the materials of the perceptible world are more subtly ordered by language. He leaves no doubt it is language that generates thought ('*Die Sprache ist das bildende Organ des Gedankens*') (66). And like his successors, Humboldt claims that every language harbours a culture-specific view of the world ('*so liegt in jeder Sprache eine eigentümliche Weltansicht*) (74). More specifically, 'every language contains the entire fabric of the concepts and ways of imagining (*Vorstellungsweise*) of a part of humankind' (75). This is why he says that when we learn a foreign language we should always try to gain from it a new perspective to modify our own *Weltanschauung* (75). Here Kant's interpretive reason lives on, and one should therefore perhaps be a little cautious in equating all Enlightenment reason only with its instrumental variety. Barring the relativity thesis in its strong version and his definition of thought as linguistic, Humboldt's observations remain attractive. What I want to revive in particular is his emphasis on the role the imagination plays in meaning.

Structuralist semantics evolved from the reconstruction of Ferdinand de Saussure's notes and writings, as well as from the work of his successors such as Hjelmslev, Benveniste or Greimas. Because it is so well known, Saussure's position can be summed up very briefly. According to Saussure, language is the semiotic master system and only linguistic signs make other signs meaningful (Saussure, 1974: 68). Saussure describes the signified as a concept or image but pays little attention to the implications of this point. The emphasis is on the arbitrariness of the linguistic sign, while meaning is regarded as a consequence solely of the differential relations of language as system. These relations are *paradigmatic* semantically in so far as they mark an associative relation either by similarity or by contrast. They are *syntagmatic* as far as their position in a syntactic chain is concerned. Saussure highlights the syntagmatic features of terms, and 'in the syntagm a term acquires its value only because it stands in opposition to everything that precedes or follows it, or to both' (123). It is likely that this emphasis is the reason why Saussure favoured the chess analogy of language, according to which 'the respective value of the pieces depends on their position on the chessboard just as each linguistic term derives its value from its opposition to all other terms' (88). For Saussure, language could be viewed as a collection of individual utterances or *paroles*, or as *langue*, an idealized system anonymized and abstracted from actual utterances. In agreement with Saussure's systemic interest, *langue* became almost the exclusive focus of his and his successors' interests. Thus, Saussure favoured the *synchronic* study of language, which pays special attention to the relations between terms that 'form a system in the collective mind of speakers' over its traditional, historically and etymologically oriented *diachronic* rival (99f.).

As far as the relation between body and meaning is concerned, Saussure's revolutionary structuralist innovations proved highly detrimental. This is so above all because of the elimination of any referential links between language and world in any sense. Having said this, however, I want to stress that Saussure himself provided a possible solution to the problem of missing reference. If we take his observations concerning general semiology at the end of the *Course* and redefine reference as a relation between different semiotic systems by which we construct our world (within constraints), then reference is mediated rather than naturalistic and allows us to exit linguistic systems to nonverbal signs. We could now theorize meaning in a quasi-corporeal manner. However, no such solution is offered in the structuralist tradition.

The Copenhagen School is dominated by the work of Louis Hjelmslev, in particular his *Principles of General Grammar* (1928) and *Prolegomena to a Theory of Language* (1953). Hjelmslev resumes the structuralist focus on *langue* as a self-sufficient system, sharpening its logical relations by a distinction between *content* plane and *expression* plane. Linguistic signs express a content by imposing a form on the undifferentiated 'stuff' or mere substance of the 'mass of thought' (Hjelmslev, 1953: 29, 31). This 'purport' is transformed by the content-form into a content-substance. Likewise, an expression-substance is the result of an imposition of an expression-form on an expression purport (32). This relation is schematized to sum up Hjelmslev's combinatory possibilities as follows:

	Form	Substance
Content	content-form	content-substance
Expression	expression-form	expression-substance

Meaning or 'purport' in this schema has no referential anchor in either empirical reality or nonverbal semiosis. From the point of view of corporeal semantics, Hjelmslev's theory suffers from several shortcomings. First, there is the assumption that language orders what is unordered. This means that humans for a couple of million years and primates, as well as a lot of other sentient beings, have lived in a chaotic world. There is no evidence for this assumption. Language is much more likely to be a sophisticated and economical way of reordering what is already ordered by nonverbal signs. Then, we note the 'violent hierarchy', as Derrida would call it, of a top-down formalism that seems to crunch everything in its way. We should not be surprised that such formalizations yield certain results. Any systemic view of semiotic relations will allow some kind of demonstrable application. With respect to language, we must remember that formal discursive moves have been derived from natural language in the first place, so it is only to be expected that we can reimport them. This point having been made, the double question of internal consistency and usefulness must be asked. Hjelmslev's scheme fulfils the consistency criterion, but only in a restricted sense. Instead of talking about language, Hjelmslev addresses only one side of language, its formal aspects. In other words, Hjelmslev's scheme is a version only of Saussure's chess analogy. To that limited extent it is internally consistent. As to the criterion of applicability, both content-substance and expression-substance are formal themselves, for they have no systemic relation to our perceptual world. Hence, the socialized body as nonverbal signifying system with its tactile, aural, gustatory and other readings is excluded from Hjelmslev's semantic. When it is applied, structuralism here commits a kind of *symbolic fallacy* in that the model does not match what actually happens. It fails the test of usefulness.

A number of other structuralist claims face similar challenges. Take, for instance, Émile Benveniste's concept of subjectivity, which is defined as 'the emergence into being of a fundamental category of language. "Ego" is he who says ego.' Here structuralism overstates its case. While it is uncontroversial to say that 'language is possible only because each speaker sets himself up as a subject by referring to himself as I in the discourse', it is quite another matter to turn this manifestation of subjectivity into subjectivity *per se* (Benveniste, 1971: 224f.). If Benveniste were right, the subjects of the Dani tribe in New Guinea who work only with two verbal colour distinctions, light and dark, yet have been demonstrated to be able to perceive the most intricate hues, would be sadly diminished creatures. And though Helen Keller's personality without doubt acquired a high degree of complexity once she was able to use language, she clearly remembers her own already rich subjectivity during her childhood when she lived in a nonverbal world.

In A. J. Greimas's *Structural Semantics* (1966) we meet an atomistic extension of earlier works in the Saussurean tradition. Building on the definition of meaning as intrasyntactically produced, Greimas offers a splitting up of the signified into *semes* or minimal semantic elements out of which larger units such as words or *sememes* are built. In turn *sememes* are argued to consist of *semic kernels*, a kind of intensional sense, and *contextual semes* according to surrounding semantic fields. As in most structuralist semantics, the anti-referential bias makes the work of Greimas unattractive for a theory of meaning oriented towards the body. Furthermore, where his inquiries do yield demonstrable semantic results they do so for reasons other than those claimed – for any insight at the level of *langue* is dependent on the undeclared ground of the systemic relations of nonverbal social semiosis.

Psychoanalytic linguistics of the Lacanian kind produces a semantics that is similarly inhospitable to corporeal semantics. In *L'Acte psychoanalytique*, a seminar series conducted between 1967 and 1968, Lacan consolidated his perspective on meaning by reiterating his preference for the signifier over the signified. Three kinds of signifiers are singled out in this period as the mainstays of our grasp of reality:

- a 'symbolic order signifier that joins the world of language to that of images and objects' and so creates the 'subject';
- 'the unitary trait which links an imaginarized-symbolic subject to others and to the world via the projections that constitute the process of identification'; and
- what he calls 'object a', described by Ragland-Sullivan as 'a falling of a piece of the real onto the vector which runs from the symbolic to the imaginary' (Ragland-Sullivan and Bracher, 1991: 1).

This is what Lacan has to say here:

> The signifier can, indeed, manipulate such material, despite the apparent hindrances the latter could cause in imaginary functioning, that is to say in the most fragile and difficult thing to grasp as far as man is concerned; not that there are not in him primitive images destined to give us a guide to nature, but, precisely since the signifier takes over, it is always very difficult to pinpoint them in their raw side. (6 December 1967; quoted in Ragland-Sullivan and Bracher, 1991: 2)

In Lacan's Saussurean emphasis on words as depending on other words we observe once more the disappearance of reference. This has more than semantic consequences. As Jacques-Alain Miller remarks, reference for Lacan shifts from the signified world to the business routine of the analyst. The referent, 'the object is the analyst himself' (Miller, 1991: 24). Miller neatly sums up Lacan's semantic as an autonomous, syntactic set:

> In a *language* [the] various signs – the signifiers – take on their value from their relation to one another. That is the meaning of symbolic order. The symbolic order is effectively a self-contained dimension and is not grounded on correspondence, but on circularity ... when Lacan proposes a definition of the signifier, it is a circular definition he gives: a signifier represents a subject for another signifier. (31)

To sustain the notion of language as a syntactic circuit can be led *ad absurdum* very simply. Consider a new language consisting of 'grinch' (S1), meaning 'blenk' (S2), which means the opposite of 'blok' (S3). Now we have a miniature language in the Lacanian sense. It is socially conventionalized by myself and a colleague. We communicate with one another in the new language. About what? Floating signifiers, is Lacan's answer. But if they float, we do not quite know what we are talking about. And how do 'symbolic order signifiers' allow us to exit the system? For Lacan must exit the circle of signifiers at one point to establish meaning. If he does not, we remain stuck in a post-Saussurean circularity, which cannot produce meanings other than formal sense (S1 = S2). Natural languages do not work like this. In natural language reference is never 'vacuous' or 'void', not even in fictions (Miller, 1991: 32). Nor do we have to accept an empiricist or naturalist definition of reference. Certainly, Lacan's claim that 'no signification can be sustained other than by reference to another signification' can be made coherent in an intersemiotic explanation, but not if we have already defined signification as consisting only of signifiers. If no reasonably stable relationship could be established between signifiers and signifieds, if signifiers were to float, then we would have a very hard time finding our way about in the world, and communication would be impossible (Lacan, 1977: 150f.). In a world where 'words are the murderers of things' (Miller, 1991: 33), we are as distant from Freud's 'talking bodies' as we are from a corporeal semantics in which reference and meaning are facilitated by nonverbal signs in fantasy and perception. One step beyond Lacan's 'floating signifier' is the idea of flickering signs.

In her paper 'Virtual bodies and flickering signifiers' (1993: 69ff.) Katherine Hayles attempts a radicalization of the weak relationship that, Lacan argues, exists between the signifier and signified. Flickering signifiers are argued to be a consequence of the shift from a concept of information based on presence and absence towards information conceived in terms of pattern and randomness. An entirely new socio-technological being emerges, the post-human of the information age. While Hayles on the whole presents a persuasive picture of new significatory attitudes, her theorization of the basis of signification is both unnecessary and incoherent. She is right to stress that 'different techno-logies of text production' and its 'embodied experience' produce new varieties of 'textual worlds'. But then Hayles redefines information as a relation between pattern and randomness, in contrast to the traditional view based on absence and presence. Information itself 'is never present in itself'. What we are acutely aware of are 'the blinking lights that comprise the text in its screen format'. As we interact with 'electronic images' we never experi-ence a 'one-to-one correspondence between signifier and signified'. As information technologies 'fundamentally alter the relation between signified and signifier', the principle of absence and presence has to compete with that of 'pattern and randomness':

> Carrying the instabilities implicit in Lacanian floating signifiers one step further, information technologies create what I will call *flicker-ing signifiers*, characterized by their tendency toward unexpected metamorphoses, attenuations, and dispersions. Flickering Signifiers signal an important shift in the plate tectonics of language. (Hayles, 1993: 76)

Hayles argues this way because she accepts Lacan's claim that signifiers are 'produced by signifiers'. She believes with Lacan that both signifiers and signifieds are part of one and the same system of linguistic relations without any exit to secondary systems of signs. Language is self-sufficient. Because of this conception of language Hayles makes the following leap from signifiers to signifieds:

Precisely because the relation between signifier and signified at each of these levels is arbitrary, it can be changed with a single global command. ... I am producing flickering signifiers on a video screen, changing the font is as easy as giving the system a single command. The longer the chain of codes, the more radical the transformations that can be effected. (*ibid.*: 77)

Yet all that has occurred is the transformation of signifiers. Font changes have no significant effects on signifieds. But since signifieds have been dismissed, the font change becomes the source of a change in language. This is unconvincing. The proof of the pudding is often to be found in an application of a claim to the very argument presented. If Hayles were right, the electronic version of her paper should show up significant differences if compared with the hard copy in front of me. The flickering signifiers on my screen should result in an argument significantly at variance with that of the hard copy. *No such changes can be observed.* The irony is that no matter how much the signifiers flicker on the screen, the signifieds, the argument presented, are relatively stable. And whatever instabilities they display as a result of the reading performance, these have little if anything to do with the technology. Rather, they stem from outside the system of linguistic signifiers, the non-verbal signs and interpretive conventions readers bring to bear on the text.

There are some other misunderstandings in Hayles's view of language that should be avoided. One is to think that absence and presence no longer play a dominant role in the digital machinery. Quite the contrary. At the level of the logic gates the 0/1 or on/off distinctions are apposite. As to the demise of one-to-one relationships between bytes and language, the ASCII coding of every space, comma and letter is entirely a one-to-one relationship. If this relationship were to flicker, we could say goodbye to word processing. There is no doubt that digital technology and its role in information technology have *semantic effects* on the social at large (Ruthrof, 1992: 161–4). However, I believe that such a claim is better made with a different theory of language, one that does not simply abandon the signified. Above all, Hayles's own interest in embodiment would be better served if her argument were not restricted to the structuralist level of the signifier.

Transformational semantics is associated with the 1950s, when Noam Chomsky advocated a radically new way of looking at natural languages. He introduced the distinction between surface structure and deep structure as a characteristic of all languages (Chomsky, 1959). By surface structures Chomsky referred to the specific ways in which a language orders its phonemes, vocabulary and syntax, whereas deep structures characterize a broadly shared underlying relationship of noun phrases and verb phrases.

By way of a transformational grammar we are able to read surface structures in terms of deep structures and so turn syntax into a semantic. At the same time, transformational relations can be reversed, so that deep structures can be turned into surface structures by generative mechanisms. According to transformational grammar, our ability to learn the mechanisms of deep structures is innate (Chomsky, 1971). In adult life, the generation of texts is typically performed by a competent speaker who is able to transform a deep structure into a variety of verbal surfaces. In a sense, Chomsky reasserts Vico's idea that 'there must in the nature of human institutions be a mental language common to all nations' (Vico, 1968: 161). Meaning in Chomsky's scheme, then, is the result of the transformation of specific linguistic surfaces into a more general deep structure.

Given its propositional and formalist leaning, it is not surprising that Chomsky's deep structure semantics is as elegant as it is barren. For one, because surface texts are not immediately related semantically with our perceptual world, because we need the detour to more general propositions of a deep structure, the singularity and importance of texts themselves are diminished. This is a dubious reductionism as far as the intricacies of social discourse are concerned and disastrous for the study of the artistic text. More importantly, from the perspective chosen in this book, even if Chomsky shows us a way of deciphering linguistic texts with the help of propositional deep structures, we now face the dual task of having to provide meaning for two different levels of language. We must know what the meanings of the surface syntax are in order to decide on the appropriate transformational pathway and we must also turn the deep-structure terms into meanings. Since we have already shown that syntactic substitutions as they appear in a dictionary have no meanings by themselves, we must exit both surface structure and deep structure and combine each, in a systemic manner, with two nonlinguistic sets of signs. As shown before, the unmediated world will not do, nor will any alternative, formalized language. Back to the process of activating empty linguistic schemata with non-verbal readings. Except, thanks to Chomsky, we now do this twice: at the linguistic surface and at the level of its deep-structure transformation. We certainly can do this, but I suggest that the Chomskyan operations are 'can' rules and not 'must' rules.

The semantics that emerges from functional linguistics is much more congenial to corporeal semantics. From its beginnings in Michael Halliday's *Learning How to Mean* (1975) to recent writings by himself and his followers, the base axioms concerning meaning have not changed significantly (Halliday, 1978, 1985). I summarize some of the principles of Halliday's approach. In functional semantics, language is regarded as a systemic meaning potential. 'Functionality' draws our attention to the observation that 'the child learns language as a system of meanings in functional contexts' (Halliday, 1975: 9). Halliday never quite gets round to giving a concise definition of meaning. Rather he lets the reader get an impression from broader descriptions, as for instance the following:

> we recognize that there are certain fundamental goals or purposes that the child achieves through the use of vocal sound. He uses his voice to order people about, to get them to do things for him; he uses it to demand certain objects or services; he uses it to make contact with people, to feel close to them; and so on. All these things are meaningful actions. (11)

Meanings are established for the child 'in terms of certain generalized contexts of language use' (15). At this stage, semantic value emerges gradually out of a situation where 'there is only content', towards the formation of 'content–expression' pairs (14). Thus the child aquires a 'system of meaningful behaviour' or 'a semiotic system', part of which is linguistic, and all of which always occurs 'always within some social context' (15):

> So the content of an utterance is the meaning that it has with respect to a given function, to one or other of the things that the child is making language do for him. It is a semiotic act which is interpretable by reference to the total range of semiotic options, the total meaning potential that the child has accessible to him at that moment. (15)

Halliday isolates three functional components in all semiotic and linguistic behaviour: *ideational* options that have to do with what is being said, *interpersonal* components that relate to the speaker and the speech situation, and a *textual* component, the mode in which something is presented, which allows the speaker to make his utterance 'operational' (17). Halliday draws a distinction between the semantics of early childhood and fully developed meaning performance. At an early stage the following functions are dominant:

Instrumental	'I want'
Regulatory	'do as I tell you'
Interactional	'me and you'
Personal	'here I come'
Heuristic	'tell me why'
Imaginative	'let's pretend'
Informative	'I've got something to tell you' (37)

In fully developed semantic performance, reference to things in the world is only one element of language use, the other being 'their relation to, and value for, the social process' (141). The world is always seen as 'processed by culture' (141). While reference to the external world becomes more and more 'indirect', the 'social matrix within which meanings are being exchanged' comes to the fore (141).

I believe that Halliday overstates the case of *intragrammaticality* when he says that 'the direct dependence of a speech situation on the perceptual environment disappears the moment he introduces the third level into his system, the lexico-grammatical level of words and structures' (142). This is so, he argues, because we now have an 'abstract' form of coding that comes between the 'reference to the situation' and language (142). My main objection has two parts. First, there never has been any 'direct' dependence. The external world is always mediated by nonverbal signs. Second, the acquisition of linguistic signification does not rule out nonverbal grasp. Nor could language mean if it were not filled with something nonlinguistic, as we have shown. To say that once we speak, we can no longer understand the world by smell, touch, hearing or sight is demonstrably wrong. As cognitivists are beginning to demonstrate more and more persuasively, our processes of mapping are not ruled by language; rather they collaborate with linguistic codes.

It would be convenient if we could point to a poststructuralist semantics in the writings of Derrida, Foucault, Lyotard, and Deleuze and Guattari. Unfortunately, there is no poststructuralist semantics, if we mean by that a fully developed theory of meaning. I use the term merely to indicate certain tendencies that we can glean from various writers associated with poststructuralist practices. No doubt meaning has undergone a number of significant transformations as a result of poststructuralist interventions. Derrida, for example, has not eliminated meaning from the chain of signs but merely robbed it of its alleged originary and stable character. Meanings are now motivated by *différance* in its various guises and metaphoricity rather than by logos. Foucault offers a new pragmatic emphasis to meaning by insisting on such features of 'exteriority' as the institutions within which discursive formations function and the question of who speaks under what conditions and from what kind of institutional status. In Deleuze and Guattari's writing, pragmatics turns political in that the semantic values of 'order-words' prevent emancipatory subjectivation by subjectification. At the same time, meaning is a potential of liberation in the form of the creation of new, critical concepts. Hence, artists and philosophers face the task of replacing the dominant semantics of a society by nomadic and minoritarian alternatives. In Lyotard's agonistic discursive universe meanings can be construed as differends, injustices that result of necessity from discursive dominance. But here too we find a liberating option. When what must be said, but cannot as yet be said, is uttered nevertheless, when the unpresentable is presented in the face of its inadmissibility, the event of a new political sublime has occurred. This too must be some sort of semantic entity to have the effect of a positive differend.

In postmodern semantics and especially in the recent writings of Jean Baudrillard, semantic assumptions have taken a dive. Meaning is not only dead but fatal to its users. Signifiers simulate signifiers. We live in a world without meaning. As I have shown, this runs into contradictions when Baudrillard wants to have it both ways. He wants to be able to describe the world as a screen that controls but he has robbed himself of any analysis of what or who does the controlling. In any case, once signifiers can be exchanged at random, Baudrillard's own writing could no longer be distinguished from a Japanese menu. Not that he is in a position to mind. He has no semantics with which to argue the case. All we can say in his defence is 'Nice metaphors'.

An approach to signification in which meaning again plays a central role can be found in cognitive science. Cognitive semantics is a fairly new phenomenon. I have already acknowledged the kind of cognitive semantics advocated by Sweetser, whose writings are indebted to George Lakoff and Mark Johnson, among others. It is the work particularly of Mark Johnson and Mark Turner that is of interest to the present study. In *The Body in the Mind: The Bodily Basis of Meaning, Imagination, and Reason* Mark Johnson offers what he calls a 'cognitive semantics' (Johnson, 1987: 190). It combines a post-Kantian view of understanding with the findings of cognitive science. What is particularly attractive about his position is that it regards linguistic meaning as largely nonpropositional. Rather it is treated as a special case of general meaning, and Johnson believes that any appropriate theory of meaning must be 'a semantics of understanding' (175). Understanding, in turn, is seen broadly, in an almost Heideggerian manner, as 'one's way of being in, or having, a world' (137). The cognitive semantics that emerges from these base axioms focuses on how an individual embedded in a culture understands things by way of public meanings (190). What are the main features of this theory of meaning?

Above all, there are various kinds of categorization or 'the way we organize our experience into kinds' (191). This takes place within the frame of 'a general theory of cognitive models' (192). Part of these models is the notion of 'schemata', especially image schemes, which 'play a crucial role in the formation of networks of meaning' (192). Another necessary ingredient is metaphor as part of the 'central projective operations' that allow us to make 'semantic connections' (192). Part–whole relations, too, or metonymy, are needed in the processes of categorization. Moreover, Johnson lists polysemy as a network of 'multiple related meanings' as well as a cognitive explanation of semantic drift, according to which 'schemata with metaphoric and metonymic extensions' are responsible for both the 'direction' and the 'nature' of semantic change (193). Above all, meaning and understanding are ultimately grounded in the human imagination.

Any theory of meaning must tell us also about the constraints which regulate the production and exchange of meanings. Otherwise, we would not be able see how communication could take place. In Johnson's semantic picture there are three main sets of constraints:

- image schemas, metaphoric entailments and metonymic relations, which provide links, pathways, scales, cycles, centre to periphery patterns and other regulative structures;
- biological constraints, such as human embodiment, perceptual mechanisms, motor programmes or bodily skills; and
- social constraints, such as our participation in culture, language, institutions and historical traditions (137).

In many ways, cognitive semantics is compatible with the corporeal semantics offered here, even though it argues its case by way of a scientific, bottom-up approach from neural excitation towards high-level, imaginative processes. Corporeal semantics takes the opposite, top-down approach, asking what kind of conditions must prevail at the base levels of the processes of understanding if language and meaning function in society as they appear to do. Apart from this strategic différance, there are also a number of specific disagreements:

1. In opposing the separation between meaning and background, as argued for instance by Searle (1984: 181–186), Johnson's account reworks, so it would seem, something that has been part of the phenomenological tradition up to Schutz and Heidegger. In particular, we are reminded of Heidegger's important idea of 'the totality of involvements' of which all meaning is a part. Furthermore, the part–whole relation, which has played a crucial role in the hermeneutic tradition from Kant's *Kritik der Urteilskraft* (1968) through the writings of Ast, Schleiermacher and Dilthey to Heidegger and is addressed also by the linguist Roman Jakobson, deserves a more central position. Johnson does acknowledge the third *Kritik* but for reasons other than to link the cognitive project with the hermeneutic tradition.

2. Questions remain as to the relation between physiological determinants of schemata and cultural specificity. When does culture kick in? What are the reasons for class, race and gender differences in our productions of image schemata? Are they all of the same generality?

3. Schemata are exclusively treated as visual or quasi-visual. And although Johnson briefly addresses other sense readings under 'Embodied schemata', they are cursorily subordinated to the visual bias. Arguing transcendentally, as much of my own work also does, Johnson writes, 'our perceptual schemata are the various possible structures that our experience must fit if it is to be coherent and comprehensible' (20f.). Two problems need to be addressed here: the intersemiotic and the heterosemiotic relations between nonverbal readings. In particular, what is missing is a discussion of the heterosemiotic, conflictual nature of various perceptual readings that have to be beaten into submission by the mind to produce meaning.

4. Image schemata are sharply distinguished from mental images by making them operate at a more general and abstract level. This looks fine for habitual meaning constructions where we are looking for a nonverbal equivalent to propositional sense. However, what this position rules out is the possibility of a scale of configurations from fairly concrete and so iconic representations to highly schematized forms. Different readings of the world as well as different kinds of readings of linguistic texts seem to demand different representational processes. It strikes me as unlikely that the habitual reading of a traffic rule 'Turn Left' engages the same level of representational schematization as the reading of a passage in a realist novel.

5. Where corporeal semantics also differs from cognitive semantics is in its emphasis on implicit deixis and, more generally, inferable modality and hence modal opacity. As things stand, Johnson's meanings are very much a referential reflection of reality. Apart from the attention given to speech acts there is no exploration of what I regard as one of the most important and intriguing features of language, namely the way in which culture instructs speakers to qualify its lexicon by modalities in the broad sense.

6. Cognitive semantics does not trace its immediate ancestry to the work of Charles Sanders Peirce. As a consequence, it does not phrase its descriptions in semiotic terms. In the absence of signs, there is always a danger of treating the perceived world as a realist rock bottom. Johnson escapes this charge by what I read as his post-Kantian approach. Nevertheless, corporeal semantics insists that the level of comparison between language and the perceived world is semiosis – that is, signs.

7.   Lastly, what precisely is language in cognitive semantics? An arbitrary or conventional sound sequence? Is it a schema itself, like visual schemata? Is it empty? Is it directional? If so, where does directionality reside? Can language mean on its own when it is not corroborated by perception?

I have paid special attention to what I think are significant differences between corporeal semantics and cognitive semantics. I have done so not because I want to show that they are incompatible but because, on the contrary, they produce similar insights. They do so in spite of their very different methods of inquiry. The one is empirical, relying on scientific experiment, the other is critical-speculative and transcendental. Cognitive semantics is mainly a bottom-up procedure, corporeal semantics a top-down approach. They meet somehow in the middle where meaning occurs. Corporeal semantics must take a hard look at its procedure should its claims contradict cognitive evidence. Conversely, cognitive science needs to remain open to the holistic demands made by the complexities of mental projections (Varela *et al.*, 1993).

Like corporeal semantics and its cognitive alternatives, all theories of meaning not only rest on assumptions concerning the nature of language but also make overt as well as covert metaphysical commitments. Some of these form the topic of the final chapter.

13. Meaning, metaphysics and representation

If we ask what sort of conditions must prevail for specific semantic assumptions to work, we are inevitably led to their stated, or concealed, or unreflected metaphysical ground. To the reader who thought we had left metaphysics behind since deconstruction, I suggest that trying to get away from metaphysics is a metaphysical move *par excellence*. Wholesale robotics may be a way out, but then we can never be sure whether robots themselves will not at a certain stage of their evolution engage in metaphysical speculation about their own destiny. (Un)fortunately we are nowhere near such a scenario. At present, certainly, every semantics yields a metaphysics. Every theory of meaning will have to own up to its underlying assumptions of how the world works in relation to human observers – how, in other words, we should relate meaning and Being. In the following pages I want to give the briefest possible sketch of some of these assumptions and conclude with a brief discussion of (re)presentation.

Empiricist and naturalist semantics (Frege, Devitt and Sterelny) regard the world as independent of sign processes, human or nonhuman. At the same time, language is controlled by conventionally agreed-upon definitions. As a result, reference is a link between syntactically ordered language signs and objects or referents, while meaning is guaranteed if those links obey truth-conditions. Here, we are linking chalk and cheese, significatory processes and objects. As a result, the metaphysics underlying this kind of semantics is flawed in the sense that it eliminates the role that signification plays in the conception of the 'world' we are talking about in the first place. The assumption here is that our observations about the world follow the right standard. Do other organisms see the 'same' world as distorted? And if they do, what general 'stuff' allows both our correct vision and their distortions to happen at the same time? Unfortunately for realists, to check this out we need some arbitration outside the universe that tells us whether we are right or wrong. In the absence of such arbitration realist and naturalist semantics rest on an act of faith. Perhaps the invention of God(s) is the acknowledgement of this failure of metaphysical realism.

Semanticists who emphasize the self-sufficiency of signifiers face a very different difficulty. I am thinking of post-Saussurean structuralists, such as Hjelmslev, Benveniste, Greimas, as well as Lyotard. Although they allow for a vague nonlinguistic ground, meaning is produced only within the confines of linguistic domains. In structuralism this amounts to a syntactic circularity, in Lyotard to a reduction of the world to the sentence. The metaphysical assumption at work here is that language is in charge. There is no reference that links up world and language. In its extreme relativist form, as in Baudrillard and his followers, such a semantics suggests that any sequence of signifiers is able to produce a viable culture. Yet why, one should ask, is there no culture that consistently claims that we should jump from the top of 20-storey buildings and survive? Or eat sand and drink mercury as a staple diet? A culture like this is, of course, thinkable, but would live only for a very short time. The Heaven's Gate community made this point rather spectacularly. 'Pain is a sign that we're out of harmony with Nature,' Diane Ackerman tells us (1991: 107). This is, of course, an inference rather than a 'direct' observation. However, even such inferential constraints are absent in relativist theories of language. As I will suggest, we do not have to return to the equally dismal metaphysics of empiricists and naturalists for an answer. Certainly, the relativist metaphysics implied in a good deal of structuralism and central to Baudrillard's picture of language cannot satisfactorily answer these questions. Pretty though they may look, they fall foul of what actually occurs.

A semiotic semantics in the Peircean tradition takes a direction somewhere between hard-headed realist and relativist semantics. This is also where the sympathies of corporeal semantics lie. We acknowledge that the 'world' exerts constraint on our signs. Importantly, however, this very world, including its constraints, is available to us only via signs. These signs are primarily nonverbal readings: olfactory, tactile, aural, visual and so on. At the same time, humans sum up their various ways of mapping the world by language. In addition, language enables humans to theorize about both the signified world and language itself. World and language, then, appear to us in the form of signs. Humans are also able to extend their signs beyond and below human scale. Still, telescopes and electron microscopes produce signs rather than noumena. In Kantian terms, these instruments extend our range of appearances. And yet we have not merely supplemented our significatory perspectives. We are in a process of epistemic multiplication. As the biologist Humberto Maturana would say, we are observers who can achieve no more than 'objectivity in parentheses' (Maturana, 1988). From this perspective, meaning is a relation between different kinds of signs guided by culture in the face of inferable deep constraints. We could characterize such meta-physical assumptions as an *abductive realism*.

Several insights by Peirce can be used to account for recent findings in various fields of knowledge, such as cognitive science. Peirce rigorously distinguishes between the fact of our experience of the world and the sort of knowledge that we are able to have about that experience. While 'we *have* direct experience', the way we realize that experience 'is entirely relative' (my emphasis). Experience is direct, knowledge is semiotic – that is, the result of interacting signs about such experiences. This also means that experiences cannot be known except as readings. Nor is the compound semiotic result that we call knowledge ever an individual accomplishment. It is always communal. It is 'independent of the vagaries of me and you'. And although it is a theoretical possibility to know the truth, this would mean to have communally understood the universe as a whole. Reality, as ground, 'is that which, sooner or later, information and reasoning *would* finally result in' (emphasis added). For Peirce, the role of the community consists largely in the affirmation of what it finds acceptable and in the rejection of what it cannot (Peirce, 1974: VI, 235; 186f.).

Combine this position with Peirce's reworking of Kant's reflective reason and we have a metaphysical scheme in which corporeal semantics makes reasonable sense. Kant's most advanced formulation of reflective reason involved the idea that when we are confronted by complex structures, such as works of art or nature, we assume a dynamic, flexible – that is, 'fallible' – telos and so invent the rules of interpretation as we go along. We read the detail against the stipulated 'teleological' whole and revise both as inter-pretation proceeds. This is one of Kant's important contributions to hermeneutics. Peirce derived his 'abductive' form of reasoning from this method. In its most abbreviated form, abduction is the process of finding general frames for specific instances. Apply this to how we think the world works and how humans act in it as observers. It would mean that we are involved in a community-steered process of projecting holistic frames for individual readings against the hard facts of bumping into the world. The circularity in this formulation is to the point. We are always already in an interpretive 'spiral', unable to step outside to a position from which to judge whether we are right or wrong. As long as we roughly follow the semiosis sanctioned by the community, we feel at home. Hence, a certain kind of hermeneutic circularity is an essential part of our metaphysical scheme. Now our meanings are about something other than language. They are about the world signified by nonverbal readings. Nor are such meanings complete, static or properly defined. Rather, they are tentative and always open to infinite regress. In the body-oriented semantics sketched in this book, meanings are at play.

Playful as the meaning process may be, the account offered nevertheless relies on some sort of notion of *(re)presentation*. The term is a can of worms which I have tried to avoid opening. Sooner or later, however, the question has to be raised as to what kind of worms we are dealing with here. First, we should note that (re)presentation functions neither as a homogeneous concept nor as mere binary oppositions. Rather, the term refers to a scale from 'representation' as a strict copying to '(re)presentation' in the loose sense of imaginative variation, including the most extreme forms of distortion. The prefix 're-' goes with the former, 'presentation' with the latter. A hard-headed realist version of re-presenting in the sense of copying is not a serious candidate for the description of language, of course. And cognitive science, where mental 'schemata' and 'mapping' have emerged as bona fide research results, carefully distances itself from any such simple notion of representation by using the term in inverted commas, if at all. However, the debate about representation and representationalism goes a little deeper than that. As Derrida reminds us, 'today there is a great deal of thought against representation' (Derrida, 1982: 304).

Davidson, who stands at the end of a long chain of critics of representation, rejects the idea of language as a 'structured medium of representation, capable of standing in determinate relations to a distinct entity called "the world"' (Rorty, 1992: 373f.). The attack here is directed at the dogmas of empiricism, which, as Davidson views the matter, rely on a 'scheme–content' distinction and point our inquiry to the wrong target. What we have instead is language and belief. Davidson's stance could be regarded as compatible with corporeal semantics if what counts as a belief consists of matters other than sentences. However, if belief is coextensive with yet more sentences, then we are back into intragrammatical constraints on their own, with corporeality turned into ideality. Though I do not think that this would be a fair description of Davidson's position, it is difficult to find out what precisely beliefs consist of. 'Beliefs are true or false,' Davidson says, 'but they represent nothing. It is good to be rid of representations, and with them the correspondence theory of truth' (Davidson, 1989: 165f.). Indeed it is, if that is what representations lead to. But how do we know whether our beliefs are true or false? Largely, according to Davidson, they are true. Most likely so. Yet meaning is not a question of truth or falsity, either in the Fregean mode or in the way they are tied to beliefs in Davidson's scheme. Meanings have to do with the relationship between verbal and nonverbal signs. And our signs are circumscribed by culture-filtered constraints.

For the purposes of a corporeal theory of meaning, Derrida's observations about representation are by far the most helpful. In 'Sending: on representation' (1982) Derrida inquires into whether there is a semantic kernel that would allow us to identify what is the same in the polysemic term 'representation'. As he frequently does, Derrida takes Heidegger as his stalking-horse and traces a picture of what is at stake in representation in French and German translations of the Greek and Latin relations of the term. Like Wittgenstein, Derrida uses the expression 'imagine', and in much the same strategic way. 'Imagine that French were a dead language' (Derrida, 1982: 295). Project a fantasy construct and think about the consequences of this thought-experiment. Derrida's strategy of moving between German and French usage opens with Bergson's remark that 'representation is an equivocal word which ought never, according to its etymology, to designate an intellectual object presented to the mind for the first time. It ought to be reversed' (295). The remainder of the paper deals with certain observations made by Heidegger. In 'Sending: on representation', Derrida cautiously helps us to slip past Heidegger's critique to a point where a disseminated form of representation as presentation can no longer be dismissed. Derrida's rationale for a semantic deconstruction of 'representation' is that 'it allows itself less than most [themes] to be detached or dissociated from its linguistic embodiment, its lexical and above all nominal embodiment' (296). Nor can we avoid, he says, addressing the 'question of Latino-Germanic translation' of the term and in particular 'the relation between *repraesentatio* and the *Stellen* of *Vorstellung* [mental projection] or *Darstellung* [presentation]' (297). For example, he asks, is the substitution of the French *représentation* for *Vorstellung* and *Darstellung* of the same order as the German–French translation practice? The answer already anticipates Derrida's general theme: such substitutions of necessity 'escape the orbit of representation' (298). If this is so, how then should we view representation? Is there a minimal 'shared semantic kernel'? There is Freud's distinction between *Wortvorstellungen* (mental images of words) and *Dingvorstellungen* (mental images of things), our representations of signifiers and signifieds, as well as his other modes of representation in 'introjection, incorporation, interiorization, idealization, and also phantasm and fetish' (311). Then there is the aesthetic use of 'representation' as 'mimetic substitution', as image which does not actually represent but merely presents something 'before our imaginative or mental gaze' (299). This is why in *The Reader's Construction of Narrative* (Ruthrof, 1981) I preferred the term 'presentation' throughout, except when referring to the copying of actual texts in certain novelistic documentaries. Likewise, Derrida rightly observes, it is highly probable that there are 'kernels of different meanings' present in the term; and if this is so, theorists of language as well as philosophers engaged in the representationalism debate are 'going to have a rough time of it' (299).

What comes to the fore here is a fundamental insight about natural language, whose 'context is never able to be saturated for the determination and *identification* of a sense' (299). A different way of arguing this situation is to say that to regard the meanings of natural language as identifiable sense is to mix up two kinds of sense, formal sense and natural-language sense, a procedure adopted by Frege and inherited by the entire analytic tradition, as I have shown in detail elsewhere (Ruthrof, 1993; 1997a: 53–76). Derrida proceeds by example, pointing to the semantic differences between the French '*représentation*', English 'representation', and German '*Repräsentation*', in contrast to *Vorstellung* and *Darstellung*. If meaning identity in a variety of contexts could be guaranteed, then, he says,

> language, every language, would be representative, a system of representatives, but the content represented, what is represented by this representation (a meaning, a thing, and so on) would be a presence and not a representation. What is represented would not have the structure of representation, the representative structure of the representative. Language would be a system of representatives or also of signifiers, of place holders substituted for what they say, signify, or represent, and the equivocal diversity of the representatives would not affect the unity, the identity, indeed even the ultimate simplicity of the represented. (Derrida, 1982: 303f.)

In order to show that this is clearly not the case, Derrida invokes Heidegger's contemplation of the meaning of *repraesentatio* in relation to *Vorstellung*, the image put before a subject by the subject. More precisely, *Vorstellung* refers to the act of 'bringing what is extant before oneself as something that stands in opposition, to relate it to the person who does the representing and to force its return to that person as the determining domain' (translation modified; 307). While in English, representation makes a claim to objectivity in its emphasis on repetition and copying, the German *Vorstellung* emphasizes both the referential side of *stellen*, or setting, positing, putting, placing, and the deictic side of referring back to the agent of representation. The reflexive verb phrase '*sich etwas vorstellen*', to imagine something, is sharply distinguished from '*etwas oder jemanden vorstellen*', to introduce something or someone. As Derrida tells us, '*Vorstellung* seems to mean simply, as Heidegger emphasizes, to place, to dispose before oneself, a sort of theme or thesis' (307), and so he highlights 'the power of a subject who can bring back to presence and make present' (308). In the notion of representation as mental representation or *Vorstellung* we are dealing with a 'double effigy, an image, a copy, an idea as a picture of the thing henceforth at hand, in the absence of the thing, available, disposed and put forward for, by, and in the subject' (308).

The repeated idea of something and the subject as the arena where this occurs are at the heart of the notion of representation. It is the eidos as a presupposition underlying the repetition of an idea in representation that would make the picture part of representation possible, its Platonism that is still sending its message to us. 'The world of Platonism would thus have given the send-off for the reign of representation' (313). On the other hand, there is what Derrida calls 'the subjective unilaterality of representation' (313). This unilateral power is curtailed, as Heidegger notes, by the regime of 'calculability'. This is what 'guarantees the certainty in advance of what is to be represented'. At the same time, 'it is towards the incalculable that the limits of representation can be transcended' (315). This Heideggerian observation is of the utmost importance, for it spreads before us a vast spectrum of possibilities of (re)presentations and presentations from technical repetition to artistic and speculative extensions or distortions: '*Der Mensch als das vorstellende Subjekt jedoch phantasiert*' (Humans as imagining subjects, however, fantasize; my trans. 316).

This is why we cannot presume a 'semantic centre' that would govern 'the multiplicity of modifications and derivations' at 'the very interior of what offers itself as the philosophical or merely theoretical usage of the word representation' (320). Instead, the notion of representation needs to be viewed under the umbrella of 'dissemination' (323). This applies as much to the rejection of representationalism, whatever that includes, as it does to the usage of 'representation' as identity. Representation has come to us from a pre-ontological world and yet there is no way back. Although 'everything begins by referring back', it never begins in the sense of a single starting-point. Rather, 'many different traces [refer] back to other traces and to traces of others' (324). From this perspective, representation as a unified concept is prohibited and a different story has to be told. As often in his writing, Derrida presents a *tertium datur* argument: we are bound neither to reject representation altogether nor to embrace its identity. Nor do we have to take a position where we are in a single sign system universe, with language unrelated to any other form of signification. Nor indeed do we have to conceive of representation as a copying mechanism. The third option is the semantic dissemination of the alleged sense of 'representation'. It harbours a vast number of incongruous readings, many of which are useful in thinking at the borderlines of orthodoxies. Above all, what is important is to trace the law that prohibits the possibility of representation in any strict sense of the term.

From the point of view of the role of the body in language, Derrida's paper is of considerable value. Although the paper does not specifically address nonverbal semiosis and its function in culture, corporeal semantics shares with his position the double critique of subjectivity and ideality. In corporeal semantics, the subjective part of (re)presentation is socialized, while representative ideality is replaced by the nonverbally signified world.

Afterword: Corporeal semantics and the obsolete body

In 'Bad futures: performing the obsolete body' (1994), Anne Marsh writes about the 'post-holocaust subject' with reference to the Australian performance robotics of Stelarc, 'the first cyborg artist'. In Stelarc's world, 'the body is recomposed' with its 'surface and interior' transformed into a 'bioelectronic triggering device'. The body, in this scenario, is 'exteriorised' (Marsh, 1994: 281). As in Donna Haraway's vision, behaviour, including signification and reproduction, is standardized (Haraway, 1991). Because the techno-body is more effective in terms of communication as well as in relation to the world, the biological body is to be discarded as 'obsolete' (Marsh, 1994: 282).

In such a fantasy, how would corporeal semantics have to be thought? It is tempting to assume that with the demise of the biological body and the subject, and hence the radical transformation of culture, corporeal semantics would be unthinkable. It is tempting to suppose that in a world under the rule of logic gates, corporeality would be superfluous. Yet robotics needs bodies. As long as action in and on the world is to be assumed, corporeality is part of the equation. Without the centrality of bodies, *Blade Runner* would not be the powerful statement about techno-capital that it is. Whether bodies are biological, biotechnical or synthetic, to be effective agents they need to be programmed. The only way this can be presently conceived is in terms of a controlled interaction between a formal program and some kind of sensor interpetation of the world. And virtual realities are sensor readings precisely in this sense. The principles of corporeal semantics then would still apply, even if in a reduced fashion. Empty signifiers, such as bytes, are activated by nonverbal signs – tactile, optical, olfactory and other readings – to interpret and act on the mediated, physical environment. Community and culture would be framing programs for the behaviour of individual robotic devices. Such cultures would be able to survive only if they respected the deep constraints of the universe that they would have to infer through their interpretations. With a little stretch of the imagination, machine intelligence would allow for the possibilities of deviance and creativity. This might happen by way of random factors introduced into programs to avoid mere repetition and vicious circularity, and so guarantee survival.

If corporeal semantics is so easily adapted to cyborg conditions, one might ask how applicable it is to human performance. Of course, the same question could be put to definitional semantics and naturalist semantics, both of which lend themselves quite readily to robotics. Such a question presupposes, however, that cultures cannot or should not be viewed as programs for humans. And why not? In evolutionary terms, this would make perfect sense. After all, the very cyborg fantasy before us is imagined not by machines but by us. If the fantasy were ever to become reality, *we* would have produced the world of cyborgs, extensions of ourselves, and *they* would remember us as their ancestral bodies.

Bibliography

Ackerman, Diane (1991) *A Natural History of the Senses*. New York: Vintage Books.

Agire, Imanol (1981) 'The origin of writing and of language', *The Epigraphic Society Occasional Publications*, 9(1), 37–48.

Aristotle (1968) *De Anima*, Books II and II, trans. D.W. Hamlyn. Oxford: Clarendon Press.

Austin, J.L. (1991) 'Ifs and cans'. In J.L. Austin, *Philosophical Papers*, ed. J.O. Urmson and G.J. Warnock. Oxford: Oxford University Press, pp. 153–180.

Baker, G.P. and Hacker, P.M.S. (1983) *An Analytical Commentary on Wittgenstein's 'Philosophical Investigations'*, vol. 1. Oxford: Basil Blackwell.

Baker, G.P. and Hacker, P.M.S. (1988) *Wittgenstein: Rules, Grammar and Necessity (An Analytical Commentary on the 'Philosophical Investigations')*, vol. 2. Oxford: Basil Blackwell.

Banting, Pamela (1992) 'The body as pictogram: rethinking Hélène Cixous's écriture féminine', *Textual Practice* 6(2), 225–246.

Barthes, Roland (1972) *Mythologies*, trans. A. Lavers. London: Granada.

Barthes, Roland (1974) *S/Z*, trans. Richard Miller. New York: Hill and Wang.

Barthes, Roland (1987) *Image, Music, Text*, ed. and trans. Stephen Heath. London: Fontana.

Baudez, Claude F. (1992) *Lost Cities of the Mayas*, trans. Carolin Palmer. London: Thames and Hudson.

Baudrillard, Jean (1979) *De la Séduction*. Paris: Denoel-Gonthier.

Baudrillard, Jean (1983) *Simulations*, trans. P. Foss and P. Patton. New York: Semiotext(e).

Baudrillard, Jean (1984) 'Nihilism', *On the Beach* 6, 38–39.

Baudrillard, Jean (1987) *Forget Foucault*. New York: Semiotext(e).

Baudrillard, Jean (1990) *Fatal Strategies*, trans. Philip Beitchman and W.G.J. Nieluchowski. New York: Semiotext(e).

Benveniste, Émile (1971) *Problems in General Linguistics*, trans. Mary Elizabeth Meek, Coral Gables, FL: University of Miami Press.

Bloomfield, Leonard (1933) *Language*. New York: Holt.

Bruner, Jerome (1990) *Acts of Meaning*. Cambridge, MA: Harvard University Press.

Chang, Briankle G. (1996) *Deconstructing Communication: Representation, Subject, and Economies of Exchange*. Minneapolis: University of Minnesota Press.

Chomsky, N. (1959) *Syntactic Structures*. The Hague: Mouton.

Chomsky, N. (1971) 'Deep structure, surface structure and semantic interpretation'. In Danny D. Steinberg and Leon A. Jakobovits (eds), *Semantics: An Interdisciplinary Reader in Philosophy, Linguistics and Psychology*. Cambridge: Cambridge University Press, pp. 183–216.

Cixous, Hélène (1997) 'The laugh of the Medusa'. In Robyn R. Warhol and Diane Price Herndl (eds), *Feminisms: An Anthology of Literary Theory and Criticism*. Basingstoke: Macmillan, pp. 347–362.

Comrie, Bernard (1986) 'Conditionals: a typology'. In E.C. Traugott, A. ter Meulen, J. Snitzer

Reilly and C.A. Ferguson (eds), *On Conditionals.* Cambridge: Cambridge University Press, pp. 77–102.

Coulmas, Florian (1989) *The Writing Systems of the World.* Oxford: Basil Blackwell.

Crossley, J.N., Ash, C.J., Brickhill, C.J., Stillwell, J.C. and Williams, N.H. (1990) *What Is Mathematical Logic?* New York: Dover.

Danesi, Marcel (1993) *Vico, Metaphor, and the Origin of Language.* Bloomington: Indiana University Press.

Danesi, Marcel and Nuessel, Frank (eds) (1994) *The Imaginative Basis of Thought and Culture: Contemporary Perspectives on Giambattista Vico.* Toronto: Canadian Scholars Press.

Davidson, Donald (1974) 'Belief and the basis of meaning', *Synthèse,* 27, 309–323.

Davidson, Donald (1984) *Inquiries into Truth and Interpretation.* Oxford: Clarendon Press.

Davidson, Donald (1989) 'The myth of the subjective'. In Michael Krausz (ed.), *Relativism: Interpretation and Confrontation.* Notre Dame Ind.: University of Notre Dame Press.

Davidson, Donald (1989) 'A coherence theory of truth and knowledge'. In Ernest Lepore (ed.), *Truth and Interpretation: Perspectives on the Philosophy of Donald Davidson.* Oxford: Basil Blackwell, pp. 307–19.

Davoust, Michel (1995) *L'Écriture Maya et son déchiffrement.* Paris: CNRS Editions.

DeFrancis, John, (1986) *The Chinese Language: Fact and Fantasy.* Honolulu: University of Hawaii Press.

DeFrancis, John, (1989) *Visible Speech: The Diverse Oneness of Writing Systems.* Honolulu: University of Hawaii Press.

Deleuze, Gilles and Guattari, Félix (1994) *What Is Philosophy?,* trans. Hugh Tomlinson and Graham Burchell. New York: Columbia University Press.

Deleuze, Gilles and Guattari, Félix (1987) *A Thousand Plateaus: Capitalism and Schizophrenia,* trans. Brian Massumi. Minneapolis: University of Minnesota Press.

Derrida, Jacques (1973) *Speech and Phenomena,* trans. David B. Allison. Evanston: Northwestern University Press.

Derrida, Jacques (1978) 'The *retrait* of metaphor', *Enclitic,* 2 (2), 5–33.

Derrida, Jacques (1982) 'Sending: on representation', *Social Research,* 49 (2), 294–326.

Devitt, Michael and Sterelny, Kim (1990) *Language and Reality: An Introduction to the Philosophy of Language.* Oxford: Basil Blackwell.

Diringer, David (1962) *Writing: Ancient Peoples and Places.* London: Thames and Hudson.

Diringer, David (1968) *The Alphabet: A Key to the History of Mankind.* London: Hutchinson.

Driver, G.R. (1976) *Semitic Writing: From Pictograph to Alphabet.* The Schweich Lectures of the British Academy (1944). London: Oxford University Press.

Dummett, Michael (1973) *Frege: Philosophy of Language.* London: Duckworth.

Eco, Umberto (1984) *Semiotics and the Philosophy of Language.* London: Macmillan.

Eco, Umberto (1997) *The Search for a Perfect Language,* trans. James Fentress. London: Fontana.

Eliot, T.S. (1963) *Collected Poems 1909–1962.* London: Faber and Faber.

Evans, Arthur J. (1909) *Scripta Minoa: The Written Documents of Minoan Crete with Special Reference to the Archives of Knossos.* Oxford: Clarendon Press.

Evans, Gareth (1982) *The Varieties of Reference,* ed. John McDowell. Oxford: Clarendon Press.

Fauconnier, Gilles (1985) *Mental Spaces: Aspects of Meaning Construction in Natural Language.* Cambridge, Mass.: MIT Press.

Fauconnier, Gilles (1997) *Mappings in Thought's Language.* Cambridge: Cambridge University Press.

Fauconnier, Gilles and Eve Sweetser (eds) (1997) *Spaces, Worlds, and Grammars.* Chicago: University of Chicago Press.

Finke, Ronald A. (1989) *Principles of Mental Imagery.* Cambridge, MA: MIT Press.

Finke, Ronald A. (1990) *Creative Imagery: Discoveries and Inventions in Visualisation.* Hillsdale: Lawrence Erlbaum.

Förstemann, Ernst (1902) *Commentar zur Madrider Mayahandschrift (Codex Tro-Cortesianus).* Danzig: L. Saunier.

Foucault, Michel (1978) *The Archaeology of Knowledge*, trans. Sheridan Smith. London: Tavistock.

Frege, Gottlob (1970) 'On sense and reference'. In *Translations from the Philosophical Writings of Gottlob Frege*, ed. Peter Geach and Max Black. Oxford: Basil Blackwell, pp. 56–78.

Froman, Wayne Jeffrey (1982) *Merleau-Ponty: Language and the Act of Speech*. Lewisburg, PA: Bucknell University Press.

Frutiger, Adrian (1991) *Der Mensch und seine Zeichen: Schriften, Symbole, Signete, Signale*. Wiesbaden: Fourier.

Fundación Santillana (1980) 'Hopi script'. Madrid: Museo de América.

Gatens, Moira (1988) 'Towards a feminist philosophy of the body'. In Barbara Caine, Elizabeth Grosz and Marie de Lepervanche (eds), *Crossing Boundaries: Feminism and the Critique of Knowledges*. Sydney: Allen and Unwin, pp. 59–70.

Gaur, Albertine (1984) *A History of Writing*. London: British Library.

Gelb, I.J. (1965) *A Study of Writing*. Chicago: University of Chicago Press.

Gimbutas, Marija (1991) *The Civilization of the Goddess: The World of Old Europe*. San Francisco: Harper.

Globus, Gordon G., Maxwell, Grover, and Savodnik, Irwin (eds) (1976) *Consciousness and the Brain: A Scientific and Philosophical Inquiry*. New York: Plenum.

Goodchild, Philip (1996) *Deleuze and Guattari: An Introduction to the Politics of Desire*. London: Sage.

Grosz, Elizabeth (1987) 'Notes towards a corporeal feminism', *Australian Feminist Studies*, 5, 1–15.

Grosz, Elizabeth (1994) *Volatile Bodies: Toward a Corporeal Feminism*. Sydney: Allen and Unwin.

Haas, W. (ed.) (1976) *Writing without Letters*. Manchester: Manchester University Press.

Halliday, M.A.K. (1975) *Learning How to Mean: Explorations in the Development of Language*. London: Edward Arnold.

Halliday, M.A.K. (1978) *Language as Social Semiotic*. London: Edward Arnold.

Halliday, M.A.K. (1985) *An Introduction to Functional Grammar*. London: Edward Arnold.

Haraway, Donna J. (1991) *Simians, Cyborgs, and Women: The Reinvention of Nature*. New York: Routledge.

Harris, Roy (1986) *The Origin of Writing*. London: Duckworth.

Hayles, Katherine N. (1993) 'Virtual bodies and flickering signifiers', *October*, 66, 69–91.

Heidegger, Martin (1962) *Being and Time*, trans. John Macquarrie and Edward Robinson. New York: Harper and Brothers.

Heidegger, Martin (1975) 'Language'. In *Poetry, Language, Thought*, trans. and ed. Albert Hofstadter. New York: Harper and Row, pp. 189–210.

Hjelmslev, Louis (1953) *Prolegomena to a Theory of Language*, trans. Francis J. Whitfield. Baltimore: Waverley Press.

Hjelmslev, Louis (1970) *Language: An Introduction*, trans. Francis. J. Whitfield. Madison: University of Wisconsin Press.

Husserl, Edmund (1966) *The Phenomenology of Internal Time-Consciousness*, ed. Martin Heidegger, trans. James S. Churchill. Bloomington: Indiana University Press.

Husserl, Edmund (1969) *Ideas: General Introduction to Pure Phenomenology*, trans. W.R. Boyce Gibson. London: Collier-Macmillan.

Husserl, Edmund (1973) *Cartesian Meditations: An Introduction to Phenomenology*, trans. Dorian Cairns. The Hague: Martinus Nijhoff.

Ingarden, Roman (1973a) *The Literary Work of Art*. Evanston: Northwestern University Press.

Ingarden, Roman (1973b) *The Cognition of the Literary Work of Art*. Evanston: Northwestern University Press.

Irigaray, Luce (1985a) *Speculum of the Other Woman*, trans. Gillian C. Gill. Ithaca: Cornell University Press.

Irigaray, Luce (1985b) *This Sex Which Is Not One*, trans. Catherine Porter. Ithaca: Cornell University Press.

Irigaray, Luce (1991) 'The power of discourse and the subordination of the feminine'. In *The Irigaray Reader*, ed. Margaret Whitford. Oxford: Basil Blackwell.

Jakobson, Roman (1971a) 'On linguistic aspects of translation'. In *Selected Writings*, vol. 2, *Word and Language*. The Hague: Mouton, pp. 260–266.

Jakobson, Roman (1971b) 'Linguistic types of aphasia'. In *Selected Writings*, vol. 2, pp. 307–333.

Jakobson, Roman (1971c) 'On the relation between visual and auditory signs'. In *Selected Writings*, vol. 2, pp. 338–344.

Jakobson, Roman (1971d) 'Quest for the essence of language'. In *Selected Writings*, vol. 2, pp. 345–359.

Jakobson, Roman (1971e) 'Results of a Joint Conference of Anthropologists and Linguists'. In *Selected Writings*, vol. 2, pp. 554–567.

Jakobson, Roman, (1979) 'On verse'. In *Selected Writings*, vol. 5. The Hague: Mouton.

Jensen, Hans (1970) *Sign, Symbol and Script: An Account of Man's Efforts to Write*, trans. George Unwin. London: George Allen and Unwin.

Johnson, Mark (1987) *The Body in the Mind: The Bodily Basis of Meaning, Imagination, and Reason*. Chicago: University of Chicago Press.

Kant, Immanuel (1965) *Critique of Pure Reason*, trans. Norman Kemp Smith. New York: St Martin's Press.

Kant, Immanuel (1968) *Kritik der Urteilskraft*, ed. Karl Vorländer. Hamburg: Felix Meiner.

Kay, Paul and Kempton, Willett (1984) 'What is the Sapir–Whorf hypothesis?', *American Anthropologist*, 86(1), 65–79.

Keller, Helen (1909) *The World I Live In*. London: Hodder and Stoughton.

Keller, Helen (1954) *The Story of My Life*. New York: Doubleday.

Kendon, Adam (ed.) (1981) *Nonverbal Communication, Interaction, and Gesture: Selections from Semiotica*. The Hague: Mouton.

King, Charles (1977) *Hieroglyphs to Alphabets*. New York: Crane Russak.

Kirby, Vicky (1997) *Telling Flesh: The Substance of the Corporeal*. London: Routledge.

Kristeva, Julia (1986) *The Kristeva Reader*, ed. Toril Moi. Oxford: Basil Blackwell.

Kristeva, Julia (1987) *In the Beginning Was Love: Psychoanalysis and Faith*, trans. Arthur Goldhammer. New York: Columbia University Press.

Kristeva, Julia (1989) *Language the Unknown: An Initiation into Linguistics*, trans. Anne M. Menke. London: Harvester.

Lacan, Jacques (1974) *The Language of the Self: The Function of Language in Psychoanalysis*, trans. Anthony Wilden. Baltimore: Johns Hopkins University Press.

Lacan, Jacques (1977) *Écrits: A Selection*, trans. Alan Sheridan. New York: Norton.

Lakoff, George and Turner, Mark (1989) *More Than Cool Reason: A Field Guide to Poetic Metaphor*. Chicago: University of Chicago Press.

Laszlo, Ervin, Artigiani, Robert, Combs, Allan and Csanyi, Vilmos (1996) *Changing Visions: Human Cognitive Maps, Past, Present, and Future*. Westport, CT: Praeger.

Leibniz, Gottfried Wilhelm (1934) *Philosophical Writings*, trans. Mary Morris and G.H.R. Parkinson. London: Dent.

Lotz, J. (1951) 'Natural and scientific language', *Proceedings of the American Academy of Arts and Sciences* 80, 87f. Quoted in Roman Jakobson, 'On the relation between visual and auditory signs'. In *Selected Writings*, vol. 2, pp. 334–337.

Lucy, Niall (1996) *Debating Derrida*. Melbourne: Melbourne University Press.

Lucy, Niall (1997) *Postmodern Literary Theory: An Introduction*. Oxford: Basil Blackwell.

Lyotard, Jean-François (1986) 'Complexity and the sublime'. In Lisa Appignanesi (ed.), *ICA Documents 4 and 5: Postmodernism*. London: Institute of Contemporary Arts, pp. 10–12.

Lyotard, Jean-François (1988) *The Differend: Phrases in Dispute*, trans. Geoffrey Bennington and Brian Massumi. Manchester: Manchester University Press.

Lyotard, Jean-François (1994) *Lessons on the Analytic of the Sublime*, trans. Elizabeth Rottenberg. Stanford: Stanford University Press.

McHoul, Alec (1996) *Semiotic Investigations: Towards an Effective Semiotics*. Lincoln: University of Nebraska Press.

Marsh, Anne (1994) 'Bad futures: performing the obsolete body'. In Nicholas Zurbrugg (ed.), *Electronic Arts in Australia*. Special issue of *Continuum*, 8(1), 280–291.

Maturana, Humberto (1988) 'Reality: the search for objectivity or the quest for a compelling argument', *Irish Journal of Psychology*, 9(1), 25–82.

Merleau-Ponty, Maurice (1962) *Phenomenology of Perception*, trans. Colin Smith. London: Routledge and Kegan Paul.

Merleau-Ponty, Maurice (1964a) *The Primacy of Perception and Other Essays*, ed. James M. Edie. Evanston: Northwestern University Press.

Merleau-Ponty, Maurice (1964b) *Sense and Non-Sense*, trans. Hubert L. Dreyfus and Patricia A. Dreyfus. Evanston: Northwestern University Press.

Merleau-Ponty, Maurice (1964c) *Signs*, trans. Richard C. McCleary. Evanston: Northwestern University Press.

Merleau-Ponty, Maurice (1968) *The Visible and the Invisible*, trans. Alphonso Lingis. Evanston: Northwestern University Press.

Norman, Jerry (1988) *Chinese*. Cambridge: Cambridge University Press.

Palmer, F.R. (1982) *Semantics*. Cambridge: Cambridge University Press.

Parnel, Laurel (1997) *Transforming Trauma – EMDR: The Revolutionary Therapy for Freeing the Mind, Clearing the Body, and Opening the Heart*. New York: Norton.

Peirce, Charles Sanders (1958) *Collected Papers*, vols 7–8, ed. Arthur W. Burks. Cambridge, MA: Harvard University Press.

Peirce, Charles Sanders (1974) *Collected Papers*, vols 1–6, ed. Charles Hartshorne and Paul Weiss. Cambridge, MA: Harvard University Press.

Ragland-Sullivan, Ellie and Bracher, Mark (eds) (1991) *Lacan and the Subject of Language*. New York: Routledge.

Rollins, Mark (1989) *Mental Imagery: On the Limits of Cognitive Science*. New Haven: Yale University Press.

Rorty, Richard (ed.) (1992) *The Linguistic Turn: Essays in Philosophical Method*. Chicago: University of Chicago Press.

Rubinger, Marcos Magalhães (1979) *Pintura rupestre: algo mais do que arte pré-histórica*. Belo Horizonte: Interlivros.

Russell, Bertrand (1973) 'On denoting'. In Douglas Lackey, *Essays in Analysis*. New York: George Braziller, pp. 103–119.

Ruthrof, Horst (1981) *The Reader's Construction of Narrative*. London: Routledge and Kegan Paul.

Ruthrof, Horst (1992) *Pandora and Occam: On the Limits of Language and Literature*. Bloomington: Indiana University Press.

Ruthrof, Horst (1993) 'Frege's error', *Philosophy Today*, 37, 306–317.

Ruthrof, Horst (1995) 'Meaning: an intersemiotic perspective', *Semiotica*, 104, (1–2), 23–43.

Ruthrof, Horst (1997a) *Semantics and the Body: Meaning from Frege to the Postmodern*. Toronto: University of Toronto Press.

Ruthrof, Horst (1997b) 'Deleuze and the body: eluding Kafka's "little death sentence"', *South Atlantic Quarterly*, 96(3), 563–578.

Ruthrof, Horst (1997c) 'The politics of desire', *Social Semiotics*, 7(2), 247–251.

Sacks, Oliver (1998) *An Anthropologist on Mars*. Sydney: Picador.

Sapir, Edward (1949) *Selected Writings of Edward Sapir in Language, Culture, and Personality*, ed. G. Mandelbaum. Berkeley: University of California Press.

Saussure, Ferdinand de (1974) *Course in General Linguistics*, trans. Wade Baskin. London: Fontana.

Schaan, Denise Pahl (1997) *A linguagem iconográfica da cerâmica marajoara: um estudo da arte pré-histórica na Ilha de Marajó – Brasil (400–1300 AD)*. Porto Alegre: EDIPUCRS.

Schlick, Moritz (1936) 'Meaning and verification', *Philosophical Review*, 45, 339–369.

Schmand-Besserat, Denise (1978) 'The earliest precursor of writing', *Scientific American*, 238(6), 50–59.

Searle, John R. (1984) *Minds, Brains and Science: The 1984 Reith Lectures*. Harmondsworth: Penguin.

Sebeok, Thomas (1986) 'Zoosemiotic components of human communication'. In Robert E. Innes (ed.), *Semiotics: An Introductory Reader*. London: Hutchinson, pp. 294–324.

Sebeok, Thomas, Umiker-Sebeok, Jean and Kendon, Adam (eds) (1981) *Nonverbal Communication, Interaction, and Gesture*. The Hague: Mouton.

Shapiro, Francine (1995) *Eye Movement Desensitization and Reprocessing: Basic Protocols and Procedures*. New York: Guilford Press.

Shapiro, Francine (1997) *EMDR: The Breakthrough Therapy for Overcoming Anxiety, Stress and Trauma*. New York: Basic Books.

Straits Times (1995) *Fun with Chinese Characters: The Straits Times Collection*, vol. 1. Singapore: Federal Publications.

Strawson, P.F. (1950) 'On referring', *Mind*, 59, 320–344.

Sweetser, Eve (1990) *From Etymology to Pragmatics*. Cambridge: Cambridge University Press.

Tarski, Alfred (1956) *Logic, Semantics, Metamathematics*, trans. J.H. Woodger. Oxford: Clarendon Press.

Turner, Mark (1987) *Death Is the Mother of Beauty: Mind, Metaphor, Criticism*. Chicago: University of Chicago Press.

Turner, Mark (1991) *Reading Minds: The Study of English in the Age of Cognitive Science*. Princeton: Princeton University Press.

Varela, Francisco, Thompson, Evan and Rosch, Eleanor (1993) *The Embodied Mind: Cognitive Science and Human Experience*. Cambridge, MA: MIT Press.

Vico, Giambattista (1968) *The New Science of Giambattista Vico*. New York: Cornell University Press.

von Humboldt, Wilhelm (1836) *Über die Verschiedenheit des menschlichen Sprachbaues und ihren Einfluss auf die geistige Entwicklung des Menschengeschlechtes* [On the Diversity of the Structure of Human Language and Its Influence on the Mental Development of Mankind]. Berlin: Königliche Akademie der Wissenschaften.

Weaver, Muriel Porter (1981) *The Aztecs, Maya, and Their Predecessors: Archaeology of Mesoamerica*. New York: Academic Press.

Whorf, Benjamin L. (1956) *Language, Thought and Reality: Selected Writings of Benjamin Lee Whorf*, ed. John B. Carroll. Cambridge, MA: MIT Press.

Wiggins, David (1992) 'Meaning, truth-conditions, propositions: Frege's doctrine of sense retrieved, resumed and redeployed in the light of certain recent criticisms', *Dialectica*, 46, 61–90.

Williams, Donna (1992) *Nobody Nowhere: The Extraordinary Autobiography of an Autistic*. New York: Times Books.

Wittgenstein, Ludwig (1953) *Philosophical Investigations*, trans. G.E.M. Anscombe. New York: Macmillan.

Wittgenstein, Ludwig (1958) *The Blue and the Brown Books*. Oxford: Oxford University Press.

Wittgenstein, Ludwig (1963) *Tractatus Logico – Philosophicus*, trans. D.F. Pears and B.F. McGuinness, introduction by Bertrand Russell. London: Routledge and Kegan Paul.

Wittgenstein, Ludwig (1972) *Über Gewissheit – On Certainty*, trans. Denis Paul and G.E.M. Anscombe, ed. G.E.M. Anscombe and G.H. von Wright. New York: Harper and Row.

Wittgenstein, Ludwig (1978) *Remarks on the Foundations of Mathematics*, ed. G.H. von Wright, R. Rhees and G.E.M. Anscombe, trans. G.E.M. Anscombe. Oxford: Blackwell.

Index

abductive realism 5, 171
abstract expressions 117–30
  and nonverbal imprints 152
  and social traces 152
achromatopsia 82
Ackerman, Diane 1, 24, 41, 47, 66, 72,
  76–7, 79–80, 102, 104, 105, 107, 115,
  128, 170
  and as-structure 47
  on dwarfism 108–9
  on tactile healing 24
Agire, Imanol 89
alphabet, iconic origins 95
appresentation 9, 10
appropriation, *see* Heidegger
arbitrariness 4, 22, 23, 91, 92, 95, 96,
  151–2
  and pedagogy 96–7
  principle of 96
Aristotle, on intersemiotic
  relations 60
as-structure, *see* Heidegger
autism 80–1

Banting, Pamela 109, 111–14
Barthes, Roland 99
Baudrillard, Jean 28, 134, 144, 165, 170
  'aleatory imputation' 29
  meaning as 'fatal' 28
  'immorality of capital' 29
  'promiscuity of concepts' 29
  'strategic resistance' 29
  without semantics 165
Benveniste, Emile 157–8, 170
Bloomfield, Leonard 17, 152, 153
body vii, 2, 4, 7, 9, 10, 11, *passim*
  biotechnical 177

gesturing 85
as grotesque 73
as ground vi, 113
haptic 73
insertion of 112
in language 14
obsolete 177–8
perceptual 84, 102, 134
'sexuate' 110
in signification 15
stylized 94
as supplement 111, 112
synthetic 177
theories of 113
body-oriented theory 57, 59,
  172
Brazilian Indian writing 92–3
Bruner, Jerome 17

Carnap, Rudolf 7
Chang, Briankle 144–5
  'voluntary mutism' 144
Chinese characters 86–7
Chomsky, Noam 161–2
Cixous, Hélène 14, 109, 111–14
code 53
cognitive
  linguistics vi, 16, 17, 19, 32, 126
  maps 17
  psychology 17
  rhetoric vi, 1, 32, 104
  schemata 101
  science 1, 12, 16, 17, 18, 32, 39–41,
    114, 128–9
  semantics 101, 143
colour
  computational processes 17